Charles Kray ⬚⬚⬚⬚⬚⬚⬚⬚⬚⬚⬚
Reggie – the K⬚⬚⬚⬚⬚⬚⬚⬚⬚⬚
property deve⬚⬚⬚⬚⬚⬚⬚⬚
ing pop groups⬚⬚⬚⬚⬚

Robin McGibbon first met Charles Kray in 1975 when, as managing director of Everest Books, he published the first edition of this autobiography.

He lives in Kent with his wife, Sue, and golden labrador, Cassie, and has three daughters and a son from his first marriage.

CHARLES KRAY WITH
ROBIN MCGIBBON

ME AND
MY BROTHERS

HarperCollins*Publishers*

HarperCollins*Publishers*
77–85 Fulham Palace Road,
Hammersmith, London W6 8JB

This paperback edition 1994
1 3 5 7 9 8 6 4 2

First published in Great Britain by
Grafton, an imprint of HarperCollins*Publishers* 1988
Reprinted ten times

ISBN 0 586 20113 0

Set in Times

Printed in Great Britain by
HarperCollinsManufacturing Glasgow

Author's Note

We all make mistakes, and I made one when I came out of Maidstone Prison in 1975 and decided to write my autobiography. I was skint and I wanted a book out as fast as possible to earn a few quid. I knew I had an interesting story to tell, about my own colourful life in the East End, as well as the twins' more spectacular exploits. But, thirteen years ago, fresh out of nick, I was more eager to cash in on the Kray name than to write a no-holds-barred blockbuster.

Not surprisingly, *Me and My Brothers*, first time round, failed to make any ripples in the publishing pond. Mostly everyone – Ronnie and Reggie included – hated it. And so did I. Like many things done for the wrong reasons, the book lacked emotion, conviction and, I have to admit, honesty.

Thanks to Grafton, I have been given a second bite at the cherry – a chance to say some of the things I didn't, or couldn't, say first time. I'm grateful for the opportunity because, quite frankly, some of the rubbish that's been said and written about me and my brothers over the years has given me the right hump.

But the book is more than just the story of how the twins ended up incarcerated for life. It is about me, too, and how the twins' waywardness affected me. Thirteen years ago, family loyalty made it impossible for me to reveal all about an event that destroyed my life. But the twins have told the truth about that and, now, so have I. I am able, also, to reveal the awful truth behind the sensational crime-and-sex mystery, involving my wife and a notorious villain, that dominated the papers in the early seventies.

Yes, I'm pleased to be given the chance to tell my story the way I should have told it thirteen years ago. I hope it now has the emotion and conviction it lacked before.

I know it has the honesty.

I would like to offer special thanks to Sue McGibbon, not only for the welcome stream of coffee that kept my memories flowing, but also for the long hours, willingly spent, transcribing then typing the finished product.

Charles Kray
South London
October 1987

This book is for my mother and father,
who will be forever in my thoughts.

Chapter One

The ringing of the phone brought me out of a deep sleep. Through half-closed eyes I squinted at my watch on the bedside table: 5.15 A.M. I took the phone from its cradle. 'Hello,' I muttered, husky from tiredness. An unfamiliar woman's voice apologized for waking me, then spoke quietly in an abrupt, businesslike manner. I heard what she said, but I couldn't take it in. Didn't want to. I thought I must be still asleep. Numb with shock, I passed the phone to Diana, lying next to me. She listened for a few moments, thanked the caller, then stretched past me to put the phone down. She looked at me and shook her head, sadly. 'I'm afraid it's true, Charlie.'

In a daze, I got out of bed and shuffled, zombie-like, downstairs into the lounge. I took a bottle of Remy Martin from the cocktail cabinet and filled a long tumbler, then I gulped the brandy fast, again and again, until it was gone. Diana came into the room in her dressing gown. We stared at each other in shock. I went to say something but no words came out. And then she moved towards me and put her arms round me and I started to sob.

That morning at my home in South-East London was the worst moment of my life. Worse than the day I was jailed for ten years for a crime I didn't commit. Worse than being charged with a murder I knew nothing about. But my tears that morning of 5 August 1982 were not only for myself; they were for my twin brothers, Ronnie and Reggie, too. And for our old man.

How on earth were they going to take it when I told

them that the woman we all worshipped, the lovely lady we thought would live for ever, was dead?

She had gone into hospital just three days earlier. We all thought it was just a check-up for pneumonia: a week or two and she'd be out as fit as ever. I'd gone in to see her that day. She was the same old Mum, bright and cheerful, full of life. She wasn't in two minutes and the nurses loved her. It was coming up to her birthday and she had all her cards by her bedside. She looked as good as gold.

Then she had the test she had gone in for and when I went in the next day she was hot and flustered. I'd never seen her like that before. She said she could never have anything like that again. I think the test embarrassed her, apart from the pain.

The next day she was lying there, her eyes closed. She wouldn't open them; perhaps she couldn't. Softly, I told her I was there. She didn't answer. One of the old ladies in another bed, who had made friends with Mum, called me over and said there was something wrong: Mum hadn't been at all well. I went back to Mum and spoke to her again and she answered me. She was hot. I put a damp cloth on her forehead. But she began to get delirious. I called a nurse who said Mum had pneumonia. I didn't believe her; she had been all right the day before. But the nurse shook her head. Then she said the doctor wanted to see me.

He broke the news as gently as he could. Mum *did* have pneumonia. But she had cancer, too. Bad. He wanted to operate, but he needed to clear the pneumonia first.

Hearing the dreaded word 'cancer' knocked me bandy. I'd thought we'd get over the pneumonia, then take her away somewhere nice to get well again. She had many years to live yet. All her family lived on: she had a brother of 88, an aunt of 102. My mum was one of the fittest. She was going to live for ever.

I gave the doctor my phone number 'in case of an emergency'. I didn't expect it to come to anything. Then Diana and I left the hospital. I was in a daze.

Early the next morning, that phone call came. The cancer had taken my mum on her seventy-third birthday.

The brandy must have done me good. I didn't feel it at the time, but it must have helped me pull myself together, helped me to be strong. I had no choice. There would be a lot to do, and with my brothers in prison and our father ill I was the only one to do it. To begin with, they each had to be told. But who first? As usual, I found myself in the middle. From the moment the twins were born, they had dominated the household and, eventually, my whole life. But on that August morning they came second. It would break him, I knew, but my old man had to be the first to know.

An hour or so later, at about seven o'clock, Diana and I arrived at Braithwaite House, my parents' council flat in Bunhill Row, in the City of London.

'What's going on at this time in the morning?' the old man wanted to know.

I'd decided there was no point in mucking about. I told him to sit down, then I took a deep breath and said, 'Unfortunately, she's just died.'

Almost before I'd got the words out he began to scream. I'd never seen him show so much emotion. It just knocked him over. He was very ill and after those first shock waves, he found it difficult to breathe. He kept panting, saying, 'I can't believe it. How can she die before me? I won't be long. It's just a matter of time. I'm waiting for it now.'

My old man, bless him, didn't have to wait long to join

his beloved Violet. That morning he lost the will to live and was dead eight months later.

I decided to tell Ronnie next. Wednesday was not a normal visiting day at Broadmoor, but I could be there in little over an hour if I was allowed to see him; the train – boat – taxi journey to Reggie on the Isle of Wight would take about five. Broadmoor's director told me to come immediately and agreed to say nothing to Ron. But I wasn't thinking straight when I asked Parkhurst to keep the news from Reggie until I got there the next day.

'That's not going to be easy, Charlie,' said a prison officer I knew from previous visits. 'He's got his radio in his cell. We can't take that away. Anyway, someone else will hear.'

I didn't say anything. The thought hadn't occurred to me.

'Charlie,' the welfare officer said, 'if you can trust me . . . I've been with Reggie for years. I'll take him somewhere quietly and tell him myself.'

I thought hard. I knew the officer quite well; I felt I *could* trust him. He was right. If Reggie heard on the radio . . .

'Would you do that for me, please?' I said.

Diana and I got to Broadmoor at about eleven o'clock. The authorities were very kind: they took us into the hospital wing, where visitors aren't usually allowed. They had got a little room for us. A few moments later Ronnie came in, looking concerned. He said later he thought it was odd, us being in that room. When he sat down I looked at him and said gently, 'Ron, our mother's passed away.'

He just broke down, as I knew he would. He leaned forward, put his head in his hands and burst out crying.

I'd had a bit of time to get over the shock, but Ronnie started me off again.

Finally he said in his quiet voice, 'I thought you were going to say our father had died.' Then a few moments later: 'We expected that. But never in a million years, Mum. Why did it happen to her?'

The three of us sat there for about an hour, remembering how lovely she had been, and then I said I had to go; I had a lot to do. As we got up Ronnie said, 'Could you ask them if I can stay here a bit? I want to be on my own.'

The nurses were very kind. 'Don't worry, Charlie,' they said. 'He won't be disturbed. We'll leave him.'

Ronnie stayed in that little room for four hours.

That afternoon the welfare officer at Parkhurst rang me to say he'd broken the news to Reggie.

'How is he?' I asked.

'Better now,' the officer said. 'He broke down. But I told him you'll be here tomorrow and he's waiting to see you. He'll feel better when you're here.'

Someone else telling him was not the same as me, though. When Diana and I met him in a private room at the prison, Reggie broke his heart. And, of course, it started Di and me off again.

Tragedy always brings people closer together and I don't think I've ever been closer to my brothers than those two days when we shared the same grief.

We didn't want a circus. We wanted a funeral our Mum would have been proud of, a funeral people would remember. George English, an undertaker from Hoxton, had buried my grandparents and I knew he would do things the way we wanted. Ronnie and Reggie were given permission to attend the funeral at Chingford Mount in

Essex. It would be the first time they had seen the outside world in fourteen years.

Crowds packed the streets from my mother's flat through the East End. The media brought out many out of curiosity, I suppose, but hundreds came out of respect; not only for my mother, but for the family as a whole. The number of wreaths amazed us: they filled eight cars. So many friends were there: from people my mum had known all her life, to some she had met through her sons in recent years. Diana Dors was there with her husband, dear Alan Lake, and Andrew Ray.

And so, of course, were the police. I don't know what they thought was going to happen, but for a couple of hours that afternoon of 24 August the village of Chingford looked like a setting for a war movie. Police on foot and on motorbikes lined the main street. A helicopter circled noisily overhead. There were even two officers in trees with walkie-talkies.

When we were all assembled in the tiny church of St John's, Ronnie was brought in, then Reggie, each hand-cuffed to a giant policeman. The one escorting Reggie was no less than six feet seven! I had reserved the front row to the right of the nave for the twins, just in front of my old man, Diana, myself and Gary. But Ronnie was led to the front row on the left. He listened to the service for his dead mother out of sight and touch of his family. Reggie sat in front of us.

After the service, the twins were led out swiftly and taken to Chingford Mount police station. While their mother was being lowered into her grave, the twins sat in a room, surrounded by fifty coppers.

The old man was marvellous that day. He was desperately ill, but he managed to stand up in the church and at the graveside. He was very proud; if anyone tried to help him, he'd pull his arm away. He wanted to do things by himself, even though he wasn't strong enough. How he managed to get through it all, I don't know.

He was terribly upset by all the police fuss; he knew it was all unnecessary. I tried to convince him everything had gone well, that Mum would have been pleased, but he felt it was too much like a circus. As we left the graveside he said firmly, 'If anything happens to me, I don't want all this.'

The twins made sure that request was granted. When the old man went the following April each one decided independently not to go to the funeral. They wanted to, of course, but they didn't want a repeat performance. At the time, officials at Broadmoor and Parkhurst rang me to say that permission would be given. I told them the twins wouldn't be going and it threw them back a bit. They didn't expect that.

But then they didn't understand the twins. They still don't. If anyone in authority had the slightest clue what my brothers are about, our mother's funeral would have been handled differently and given the dignity and respect that she deserved and we all wanted.

How daft and unnecessary to separate the twins from each other and their family, and to handcuff them to strangers throughout the most harrowing ordeal of their lives. How irresponsible and wasteful to employ enough men to control a football match. And how crazy and insensitive to banish the twins from the graveside and guard them with *fifty* men in a police station while their mother was being buried.

The government and its servants were more concerned that August day with a massive, well-orchestrated propaganda exercise; a show of strength to the nation for reasons known only to themselves. I don't know how much the whole business cost the taxpayer: £30,000 has been mentioned. But what I do know – and what the

13

authorities themselves should have known if they truly believe in penal reform – is that Messrs Ronald and Reginald Kray could have been trusted to go to that funeral on their own. And to return afterwards.

They respected and adored their mother too much even to consider doing anything else.

Chapter Two

Respect was something Mum had always commanded. She had a wonderfully sunny attitude to life, always laughing, always happy. I never once heard her criticize anybody or complain. As a woman she was immensely popular: always upbeat and chatty, but never gossipy. As a mother she was unbeatable, simply the tops. And I have her to thank for giving me a wonderful, happy and secure childhood in an East End that suffered as much as anywhere from the Depression that bit in to Britain in the late twenties and thirties. Hungry children roamed around Hackney in rags, stealing food from barrows and shops. But I was always well fed and dressed in smart, clean clothes; one vivid memory is of being taken for a walk in a strikingly fashionable sailor suit and noticing other children with holes in their trousers.

Millions throughout the country were penniless, but my old man made sure there was always money in our home in Gorsuch Street, off Hackney Road. He was a dealer who called on houses buying up gold and silver – anything of value, in fact. 'On the knocker' it was called. And he was good at it. The job meant he was away from home a lot; when he wasn't 'on the knocker' he was selling the goods on the street stalls that had been in his family for fifty years. And even when he was at home he went down the pub nearly every night, like most men at that time. It didn't bother Mum; she seemed happy to stay at home looking after me and go out with him just once or twice a month.

The old man was sport-mad and was chuffed when I

was picked to play football for Laburnum Street School. He always made sure I had the right gear, and when he came to watch I'm sure he took an extra pride in seeing that his kid was one of the best-dressed players on the pitch. Boxing was his passion, though, and when he wasn't in the pub he would go to professional contests at nearby Hoxton Baths, or other venues. Sometimes, he would take me. I can remember sitting in the crowd in my sailor suit, entranced by the sight of giants thumping hell out of each other.

The old man's father, who ran a stall in Hoxton, could handle himself. He was known as 'Big' Jimmy Kray and was afraid of nobody. I used to sit on his knee at home as he told me thrilling stories of famous boxers he had known, including Hoxton's own hero, Ted 'Kid' Lewis, who became world lightweight champion. Often I'd go to bed, my six-year-old head filled both with these stories and with the real thing I'd seen with Dad, and I would dream of standing in a ring, the treasured Lonsdale belt round my middle, as the cheering crowd hailed me Champion of the World.

The brutality of East End life, where most disputes were settled with fists, rubbed off on the children: it was not uncommon for two tiny tearaways to slug it out with the venom of the fighters I'd seen in the ring. I was one of them. I didn't get involved too often but I quickly learned how to handle myself. Mum didn't approve of fighting, however, and wasn't too impressed that I'd inherited Grandad's natural boxing ability. Whenever I had a scrap at school I made sure I tidied myself up before going home.

In 1932, we moved to Stean Street, the other side of Kingsland Street. Just along from our new home was a stable yard, and the old man who looked after it let us kids play there. It was an exciting place and I spent a lot of time sitting on a wall, watching the man mucking out and grooming the horses when they came in after hauling the delivery carts. I would go home smelling of manure and with muddy shoes. Mum would tell me off, but in a nice way. She never screamed and yelled like other women in that street . . .

One day a year later, when I was seven, I was encouraged to go out and play and not come back until called. Curious, and not a little put out, I watched the house from my wall for most of the day. There was a lot of coming and going and then, in the early evening, I was told I could go in. I went up to my mum's bedroom and there they were.

'Where did they come from?' I asked.

'I bought them,' my mum replied.

'But, Mum,' I said. 'Why did you buy two?'

She laughed.

It was a little after eight o'clock on 24 October 1933. My twin brothers had arrived.

Suddenly my aunts May and Rose started coming round to the house more than usual. They adored the twins and begged Mum to let them take them for walks in their brand-new pram. Mum usually agreed and May and Rose would fuss over them like mother hens with their chicks. When Mum was busy I would take them out too, and, like my aunts, I would feel a surge of pride when neighbours stopped to lean over the pram, enthusing about how gorgeous they were. The twins, of course, lapped it up. It did not take long for them to expect to be the centre of attention all the time. And to show their displeasure when they weren't.

The Kray family was already well known. Big Jimmy Kray, and Mum's dad, Jimmy Lee, worked for themselves, and their independence was envied by less

17

ambitious people who were forced to do what they were told.

Jimmy Lee was a legend in his own time. He had been a bare-knuckle fighter with the nickname 'Cannonball' and he later became a showman and entrepreneur. In an area where competition was tough he was an outstanding personality. He was teetotal, which meant he didn't hit it off with the old man, but he was very fond of me and the twins. He loved entertaining us: his favourite trick involved a white-hot poker which he would lick without burning his tongue. He gave us a scientific explanation – something about the saliva making contact with the hot metal – but it went over our heads. To us it was just pure magic.

He'd always been an amazing athlete. Once, one of his sons – my Uncle Johnnie – drove a coach party forty-two miles to Southend for the day. As he was preparing to bring them back again, Grandfather Lee turned up – on his bike. He'd cycled there just for the fun of it and was eager to do the return journey, until Uncle Johnnie insisted he took the coach. Grandfather Lee was seventy-five years young at the time.

In those early thirties, the Kray family had a sort of local fame. And in their own way the beautifully dressed, scrubbed-clean twins, sitting up in their big double pram, beaming into the faces of all their admirers, were just as famous as their grandfathers.

I was thrust into the background but I didn't resent my brothers. If anything I was pleased, because Mum was obviously overjoyed at having them. At night I shared the same upstairs room with them, because Mum's brother and his family were living downstairs. But neither twin cried much at night and they never disturbed my sleep. When they were put in their cots I would stare at them, trying in vain to tell which was which. Sometimes they

18

looked up at me in a strange, adult sort of way, and I'd have this weird feeling that they knew all about me and what was going on around them. Their dark eyes seemed to lack that childlike innocence. It was as if each boy knew more than he ought to.

The mental and physical relationship between them was intense. Nobody was more aware of it than Mum – the only person who could tell them apart – and she demonstrated this when Reggie became ill at the age of two. Whenever he got excited his face would turn blue and sometimes he would fall down, screaming in pain. The doctor diagnosed a double hernia and sent Reggie into hospital for an operation. It wasn't long before Ronnie started to get ill himself at being separated from his twin. And when Reggie failed to improve after the operation, Mum took matters into her own hands. One day she marched into the hospital and announced she was taking Reggie home. Shocked doctors and nurses told her he was not ready to be discharged and insisted he would be better off in trained care. But Mum was adamant; she said quietly but firmly that the child needed to be with his mother and twin brother and that was that. She was proved right. Within days of being reunited, both boys were back to normal.

While my brothers were toddling about that house in Stean Street I spent most of my spare time running. Like Grandfather Lee I was sport-crazy and as well as soccer I was involved in athletics then boxing. At my senior school in Scawfell Street, off Hackney Road, I was a tiddler in a big pond, but a marvellous all-rounder called Gregory helped me achieve a sporting triumph I'll never forget. He was the school goalkeeper and wicketkeeper, and it was largely due to him that I got in the school football team that won the district finals. Gregory boxed well, too, and gave me tips on how to improve my ring-craft.

In the East End in those days, violence was never far below the surface; settling a disagreement with fists was the accepted thing. I forget the name of the boy I swapped punches with in my first serious street fight, but I do remember a crowd of adults loved every bruising minute of it. They formed a circle and watched us slug it out for nearly an hour. Afterwards they made us shake hands, as though we'd been fighting purely for their entertainment.

There was a wood yard in Hackney Wick where local villains settled disputes between rival gangs. Sometimes the punch-ups would not take place and the gangs would drift off to a pub together. Often, though, a chance remark would upset somebody and fighting would break out. Razors and broken glasses would be used as weapons and blood would flow.

That was the way of East End life in 1938 as we began to hear stories of a little thin-faced German madman with a moustache who wanted to conquer the world.

The old man's business boomed at that time. The factories and docks took thousands off the dole queues and there was more money about. Cash registers sang in the pubs as people talked over their pints about the prospect of war. And householders eagerly chucked out their old gear to make way for the new.

Oswald Mosley's fanatical Blackshirt mob marched noisily through Mile End and Whitechapel, striking terror into the Jews. But for me football, as usual, was far more important. One day the old man came home with a new pair of football boots for me; they were the latest style and very expensive. We had a game at the local recreation ground that afternoon and I couldn't wait to try them out. I trotted off excitedly, the boots dangling by the laces over one shoulder. Suddenly, as I walked under a railway arch, three kids grabbed the boots and ran off. I sprinted after them, shouting as loudly as I could. They dodged round corners, clambered over walls, crossed roads, but I kept after them. It was worth it: first, they dropped my socks, which had been inside the boots, then the boots themselves. I picked them up then dashed back to the park, making it in time for the game.

When I got home, I told the old man what had happened. He listened intently, then patted me affectionately on the shoulder. 'You're a real trier, son,' he said. 'A real trier.' At that moment, I'd never felt closer to him.

Don't get me wrong. Although the old man was away a lot, he was a good father. He loved the booze, but he never put that before his wife and kids. Unlike many East End wives Mum never had to go out to work, which meant that the twins and I were never left to roam the streets like other children.

I can remember only one time when she had the hump with me. I came running along the courtyard where we lived and crashed through the front swing door frightening the life out of her. I was twelve at the time and thought it was a funny practical joke. But Mum was angrier than I'd ever seen her. Her blue eyes hardened and she shouted, 'I'm going to whack you for that, Charlie!'

This terrified me because Mum always spoke in a soft, calm voice. But she didn't hit me; she would not have known how to. The old man handed out a few whacks, but I was a bit of a mummy's boy and she would always step in and put it right for me.

Mum had great will-power. Once she had set her heart on getting something she would persevere until she got it. She had no ambition in life but to bring up her children as well as possible, and she placed a lot of importance on having her own house, with a back garden and a front door that wasn't shared. One day, Aunt Rose came round excitedly, saying her next-door neighbours were leaving.

Something in Mum's reaction told me we would soon be on the move ourselves – to that house. I was not mistaken.

Vallance Road runs between Whitechapel Road and Bethnal Green Road for about half a mile and is roughly parallel to Commercial Street, which lies to the west. Number 178 was a terraced house with two rooms, a kitchen and a scullery downstairs, and an outside loo. Upstairs there were three rooms and out of two of them we could see the trains thundering along a raised track between Liverpool Street and Bethnal Green stations. When we moved in late that summer of 1939 it was just a humble East End house. But it was not long before Mum made it into a warm, happy and secure home.

With the excitement of moving, the outbreak of war meant little to the twins and me. We'd been told that enemy planes would be dropping bombs on to our home, but all we could see around us were sandbags being packed around public buildings, gas masks being handed out, and men in makeshift uniforms dashing about. When I wasn't at school, I was playing football, running or boxing. The twins, coming up to their sixth birthday, spent their time either with Aunts May and Rose, Grandpa and Grandma Lee, nearby, or in Uncle Johnnie's cafe across the street. If it was time to eat, they would be at home. They loved Mum's cooking.

The twins were fascinated by Grandfather Lee's stories of when he fought bare-knuckle in Victoria Park for a few shillings on Sunday mornings and whenever I knelt down to spar with them they shaped up like miniature prize-fighters. Even at six, they were tough and incredibly fearless, and sometimes they would catch me with a punch that surprised me with its speed, accuracy and power.

When the bombs began to fall and the anti-aircraft guns opened up, the twins showed no fear. They had always been content in each other's company and in the Blitz

22

that contentment deepened into security. While other kids cried in terror as the shells dropped, the twins just clung on to each other's clothes and shut their eyes. And when Mum said she was taking us to the shelter under the railway arches they would toddle along unconcernedly, hand in hand, more excited than afraid.

But the East End in the Blitz was no place for kids, and soon someone somewhere decided women and children should go away until it was all over. Mum didn't fancy the idea much; she had only just moved into her long-sought-after house. But as usual the twins and I came first, and she prepared for our evacuation. The old man wasn't coming. His business was still booming and he needed to stay in London. He would be recruited into the Army, of course. But he had other plans for when his call-up papers arrived.

We had no idea where we were going. All we were told was that we would be living in a house in a country village, fifty miles further east of London. To many, the massive exodus from Liverpool Street Station that January in 1940, was The Evacuation. But to the twins and I, who had seldom left the narrow, crowded streets of Bethnal Green, it was An Adventure.

The village was Hadleigh, in Suffolk, and the house was a huge Victorian building belonging to a widow called Mrs Styles. After the cramped terraced house in Vallance Road it was a palace, and Mrs Styles went out of her way to help us adapt to the traumatic change in our lives.

I quickly got a job in the local fish-and-chip shop and later worked full-time as a tea boy in a factory making mattresses. The people there were friendly, but we didn't have much in common and I missed the East End, particularly my football and boxing. The twins, though, were happier than ever. In fine weather they would spend hours scouring the fields and woods for miles around, revelling in the fresh air and boundless freedom of country life. When the snow came, Mrs Styles's nephew lent me his sledge and I'd take the twins to the nearest hill. I'd lay full-length on the sledge with the twins on my back and push off. We nearly always ended up in a heap of tangled arms and legs, laughing. It was great fun.

Mum, however, was not enjoying being away from her family and friends. She never complained, but I sensed her unhappiness, especially when the old man visited us. He was popular in the local pub, with his news of what was going on in London, but he was always keen to get back after a day or two.

We'd been in Hadleigh for about a year when rumours of a German invasion on the east coast started sweeping the village. Mum got more and more worried until one day she announced that she was taking us back to London.

Mrs Styles tried to dissuade her, but Mum said she had given it a lot of thought and her mind was made up. Later, it was found that the rumours were unfounded, but by then it was too late: Mum and I and the twins were back in Vallance Road. I was pleased; I couldn't wait to see my mates and take up boxing again. But the twins were not. They had fallen in love with the countryside and preferred green fields and animals to teeming streets and noisy traffic.

The old man's call-up papers finally arrived. He'd made up his mind that he wasn't going to serve, and promptly went on what was called the 'trot'. He reasoned that he didn't start the war, so why should he help finish it? The police called at the house from time to time looking for him, but the twins and I had been told to say nothing. Lying for the old man didn't bother me; he was my dad and he'd done his best for all of us all his life. Now I was

24

in a position to do my best for him, and I lied without so much as a blush.

It did affect the twins, though. Soon they started seeing the coppers' uniform as The Enemy. Aunt Rose didn't help; if she was around, she'd have a right go at the officers, four-letter words and all. If the twins were there, they would stand side by side, gravely taking it all in. Whatever they thought, they kept to themselves, but I had a feeling then, even though they were just eight, that they were beginning to distrust uniformed authority.

With so many men in the Army there were plenty of jobs, and I became a messenger boy at Lloyd's in the City, within walking distance of Vallance Road. For five and a half days a week, I was general dogsbody for eighteen bob. In the old man's absence, I wanted to do my bit as the man of the house, so every Friday night I proudly gave Mum my wages. She didn't need the money, but she took it to make me feel good. Needless to say, I got most of it back during the week, one way and another.

Boxing now dominated my spare time. I went to the local institute for training three nights a week and Grandfather Lee fixed up a punchbag in the top back room of our house. The twins would watch me hammering away, and now and then I'd stand them on a chair so they could have a go. Mum wasn't that keen on the preoccupation with boxing; she probably remembered her dad coming home from Victoria Park, looking the worse for wear after his bare-knuckle scraps. But when I told her amateur boxing was safe and the gloves were like feather pillows, she seemed satisfied. Anyway, she didn't put up much of a fight. I suppose she thought boxing was the lesser of two evils: if I wasn't down the institute, I'd more than likely get into bad company – or worse, start showing an interest in girls. Both had their dangers: if boys of my age weren't breaking into shops or factories, they were going too far with girls and walking down the aisle almost before they'd drawn their first pay packet. I think Mum was secretly pleased that my only passion at that time was not for kissing the opposite sex but for belting the daylights out of the boy in the opposite corner.

I had not touched alcohol or smoked a cigarette. I was as fit as a fifteen-year-old can be. And then suddenly I was whipped into hospital with a mystery illness that was to terrify me so much I thought of killing myself.

It started with a sore throat. Gargling with salt water did no good, so Mum took me to hospital where doctors wasted no time taking me in. I was put in a bed and told to do nothing but lie still; I wasn't even allowed to get up to go to the toilet. The illness was diagnosed as rheumatic fever and it kept me in that hospital for four weeks. The enforced idleness was maddening and I counted the minutes and hours between the visits of Mum, my aunts and my friends. Lying on my back helpless for a few weeks was one thing, but then I learned that I might become a permanent invalid with a heart condition. I was terrified. For someone so energetic the thought was too much to bear and it was then that I seriously thought about doing myself in.

In the end, the Germans saved my life. They scored a direct hit on the hospital and in the pandemonium I walked, unsteadily and unnoticed, out of the ward and down the stairs. In view of the things I'd heard, I expected to drop dead any minute, but nothing happened and the next day Mum took me home. For the next week or so the old man – still 'on the trot' – took a risk and stayed with me day and night. And then, one morning, I felt well enough to get up. Touch wood, I've been as right as ninepence ever since – a walking miracle, according to the doctors.

Before I was taken ill, I'd graduated from the Coronet

junior club to Crown and Manor youth club in Hoxton, and as soon as I'd recovered from the rheumatic fever I took up boxing again. I also joined the naval cadets at Hackney Wick, where the training facilities were good, and it wasn't long before I started taking the sport very seriously. I'd been a very useful welterweight, and the idea of turning pro appealed to me: a good crowd-pleaser could earn as much as ten quid for four three-minute rounds. There was also the handy bonus of 'nobbins' – coins thrown into the ring by satisfied customers – although boxers often came off second best to their helpers. Try picking up a handful of coins wearing boxing gloves and you'll see what I mean.

When the twins saw some of the cutlery, glassware and trophies I won as an amateur they felt boxing might be for them, too, and they joined me in my early-morning road running, copying my side-stepping and shadow-boxing in the streets around Vallance Road. They were so enthusiastic that I turned an upstairs room into a sort of gym, with a speedball, punchbag, skipping ropes and weights. I found some boxing gloves to fit the twins and started to teach them. We were at it every day. It used to drive them mad, I suppose: keep that guard up, shoot out that left, duck, weave, watch that guard now, keep the left going . . . Ronnie was a southpaw; he led with his right. I corrected this by tying his right arm down, so that he couldn't move it.

The twins loved that little gym and it wasn't long before they started inviting their mates round for some sparring. I'd come home in the evenings to find the room full of kids, all waiting for me to get them organized. After a while, I started arranging contests and bought books and things to give the winners as prizes. The kids adored it. That gym was like their own little club.

Mum made sure all our gear was the cleanest by

washing it every day, and the old man even cleaned and ironed the laces on our boxing boots. Mum didn't come upstairs much, except to bring the boys tea and sandwiches. But as long as no one was getting hurt she didn't mind all the noise and running around. She loved having kids in the house and the Kray home got a reputation for always being full up.

A year later the twins showed so much promise that I took them to the Robert Browning Institute in Walworth, near the Elephant and Castle in South London. One of the resident trainers watched them in the ring, a look of amazement on his face. 'How old did you say they were, Charlie?' he asked.

'Ten,' I said.

'Are you sure they haven't been in the ring before?'

'Absolutely,' I replied proudly.

'They're amazing,' the trainer said. 'Bloody amazing.'

'So you want them in the club?'

'Definitely.'

And so the short-lived but sensational career of the young Kray twins was born.

My own career in the ring was about to take off, too – courtesy of the Royal Navy. I decided to volunteer for the Navy before being called up and sent into the Army, which I didn't fancy. I joined towards the end of the war, but my boxing reputation preceded me, and I spent most of my active service representing the Navy as a welterweight against the Army and Air Force.

After the war, contests were arranged to keep the men entertained while they waited to be demobbed. I found myself boxing roughly twice a week in various parts of the country. Whether it was the pressure of these fights or the legacy of my rheumatic fever I don't know, but I suddenly developed chronic migraine and was discharged from the Navy on health grounds.

I was thrilled to return home to find that my little twin brothers had become quite famous locally with their spectacular triumphs in the ring. They had fought locally and nationally with outstanding success. In the prestigious London Schools competition they got to the final three years running and had to fight each other.

I shall never forget the third encounter at York Hall in Bethnal Green; it was a classic. I went in the dressing room beforehand and told them to take it easy and put on a good show. Ronnie was as calm as ever, but Reggie was extra keyed up. He had lost the previous two fights and I sensed he'd made up his mind he was going to win this one.

The announcements ended. The bell rang. And to the deafening roar of a thousand or so school kids the tenacious thirteen-year-old twins came out of their corners to do battle: Reggie the skilful boxer, Ronnie the fighter, who never knew when he was beaten. For three two-minute rounds they were totally absorbed, both committed to winning. They were belting each other so hard and so often that Mum and the old man wanted to get in the ring and stop it and it was all I could do to restrain them, although the battle got so bloody in the final round that I nearly shouted 'Stop!' myself.

The judges found it difficult telling the twins apart in the first part of the fight but they had no trouble towards the end: Ronnie's face was a mess and Reggie got a unanimous verdict.

Afterwards, in the dressing room, Mum laid into them. She was horrified at the sight of her two babies knocking the daylights out of each other and told them in no uncertain terms that they would never appear together in a ring again as long as she was alive.

The twins burst into tears. But they never did fight each other again.

Back in civvy street again, I teamed up with the old man on the knocker, and dedicated myself to boxing. The Kray fame began to spread. Three brothers – two of them identical twins – chalking up one victory after another was hot local news, and suddenly our photographs were all over the *East London Advertiser*, with reports of our fights.

Mum hated boxing, but she always came to our fights with her sisters; she felt she had a duty to be there. We used to laugh at her because she admitted that half the time she didn't look. She tried to talk us out of it, saying, 'Do you really want to end up disfigured?' And if one of us got hurt, she'd say, 'You've got to stop – it's no good for you.' But in the end she gave up because she realized we loved the sport.

As boxers, the twins were quite different from each other: Reggie was the cool, cautious one, with all the skills of a potential champion and, importantly, he always listened to advice. Ronnie was a good boxer too, and very brave. But he never listened to advice. He was a very determined boy with a mind of his own. If he made up his mind to do something, he'd do it, no matter what, and unlike Reggie he would never hold back. He would go on and on until he dropped.

A trainer told me, 'I know Ronnie doesn't listen half the time. But he's got so much determination that he'd knock a wall down if I told him to.'

Once, at Lime Grove Baths in West London, Ronnie was fighting a boy Reggie had knocked out a few months before. In the dressing room, I warned Ronnie, 'This lad can punch. If he catches you, you'll be over, I promise.'

Ronnie nodded. But I sensed he wasn't listening.

In the first round, his opponent threw a huge overhead punch. Everyone round the ring saw it, but not Ronnie. He almost somersaulted backwards on to the canvas. It seemed all over, but Ronnie rolled over and crawled to his knees, then slowly to his feet. He didn't know where he was, but he survived the round. He was still in another world when he came out for the second and he took a hammering. But when the bell went for the third, his head suddenly cleared and he tore into his opponent, knocking him out after a series of crushing blows to the head.

In the dressing room afterwards, I said, 'That was very clever.'

Ronnie barely looked at me. 'What did you want me to do?'

'I told you to keep your chin down otherwise you'd get knocked over.'

Ronnie looked pained. 'Oh, stop nagging. I won, didn't I?'

Another time, at a dinner-jacket affair at the Sporting Club in London's West End, I took a look at Ronnie's opponent – a tough-looking gypsy type. I knew what to expect and I said to Ronnie, 'He'll be a strong two-handed puncher and he'll come at you from the first bell trying to put you away. So take it easy. Keep out of trouble for a bit.'

But, as usual, Ronnie wasn't too interested in what I had to say. In sport, it's good to have some nerves, it gets you keyed up, helps you perform well. But Ronnie didn't have any nerves. He didn't care.

When the bell sounded the gypsy almost ran from his corner and then started swinging at Ronnie with both hands. Ronnie looked totally shocked. He was battered about the head and forced back against the ropes taking massive lefts and rights to the head.

The gypsy's brothers, sitting near me, grinned. 'That's it. It's all over,' they said triumphantly.

Suddenly Ronnie found his breath. He started ducking out of the way of the gypsy's punches, then got in a few of his own. The gypsy's onslaught stopped. It was all Ronnie needed; he was in, smashing rights and lefts into the face and body as though he was possessed. It was quite devastating.

I knew the signs, and turned to the brothers. 'Yeah. You're right. It *is* all over.'

Less than a minute later the gyspy was being counted out.

I think Ronnie was secretly annoyed with himself for being caught cold because in the communal dressing room afterwards, he acted out of character. He overheard the gypsy moaning to his brothers about being caught unawares. It would never happen again, he said.

Before I could stop him, Ronnie had walked over to them. 'Stop making excuses,' he told the gypsy quietly. 'If you want, I'll do it again. I'll catch you unawares again.'

I stepped in and took Ronnie away. But that was him all over: he always believed that what was done was done and there was no point whingeing or trying to change it. Reggie would always be prepared to discuss matters, but Ronnie was withdrawn and would say, 'I don't want to talk about it.' And he was always right: there would be no argument, no discussion, no possible compromise.

Once, as boys, the twins were due to box at Leyton Baths, and Ronnie did not turn up. Reggie and I waited for him at home, but in the end had to leave without him. We were worried about his safety, naturally, and about the inquiry that would be launched by the boxing board: it was bad news not to turn up for a bout.

A few minutes after we got back home, Ronnie walked in with a school pal, Pat Butler.

'Where the hell were you?' I wanted to know.

'I had to go somewhere with Pat,' was all Ronnie replied.

'You know you could lose your licence.' I was livid.

' I don't care,' Ronnie said. 'Pat was in trouble with some people.'

'You're out of order, Ronnie. You should never not turn up for a fight.'

But Ronnie just shrugged. 'I don't care about not turning up. This was more important to me.'

Then Reggie chimed in. 'You could have helped Pat out tomorrow.'

'No,' Ronnie said, quietly but forcibly. 'It had to be done tonight.'

Reggie and I continued to argue with him, but Ronnie just said, 'Anyway I had to do it and it's done now. I'm not apologizing.'

We pointed out that Mum had stayed at home because she was worried about him. Ronnie was sorry he'd caused her to miss the fight, but otherwise he couldn't care less.

The twins seemed unaffected by their local Press coverage and the local fame that went with it. They still went to school regularly, didn't throw their weight around and were never loud-mouthed, like some kids in the neighbourhood. If anything, they were quiet and modest and always respectful. Someone who saw this side of their character was the Reverend Hetherington, vicar of St James the Great, in Bethnal Green Road. The church youth club, which the twins belonged to, ran jumble sales and other fund-raising functions, and they were always keen to help set up stalls and so on. The twins admired the vicar and went out of their way to oblige him whenever he wanted a favour. He liked them too, and always spoke well of them. That friendship was to last a lifetime.

One night, the vicar was standing in the doorway of the vestry when the twins walked up.

'Can we do anything for you, Father?' Ronnie asked.

Mr Hetherington was a heavy smoker and had a cigarette going at the time. He drew on it. 'No, I don't think so, Ronald.' he said. 'But it's very kind of you to ask. Thank you.'

He asked them one or two questions about what they were doing with themselves and was generally as pleasant and friendly as usual. Then he said good-night and went into his vestry.

Half an hour later he felt in his cassock for his cigarettes and was amazed to find an extra packet. The twins had bought the cigarettes for him. But they knew he would not have accepted them had they offered. So they slipped the packet into one of his pockets without him knowing.

Later, I learned that Mr Hetherington said no when the twins asked if he wanted anything because he always wondered: 'What on earth are they going to do to get it!'

That immediate post-war period in the East End was a happy time. Life was getting back to normal after the horrors of the Blitz, and the family atmosphere Mum created at Vallance Road was warm and cosy and very secure.

As boys, the twins were very disciplined about their boxing. They went to bed early, ate well and regularly, and were almost fanatical about their fitness; they were always pounding the streets early in the morning.

Just after their fourteenth birthdays, however, the twins started to change. For the worse. Suddenly they started staying out late and neglecting their morning roadwork. They became very secretive about where they were going, what they were doing, who they were seeing. Mum was very concerned but she bit her tongue. She put it down to their age: they were probably going through that 'growing up' stage and she didn't want to appear a moaner. But then I discovered the twins were calling in at Aunt Rose's house late at night to clean themselves up before coming home.

The reason for their secrecy was suddenly very clear. They had been fighting in the street and knew that Mum would give them hell if she found out.

The East End had been relatively free of violence during the war and the couple of years after it. But now that the wartime controls were being relaxed, teenagers roamed the streets looking for excitement. It was, perhaps, inevitable that the twins, tough, utterly fearless and locally famous, would be involved, and with their flair for leadership it was hardly surprising that they were out in front when the battles began.

An incident that stands out involved a Jewish shop-owner, aged about seventy who made a point of coming round to our house to say how wonderful the twins were. Apparently they were walking home one night when they saw some boys smash the old man's shop window and help themselves to some of his goods. As they ran off, the twins chased them – not to have them arrested, but to give them a good hiding and to get back what they had stolen. They didn't catch them, but the thieves never came back. The shopowner was very grateful to the twins, but it was nothing to them; they were always eager to help someone in trouble. Once Ronnie pawned a gold ring for a couple of quid to help a kid out. Another time he came home with no shoes. When Mum asked where they were, he said, 'I've just given them to a poor kid who didn't have any.'

They could not stand bullies, especially if our family was involved. When they were fifteen they heard that the old man had been slagged off by a crowd of young blokes in a pub. The old man and some friends were having a singsong when the crowd started taking the mickey out of them.

'Leave us alone,' the old man said. 'We're enjoying ourselves.'

'Who are you, you old bastard?' one of the youths replied, and he went to give him a smack.

One of the old man's friends warned, 'I wouldn't do that if I were you,' and the trouble was stopped.

But a few of the bullying crowd said, 'We're not finished here.'

The next day the old man told Ronnie and Reggie what had happened. 'Who were they?' the twins wanted to know. The old man thought they worked for a chap called Jack Barclay, who owned a big East End store. The twins were round there like a shot.

'Hello, Mr Barclay,' Ronnie said respectfully. He asked for two people by name.

'They're out the back,' replied Mr Barclay.

'Thank you,' said Ronnie. And he walked straight through with Reggie and confronted the two bullies.

'You had a go at our old man last night. And we don't like it.'

With that, Ronnie floored one of the guys and Reggie did the other. Then they went out, saying goodbye to Mr Barclay on the way.

Several times in that long hot summer of 1948, I talked to the twins. I tried to tell them what fools they were; that the only place they should be fighting was in the ring, where they could made a *good* name for themselves. I should have saved my breath. My twin brothers were not interested in what I had to say or what I felt. They were not fifteen yet, but almost overnight they had become men and nobody, not even their elder brother, was going to tell them what to do.

Adolescence, tragically, had passed the Kray twins by.

Chapter Three

My own life as I entered my twenties was going along nicely. I was earning a few quid with the old man. My boxing was fine; I was winning most of my fights and thinking seriously of turning pro.

And then I fell in love.

I was dedicated to fighting. I trained hard and nearly always went to bed early. But every sportsman needs a break some time, a chance to unwind, and one of the favourite places to do that in the East End was the Bow Civic dance hall. It was there that I met a stunning blonde who lived in nearby Poplar, the youngest of four sisters and a very talented dressmaker. She was two years younger than me and we hit it off immediately. We soon started going out seriously together.

Her name was Dorothy Moore and we felt we were destined to get married.

Mum and the old man approved of Dolly, and wedding bells rang out for us on Christmas Day 1948. Mum solved our housing problem by dismantling the gym in Vallance Road and redecorating and furnishing the room for us. We spent our honeymoon there. A week later I was in the ring at Leyton Baths, cruising to a points win in my first professional fight.

After that, I was much in demand and picked up between five and ten quid a fight. I trained hard and took everything that came my way, hoping to catch the eye of a leading promoter. The twins came to watch me fight at Hoxton, Stepney, West Ham and the famous Mile End arena, eager to pick up tips that might help them in the ring. I gained a reputation as a useful and reliable fighter, and although I didn't have that extra touch of class that makes a champion, I was proud of my skills and my considerable local fame.

Certain necessities were still rationed, but life had more or less got back to normal after the horrors of war. We ate and slept well, and the family atmosphere Mum created for us all at Vallance Road was warm and cosy and very happy.

It seemed too good to last. And it was.

One evening in March, the old man and I came home after working in Bristol and found Mum dreadfully upset. There had been a nasty fight outside a dance hall in Mare Street, Hackney, and a boy had been badly beaten with a length of bicycle chain. The twins had been arrested. Mum couldn't believe it; neither could the old man and I, because the twins had never once needed to use anything other than their fists to settle an argument.

The case went to the Old Bailey. The twins were innocent of the offences with which they were charged and they were rightly acquitted. But they had come face to face with that uniformed authority which they neither respected nor trusted. Just seven months later there was to be a more far-reaching and damaging confrontation.

It was a Saturday evening in October. There had been a fight near a youth club in Mansford Street, off Old Bethnal Green Road, and Police Constable Donald Baynton wanted to know about it. He went up to a group of youths on a corner outside a restaurant. Picking one out, he asked if he had been involved in the fight. The boy shook his head. 'Nothing to do with me.'

PC Baynton went up to the boy and pushed him in the stomach. The boy told him to leave him alone; he said again the fight had had nothing to do with him. The officer poked him in the stomach again.

It was a mistake. The boy was Ronnie. He didn't like the PC's manner one bit.

And he lashed out with a right hook to the jaw.

It wasn't a hard blow; PC Baynton didn't even go down. Ronnie ran off, but not very fast, and Baynton caught him. There was a brief struggle and Ronnie went quietly to Bethnal Green police station.

What happened inside that station during the next few minutes almost certainly changed Ronnie's life for ever.

Reggie heard about the incident from one of Ronnie's friends. Immediately, he went to the police station and waited outside. After a while, PC Baynton came out. Spotting Reggie, he grinned mockingly. 'Oh, the other one now,' he said. 'I've just put your brother in there and given him a good hiding. He ain't so clever now.'

Reggie sneered. 'You won't give me one,' he said. Then he darted into a side street, but not too quickly.

Thinking Reggie was running away, Baynton chased after him. It was his second mistake of the evening. When he turned the corner, Reggie was waiting, and he slammed into the surprised officer's face with a few right- and left-handers then walked away.

I was at home with Mum when someone knocked at the door and told us what had happened. When I got to the police station I couldn't believe it. Ronnie was in a terrible state: blood all over him, his shirt ripped to pieces.

'What the hell happened?' I asked.

Ronnie was still defiant. His eyes hardened. 'They got flash. A load of them came in the cell and gave me a hiding.' He glanced over to some of them watching. 'They all think they're big men. If they want a row it's ten-handed.'

I turned round on them angrily. 'Aren't you lot clever?'

I said sarcastically. 'Not one of you is man enough to fight him on your own.'

'Look, Charlie,' one of them said in a friendly tone. 'We don't want any trouble – any problems.'

'No problems!' I yelled. 'I'm going to cause you plenty of problems. This is diabolical, what's happened here. You're not getting away with beating up a sixteen-year-old kid!'

I started ranting and accused them again of being cowards. They threatened to arrest me and suggested I left. Finally I agreed but I warned them I was taking Ronnie to a doctor.

Later that evening it was bedlam at Vallance Road. Mum was crying her eyes out at the sight of Ronnie's smashed face; Ronnie was trying to console her, saying he was all right and he hadn't hurt the policeman anyway; the old man and I were wondering if we could take legal action. Then there was a knock at the front door. It was an inspector the old man knew from the local nick. PC Baynton was with him, looking the worse for wear. The Inspector wanted to speak to Reggie.

When I said he wasn't in, the Inspector motioned towards Baynton. 'Look what he's done to him,' he said.

'Oh, yeah,' I replied scornfully. 'Come in and have a look at what your officers have done to Ronnie.'

'I don't know anything about that,' the Inspector said.

I made them come in and see Ronnie anyway. 'You're dead worried because one of your men copped a right-hander,' I said. 'Ronnie got more than that – from half a dozen of them.'

The Inspector didn't want to know. All he wanted was to arrest Reggie and charge him with assault. A few minutes later Reggie walked in. After a brief chat I advised him it was best for everyone if he gave himself up, and he did. But I warned the Inspector that if Reggie was so much as touched, I'd blow the whole thing wide open to the papers.

A day or so later, the old man was told the police didn't want to make a song and dance about it unless they were forced to. The twins had to be charged because they had unquestionably assaulted a policeman, but they would be treated leniently – probably just put on probation – if I kept quiet about Ronnie's beating. If I didn't, the police would make it unpleasant for the whole family – starting with nicking the old man for dodging the call-up. I decided to swallow it.

A few days after their seventeenth birthday the twins appeared at Old Street in North London, accused of assault. For some reason, the magistrate, Mr Harold Sturge, praised PC Baynton's courage in a 'cowardly attack'. No mention, however, was made of the cowardly attack behind closed doors at Bethnal Green police station.

Not long afterwards Baynton was moved to a different area. But the PC had fuelled the twins' resentment and distrust of uniformed authority and the legacy of his arrogance that autumn evening was to last a lifetime.

The Baynton episode did nothing to destroy the myth that was growing up around the twins. They were tough and fearless and, in the tradition of the Wild West where the 'fastest guns' were always the target of other sharpshooters, they became marked young men in the East End. Hard nuts from neighbouring districts came looking for them in search of fame and glory as The Kids Who Toppled The Krays. Like the police, they came mob-handed. But they never came back.

One evening Reggie walked into the house at just after ten at night. I told him Ronnie had left a message saying he was in the Coach and Horses with his friend, Pat Butler. It was nearly closing time and I said it was a bit late to go, but Reggie had a strange feeling he ought to. He left quickly. What happened when he got there became the talk of the East End for months.

Ronnie was in the saloon bar with Pat. As Reggie walked in, Ronnie said, 'Just in time.' He nodded to nine youths at the other end of the bar. 'That little firm are looking for us.' ·

A few minutes later, the twins told Pat to make sure he stayed out of the way, then dashed out of the door, as though they were scared. But it was only a ploy to reduce the odds a little. As four of the rival gang followed them into the street, the twins doubled back into the saloon, through the public bar, taking the remaining five by surprise.

It was an almighty battle. Fists flew, chairs were thrown, tables overturned. Although the twins were out-numbered by more than two to one, they floored the whole lot. And when the other four ran back in, they knocked them out too. Amazingly, the twins came out of that scrap virtually unscathed. But one of the kids, Bill Donovan, who Ronnie had hit with a chair, was taken to hospital with a badly damaged eye.

The twins were very concerned about Bill and asked me to ring the hospital. I pretended to be a relation and asked how he was. A nurse said he was stable, but nobody knew if the eye was going to be permanently damaged. It was a worrying few days. The twins kept telling me to ring and eventually, to the twins' relief, we learned Donovan was going to be all right.

Pat Butler told me later that he was in the street after the fight had ended and an old man had asked him who the twins were. He'd never seen anything like it; it was like a scene from a Western.

42

One night a few weeks later the twins were spotted going into a café in Commercial Road. When they came out, they found themselves facing ten members of the so-called Watney Street Gang who, it seemed, were intent on teaching them to stay in Bethnal Green. The twins did not want to risk waiting for the usual preliminaries to a punch-up; they waded into the mob, laying six of them out on the pavement. The rest, not fancying the new odds, ran off.

Incidents like this built up the legend that the twins were tough guys who went around the East End looking for people to punch. That is far-fetched and unfair. What *is* true is that they were tasting power for the first time. They had been accustomed to victory in the ring against one opponent but now they knew they were hard and tough and skilful enough to take on, and beat, eight or nine between them.

And they enjoyed the feeling.

The Albert Hall was packed that night, 11 December 1951. Tommy McGovern, one of my contemporaries at the Robert Browning Institute, was defending his British light-heavyweight championship. And five of the other seven bouts involved Bethnal Green fighters – including the three Kray brothers. It was the first time we had appeared on the same bill together, and it was to be the last.

In those days, a boxer had really arrived when he appeared at the Albert Hall or Harringay Arena; it had taken me eighteen victories in twenty contests. But the twins, who had turned pro in July, had made it there after just six fights – and six wins. That's still a British boxing record.

My appearance almost never happened. I had decided to quit boxing and hadn't been in the ring for several months. But I wanted an extra bit of money for Christmas and agreed to take on an unbeaten Aldgate welterweight called Lew Lazar for twenty-five quid.

We were the first three fights on. First, Ronnie lost to a clever boxer from King's Cross named Bill Sliney, whom Reggie had outpointed two months before. Sliney was not too keen to continue after a first-round mauling by Ronnie, but he was persuaded to, and won a points verdict. Reggie's cool, scientific style earned him an easy points win over Bob Manito, of Clapham, and then it was my turn.

Unfortunately, it was a night when the deafening cheers of the Bethnal Green faithful could not help me. I'd been out of action too long and my timing was haywire. My pride got me to my feet after two counts of nine in the first two rounds, but a left hook in the guts finished me in the third.

I spent some of the twenty-five quid on a white fur coat for my baby son, Gary, who had been born two days after the twins turned pro. But it was my last boxing pay-day. I never put the gloves on in public again. Neither did the twins. For the next two years they were to pit their strength against a very different opponent.

The Army.

The twins filled in their time between call-up and reporting by joining the old man and me on the knocker. But they didn't show much enthusiasm, and it was a relief to them when they were ordered to report at the Tower of London for service with the Royal Fusiliers. They left Vallance Road early one March morning in 1952.

And were back in time for tea.

Mum asked what on earth had happened, but the twins were in a foul temper and refused to tell her. They went out and didn't come back until the early hours when we'd

44

all gone to bed. Later that morning, they were arrested for deserting.

They had, it transpired, reacted badly to uniformed authority once again. An NCO had shouted some orders to them. The twins didn't like his attitude, his lack of respect, and one of them had thumped him. Then they had walked out, deciding Army life wasn't for them.

And after an uncomfortable week's punishment in the guardroom, they walked out again.

To me, it all seemed a terrible waste. Just four months before, they had been promising young boxers with just one minor blot on their record, for which they had been treated leniently. Now they were wanted men facing serious disciplinary action and, almost certainly, jail. I went to see them in hiding in various parts of London, and tried to persuade them to give themselves up. I told them the Forces favoured sportsmen; they could do well with their boxing talent. But it was a waste of breath, as usual. The twins were not going to serve in the Army and that was that.

They stayed on the run until early November, two weeks after their nineteenth birthday. Then one cold, snowy night Reggie suddenly turned up at Vallance Road. Mum was desperately worried for him but Reggie assured her he was all right. He stayed with her for about an hour then left. As he walked into the street, a voice called out, 'Hello, Reg. I'm going to take you in.' It was PC John Fisher, who knew the twins by sight.

Reggie asked him calmly to do him a favour and go away; he didn't want a row. But PC Fisher said he couldn't do that and lunged forward to grab him. Reggie ducked and threw a right hand. PC Fisher fell to the ground and Reggie hurried away in the snow.

It was only a matter of time. The police knew both

twins were in the area and they were picked up a few hours later.

At Thames Street Court that morning the magistrate, Colonel W. E. Batt, jailed them for a month. It was the first time they had seen the inside of a prison as convicted persons.

After their sentence, a military escort took the twins to Wemyss Barracks at Canterbury, Kent, where they were court-martialled for desertion. They escaped yet again, but it was a short-lived freedom and on 12 May 1953 the twins found themselves serving nine months' detention in the notorious military prison of Shepton Mallet in Somerset.

It was to be a tough nine months . . . for the Army! The prison staff at Shepton Mallet had never seen anyone like the twins before, and several sergeants were replaced because they couldn't handle them. The twins were so uncontrollable that the Commanding Officer sought my help. He wondered why it was impossible to get through to the twins with words, why they resolved everything with violence. I tried to explain that life was like that in the East End; if anyone tried to threaten you, you hit them first. It was a world which that polite, charming CO would never understand, and he asked me to have a quiet word with the twins. I agreed to try.

The twins were unimpressed that I'd been having a cosy chat over a cup of tea with the CO; all the guards understood was a punch in the face, they said, and that was what they'd get. Nothing I tried to say cut any ice with them. They simply would not tolerate being ordered around. Tell them to do something and they'd rebel. Ask them, in a civil tone, and they would be fine. Ronnie, particularly, would rebel against a strong person, unless he had reason to respect him. There was one sergeant

46

there they *did* like: he was firm but courteous, and they did what he told them.

The twins didn't always use violence to make their point. One day a military policeman who had been giving Ronnie a hard time was standing outside the cobbler's shop where Ronnie was working. Suddenly Ronnie rushed out, blood all over his face, screaming, 'That's it! I've done it now! It's all over! Better get in there!'

The guard, convinced there had been a murder, dashed off to get reinforcements, but by the time they arrived everything was calm. Ronnie, who had smeared the blood over his face after cutting his hand slightly while working, was back at his bench.

'What the hell happened here?' demanded a senior officer.

Ronnie looked at him blankly. 'Nothing,' he replied. Then he looked at the embarrassed MP. 'He must be going round the bend. Been working too hard or something.'

It is a pity that the NCO at the Tower of London rubbed the twins up the wrong way that March morning in 1952, because I'm sure they could have made something of themselves in the Army. They were fit and strong, and they would have loved the physical side; I'm sure they would have become physical training instructors in no time. They both had a lot of guts, too: once, on an assault course, Ronnie jumped from something and landed awkwardly, crashing his knee sickeningly into his chin. But he forced himself to carry on; he had unbelievable determination and hated quitting anything. They both had a gift for leadership, too, and had it been wartime I feel it would have been a very different story. They were the type who could so easily have distinguished themselves with courage in the face of extreme danger.

As it was, the twins spent what should have been the rest of their National Service giving the Shepton Mallet staff a very hard time. And when they were thrown out on to Civvy Street towards the end of 1953 each of their records bore that ugly scar: Dishonorable Discharge.

What, I wondered, were they going to do with the rest of their lives?

Chapter Four

What they could have done was box for a living. They were both above average, particularly Reggie, and I'm sure they could have earned a few bob. I'd seen what boxing in the Forces had done for me and I'd urged them to give it a go in the Army. But, as usual, the twins felt they knew best. When they found themselves back in civvy street, Ronnie had lost interest in fighting and Reggie used the excuse that he would not get a licence because of his Army record. He did train with me, though, and the fitter he became, the more he felt he would like to box professionally.

Finally he did apply for his licence. However, the Christmas incident with PC Fisher was on his record and would have gone against him but for a lovely gesture by the policeman. He wrote to the boxing board explaining that Reggie's punch that night was thrown under provocation. 'Reggie told me to walk away, but I didn't accept his advice,' PC Fisher wrote. 'I tried to grab him, thereby provoking him to hit me to evade arrest.'

That letter swayed the decision in Reggie's favour and he was granted his licence. But within a few months he had lost all interest in the sport: he felt that all the managers and agents were too ruthless and only wanted to know those fighters who were going to become champions. The irony was that Reggie was good enough to become a champion; I didn't doubt that for one moment. But he didn't like the atmosphere and that was the end of that. Reggie never went in the ring again, although I believe he knew in his heart that he was good enough.

It quickly became clear that the twins were not cut out for a life on the knocker. I lent them some money and they did spend several weeks trying to generate some business, but they were always looking for something else. It came in the form of a filthy, neglected billiard hall in what had once been a small cinema in Eric Street, off the Mile End Road. The takings were low, mainly because the manager preferred playing snooker himself rather than encouraging business. But the twins saw the potential and put a proposition to the owner: they would take over the place, smarten it up and make it pay; in return, they would give him a weekly cut of the takings. Since the owner was receiving next to nothing, he accepted the deal. The manager was fired, the former 'flea pit' spruced up and, at just twenty-one, the twins were in the entertainment business.

They had the Midas touch. Word spread that the twins had taken over the billiard hall and business boomed. One aspect, however, I found disturbing: the clientele. No one expects an East End billiard hall to look like a church fête in Cheltenham, but I was shocked at the number of young tearaways and villains who gathered there, simply idling their time away. Some, who had been with the twins in Shepton Mallet glasshouse, should have been given a cool reception. But that wasn't in the twins' nature: it is a family characteristic that we accept people for what they are, not what they have done. Others who came to regard the billiard hall as a regular meeting place were hard people, who were not fussy how they earned a few bob.

I had no idea Ronnie was homosexual until he told me himself a few months after the billiard hall opened. As well as all the tough nuts, a lot of younger, very good-looking guys used to congregate there and I noticed they always stopped laughing and joking whenever I walked in.

After a while I got a bit paranoid. 'Why have you suddenly gone quiet?' I'd ask.

Someone would snigger. And I'd say, 'I don't find it funny.'

They would say they meant nothing by it. But it would happen again and I'd get really annoyed.

Finally, Ronnie said to me one day, 'You don't know, do you?'

'Don't know what?'

'That I'm AC/DC,' Ronnie said.

'Leave me alone,' I scoffed.

'It's true. That's what I am, whether you like it or not.'

I didn't know what to say. I just stared at him, shocked. I knew he had not had many relationships with women, but I certainly hadn't given a thought to him being the other way.

'That's what we'd be talking about when you walked in,' Ronnie said. 'They all knew and would be laughing about it. Then I'd say, "Sssh, here's Charlie." And they'd all shut up.'

All I could think to say was: 'I can't believe it.'

'Well, it's true,' Ronnie said. 'That's how I am and you're not going to change it.' He went on to say he'd always been that way and could not care less who knew. He could not understand why so many people took a pop at homosexuals. 'They can't help what they are,' he would say.

In the main, though, the billiard hall was a place for hard, tough men. One such man was Bobby Ramsey, and he, more than anyone at that time, was to influence the course the twins' lives would take.

Ramsey was an ex-boxer who could have made a good living from the sport. But he fell into bad company and had settled for being 'minder' for the notorious Jack 'Spot' Comer, one of London's underworld kings of the fifties. Ramsey, several years older than the twins, had been around and the twins admired him; they listened in some sort of awe as he described the high life the likes of Comer enjoyed through controlling clubs and spielers.

I didn't like Ramsey. I had a feeling he would cause the twins problems and I told him, 'If you've got trouble, don't take the twins with you.' He promised he wouldn't. I warned the twins about him, too, but they scoffed. They were quite capable of handling Ramsey, and half a dozen like him, they said. It hit home to me then that they were probably right. They were not my little kid brothers any more: they were men in a man's world, and formidable men at that. They were identical twins, with identical thoughts and opinions – a language of their own. They had proved their strength, power and tenacity, both in the ring and against heavy odds outside it. They had taken on the police and the Army and had not been intimidated. They had survived a short spell in prison and a longer spell on the run. And now, at just twenty-one, they were running their own business – not an empire by any means, but it was their own and it was profitable. They ate, drank, and dressed well. And there always seemed to be enough money around to give to others who were not so well off. The East End may have been a small pool, but the twins were very big fish in it. Perhaps they were right. Perhaps they *could* handle the problems I feared Ramsey might create.

Over the next eighteen months the Regal billiard hall became more and more popular. The twins ensured there were no fights or disorders of any kind that might bother the police, and the business still made money. Inevitably, though, it became a meeting place for thieves where robberies were planned. The twins were never involved, I know; but if any of the pals they helped out had a good tickle, I'm sure the twins made sure their debts were repaid with interest.

All was going well. The twins – particularly Reggie – were becoming more ambitious and thinking of opening a more respectable club where decent East End families could go.

And then Bobby Ramsey turned up. He hadn't been at the billiard hall for several weeks and when he arrived one hot August night in 1956, I learned why: he had been hit on the head with an iron bar during a fight with a gang from the Watney Street area, the other side of Commercial Road. Now that he had recovered, he wanted revenge. He'd come into the billiard hall with a pal, Billie Jones, and asked Ronnie to go with them to a local pub called the Britannia. A villain called Charlie Martin, who had wielded the iron bar, was drinking there with Jimmy Fullerton, a local tearaway who'd helped in the attack. Ramsey was in a dangerous mood: he said he had several weapons in his car, including a bayonet. He asked Ronnie to go with him. Before they left, Ronnie went behind the bar. He opened a drawer and took out a loaded revolver.

Martin and Fullerton were not at the Britannia, but Martin's younger brother, Terry, was. On the principle that one of the Watney Street mob was better than none, he was dragged outside. Ramsey, his bayonet tucked in his trousers, laid into him, then pulled out the bayonet and stuck it up the young man's backside.

At that time, East End gang feuds were commonplace. Normally, a victim was carted off to hospital, mouths were kept shut and the police never got involved. But that night Ramsey was a reckless fool: as he drove away from the Britannia, he got stopped for speeding. The officers in the patrol car couldn't believe their luck when they found a blood-stained bayonet, a crowbar and an axe in the car. Ramsey, Jones and Ronnie were arrested.

At the station, the gun was found in Ronnie's pocket. It had not been fired, but that made little difference.

While the three of them were being questioned, a report came in that a man had been taken to the London Hospital with serious stab wounds. The police put two and two together and spoke to Terry Martin, who confirmed he had been attacked. The case against Ramsey, Jones and Ronnie was cast-iron and on 5 November 1956 they appeared at the Old Bailey charged with causing grievous bodily harm. Reggie, too, was charged, even though he wasn't aware of the attack until afterwards.

Ramsey was jailed for seven years; Jones and Ronnie got three each.

Reggie, thankfully, was justly acquitted. But the immediate future would be difficult for him, too. As identical twins, he and Ronnie had lived virtually in each other's pockets all their lives. Now, for the first time, they were going to have to exist separately.

Dolly and I were still living at Vallance Road but were desperate to find a place of our own. Mum was kind and understanding, as usual, and treated Dolly like a daughter, and the old man, bless him, was a diamond. But a house – no matter how warm and friendly – is not the same unless it's your own, and I was always on the lookout for a place where Dolly and I could live a proper and private family life.

In those early days Dolly was a good wife. She didn't make friends easily and was extremely possessive and money-mad; but she seemed to care for me and Gary and was very neat and clean about the house. She was a highly strung woman with a vivid imagination, though, and when

Gary needed surgery to correct a squint, she convinced herself he would be blind for the rest of his life.

I'd had a couple of insights into her strange behaviour when we were courting. Often Dolly would stay overnight at Vallance Road, sleeping with Mum upstairs while I shared the twins' room downstairs. Once, at about three in the morning, there was an almighty crash and I found Dolly staggering around in the hall, covered in blood. She'd had a nightmare and thrown herself through a closed window on to the scullery roof. Amazingly, she escaped with just a badly cut face.

The other occasion was when I was boxing in a competition in Watford. Dolly was at the ringside, having seen me qualify for the semi-final. But when she saw the man I was to meet knock out his opponent in the first round, she fled. She came back after I'd won the competition, but I don't know to this day whether it was the prospect of seeing me hammered that made her run – or the thought that I wouldn't win the £15 prize money.

Life on the knocker did have its moments, and I'd get a terrific buzz coming home with a load of gear that would fetch ten times as much as I'd paid, but I was eager to better our standard of living. The chance came when Reggie and I became closer in Ronnie's absence.

Reggie was a real go-getter and when he came across a dilapidated old house near Poplar Town Hall, only two hundred yards from Bow police station, he saw the potential immediately. He asked me to help him renovate it and, with the help of a few mates, we transformed that house into a sparkling club with a stage and dancing area – the East End had never seen anything like it before. We called it The Double R, after the twins.

The only clubs around at that time were 'dives': dark and dingy 'Men only' drinking places where pints were pulled but punches were not. We wanted The Double R to be different. We didn't want the billiard-hall clientele – layabouts and villains who liked a bit of trouble. We wanted the club to have a family atmosphere, a club where respectable working men could enjoy a quiet drink and listen to a band with their wives and families.

It took us six months to make our point.

The local tearaways had never seen anything like The Double R and assumed it was a 'dive' like all the other places in the area. And they treated it as such.

Few unwanted visitors got by our twenty-two-stone doorman, 'Big' Pat Connolly, but one quiet afternoon when security was relaxed three burly coalmen barged in. They were covered in coal dust and leaned against the newly decorated wall, demanding drinks. Reggie quietly asked them to leave. They started to argue and one of them aimed a punch at Reggie. I was serving behind the bar and raced round to give Reggie a hand. It wasn't necessary. By the time I arrived all three were laid out.

Reggie was extremely swift to nip problems in the bud. He hit first and did not bother to ask questions afterwards. One night an over-enthusiastic customer made the mistake of trying to take the microphone from a woman singing on stage. Reggie took the mike away and handed it back to her. The customer's second mistake was trying drunkenly to pull our mum up from her table to dance when she was happy minding her own business. Reggie felled him with a right hook then ordered him to be carried out. Two days later the customer came back and, rather sheepishly, apologized.

I'd always settled disputes with words, not fists. And up to the day we opened The Double R, I'd never had a fight outside the ring. I had had arguments with the twins over this when they resorted to violence. I told them they should not get involved in fights, but they would sneer

56

and say I had no idea what was going on, what it was like when someone was spoiling your business.

I found myself taking a different view when the trouble-makers started getting busy at The Double R. After all the hard work that had gone into transforming that Bow Road house I was damned if I was going to stand by and watch some mindless Jack the Lads ruin the venture before it had properly started. So: when there was no other way out I met violence with violence. I spoke to the idiots in the language they understood and, since I was fit and technically well equipped, I was able to handle myself more than adequately.

Reggie was amused and quietly pleased by my attitude. The afternoons were worst; if there was going to be trouble, that was the time. I had asked Dolly to stay away during the day but one afternoon she came in for something. Three blokes were drinking at the bar and one said, 'Hello, darling.' I let that pass because I was all for being friendly, but then they all started making stupid, unsubtle remarks, generally being lairy and showing a lack of respect to a woman. I was serving behind the bar and politely asked them to be quiet because Dolly was my wife.

Unfortunately, they took no notice and finally I went round the other side of the bar to show them the door. One of them threw a punch and before I knew it I was having a row with all three.

Bill Donovan, who had been badly hurt in the Coach and Horses battle several years before, was on the door, and helped me out. We finally sent the troublemakers on their way with a message not to come back.

When Reggie heard about it he said, 'Now you know. Sometimes you've got to fight.'

I could not argue. But all the aggro got on my nerves and made me sick. I found it hard to understand the mentality of people who took a delight in smashing up something that was nice.

We turned the room above the club into a gymnasium and, although I left it very late to ask him, Britain's favourite boxing champ, Henry Cooper, came along with his manager, Jim Wicks, to open it. This helped publicize The Double R and more and more people came along to see what it was like. The message finally got home to the sort that took pleasure in trouble, and gradually the club became the sort of establishment we had wanted in the beginning. The twins attracted all sorts – good, bad and indifferent – but everyone knew the rules and respected them. Some hard gangland men from South London crossed the water to drink there. They may have been enemies with some of the East End clientele but after those first six months there was hardly any hint of bother. The Double R, it seemed, was welcome neutral ground, a 'Little Switzerland' in the middle of Mile End.

Reggie, who had a natural flair for mixing with all types, was the perfect host, and I ran the bar with Barry Clare, an engaging homosexual, who also doubled up as compere, calling up amateur talent from the customers.

One night a lady asked Barry if she could sing a number. It was a beautiful blues song and she was so good I asked her if she would come along and sing a couple of times a week. She was thrilled and said, 'I'd be delighted.'

'How much do you want?' I asked.

The lady laughed. 'I don't want any money for singing.'

But I insisted and she finally gave in to shut me up. I forget how much we agreed; it was probably a fiver.

After her first performance I went up to her and tried to give her the money. She refused, but I forced her to take it: she had been excellent value and had earned it.

She immediately went to the bar and put the money on the counter.

'What are you doing?' I said.

'You've paid me, Charlie,' she replied. 'I can do what I like with my own money. And what I'd like to do is buy everyone a drink.'

And she did. Not just then, but every time she came in. She was a lovely woman who just loved to sing, and her name was Queenie Watts.

For the rich and famous, the West End had always been the place for a night out. But in the middle fifties the other side of the river became fashionable, and wealthy, titled gentlemen and showbusiness stars – including Danny La Rue and Joan Collins's sister Jackie – started coming to The Double R.

For me, the work was tiring. But it was our own business and the financial rewards were worthwhile. Most of the time, too, I was meeting very nice, genuine people. It certainly beat life on the knocker.

With business booming, Reggie and I decided to expand into gambling. At that time it was illegal: bookmakers were not Turf Accountants with shops in the High Street; they operated on street corners and anyone who wanted to put a couple of bob on a horse risked being nicked. Card games, too, were against the law. Anybody who wanted to play for money had to go to a spieler – a club, normally in a basement, where chemin de fer and poker were played away from the prying eyes of the police.

Reggie and I saw the financial possibilities in spielers and we acquired one across the road from The Double R. Within a couple of months, we opened two more. Money, suddenly, was coming out of our ears.

To make life even sweeter, a member of The Double R tipped me off about an empty flat in Narrow Street,

Wapping. It was a two-bedroomed flat on the second floor of a shabby block called Brightlingsea Buildings, built for dockers and their families nearly a hundred years before. A palace it wasn't. But it *was* a place Dolly, Gary and I could call ours at last and I snapped it up the same day. I had the money to move to a posher pad away from the manor, but the thought didn't occur to me. The East End was in my blood, and anyway, that was where we were making a very good living.

Dolly adored the new lifestyle. She had always dreamed of being rich, and now that there was a few bob around, she made the most of it with lots of new clothes and regular hair-dos. We went to West End clubs with upper-crust patrons of The Double R who accepted us as friends, cockney accents and all, or we enjoyed ourselves with old friends in the East End. Wherever we went, Dolly always looked lovely and attracted a lot of attention. I was proud of her.

One bloke at The Double R seemed to be taking more than a passing interest in Dolly but I felt secure in our marriage and didn't think much of it. She was a stunning looker and it was hardly surprising that other men found her attractive. My life was full to the brim with money and excitement and plans for the future, and I didn't give George Ince another thought.

In Wandsworth Prison Ronnie was delighted that business was going well on the outside; he knew he would have a share in it when he was released, and because he'd earned full remission through good behaviour in his first year it seemed he would be home in time for Christmas 1958.

In one day, however, the whole situation changed. From being more or less a model prisoner without one black mark on his record, Ronnie found himself in a tiny, concrete cell in a strait-jacket. Dreams of freedom vanished. The nightmare from which Ronnie still hasn't escaped had begun.

During the year he'd been in jail, Ronnie had been a loner. He had had his place in the prison hierarchy and made sure everyone understood it, but he had made it plain that he wouldn't cause trouble if he wasn't bothered. Ronnie has an overpowering manner, bordering on hypnotic, and often sounds as though he's demanding when in fact he's merely asking. Whether this led to the problems in Wandsworth I don't know, but a prison officer reacted badly to something he said and Ronnie snapped. The officer went down but within seconds other officers were on Ronnie who, strong as a bull, chinned a couple and they went over. An almighty fight broke out with fists flying, boots kicking. More officers, some armed with truncheons, joined in. Ronnie laid into them until they grabbed his arms and pushed them behind his back. Then they forced Ronnie's head down and rushed him along the cell corridor into a post. Someone came running with a strait-jacket. Somehow they got Ronnie into it. Then they dragged him along to a concrete cell they call the 'chokey' block. They held him down while an officer injected him with a drug, then slammed the door. Ronnie was left in that cell for a week.

Then they transferred him to the psychiatric wing at Winchester Prison in Hampshire.

And a doctor certified him insane.

The family all reacted differently. I was very worried and disturbed because I realized the implications: Ronnie could be kept in jail indefinitely. Mum couldn't believe it, but she tried to keep cool about it and was as optimistic as usual, saying everything would be bound to sort itself out in the end. The old man *wouldn't* believe it. Ronnie was being clever, he said; he was getting the authorities at it, working his ticket. No way was Ronnie mad.

And Reggie? Reggie was beside himself with fury and worry. If his identical twin, the man who shared his innermost thoughts, had been officially declared a nutcase, what on earth did that make him?

The news from Winchester that spring of 1958 shattered us all and for weeks we tried to change the prison rules that did not allow us to have a second opinion. Meanwhile, Ronnie was given massive doses of a tranquillizing drug called Stemetil. We were told this was to stabilize him and curb his violent tendencies. But it dulled his mind and affected his memory, and we were powerless to do anything about it. We watched him deteriorate before us to a point where sometimes he didn't even recognize us.

Out of my mind with worry, I decided to find out just what Stemetil was. When I did, I was horrified. A Harley Street specialist confirmed that Ronnie was being treated for schizophrenia with a drug normally used for treating vertigo and vomiting! To make matters even worse he said, 'The precise mechanisms of the action of this drug are not yet fully understood.'

It was too much to take. Reggie and I decided that Ronnie was coming out of Winchester even if we had to blow a hole in the prison wall to get him. Happily, this wasn't necessary. A week or so later, in May 1958, Ronnie was transferred to a mental hospital just fourteen miles from London. It was Long Grove near Epsom, Surrey. And springing him from there was going to be a doddle.

The Strange Case of the Vanished Twin hit the headlines later the same month. Millions probably thought it was just another piece of Kray skulduggery, another cheeky swipe at authority, but we removed Ronnie from that hospital because we were far from convinced of his unbalanced mind. Also, we were very concerned at the bad effect the drugs were having on him.

One thing the drugs hadn't done was change Ronnie's appearance; he still looked like Reggie. When Reggie put on a blue suit, white shirt and blue tie, similar to those Ronnie wore in hospital, only those who knew them well could spot the difference. When Reggie had his hair cut as short as Ronnie's and put on a pair of glasses, even I had trouble telling them apart.

The switch was a simple operation. Leaving some friends in a couple of cars outside the hospital grounds, Reggie went in to see Ronnie as though it was just another routine visit. They sat chatting at a table in the small visiting hall and waited until a patrolling male nurse's back was turned. Ronnie whipped off his glasses; Reggie slipped his on. Then they quickly but discreetly changed places.

When they were sure no one had noticed the change-over, Ronnie got up and sauntered over to a door which visitors were allowed to go through to fetch tea and biscuits. The nurse, assuming he was Reggie, opened the door and Ronnie walked out. But he didn't go for tea; he walked straight out of the hospital into the grounds. One of the hospital staff came towards him on a bike and Ronnie tensed. But the man merely nodded a greeting and rode past. Ronnie walked on and on until he reached the gate, and then he spotted the cars Reggie had told him about and he was gone.

Reggie waited for about half an hour, then he went up to the nurse on the door and said, 'Excuse me, Ron's been a long time getting the tea. I didn't think they were allowed to get the tea.'

The nurse looked puzzled. '*You're* Ronnie,' he said.

Reggie shook his head. 'I'm Reggie. Ronnie went to get the tea. I'm getting worried.'

The nurse stared at Reggie closely. He must have believed him, because he ran off, a worried look on his face. Then all hell broke loose. An alarm bell went off. Hospital staff started running around. And then the police arrived.

Someone said to Reggie, 'This is all down to you.'

But Reggie pleaded innocence. 'I just came to see him. He went to get the tea, then everyone got excited.'

To confirm Reggie's story, the police took his fingerprints and checked them with the Criminal Records Office at Scotland Yard.

'You *are* Reg Kray,' someone commented.

'That's what I've been trying to tell you for the last hour,' said Reg. Then he added, straight-faced, 'I'm worried. What's happened to him?'

'Do us a favour,' one copper said impatiently. 'You know what's happened.'

But Reggie kept saying he didn't. And they kept him there for a couple of hours before letting him go.

By then, Ronnie was in a beautiful, expensive flat in St John's Wood. Not for long, though. When he arrived, he took one look round and said, 'I don't like this. You can get me out of here.' And we did – the next morning. Ronnie was like that. It wouldn't have occurred to him that we'd gone to a lot of trouble and expense to get him a 'safe' house. He just didn't like the place and that was that.

That day, the Superintendent of Long Grove got in touch with us and asked us to see him at the hospital. He said we'd made a serious mistake: Ronnie wasn't well and should have stayed there for treatment. We played dumb, but the Superintendent laughed. He said he admired how it had been done: there had been no trouble, no one had been hurt. But, nevertheless, we had made a mistake. And he warned us that we would find out he was right.

For the next few months Reggie and I had our work cut out running our businesses while keeping Ronnie ahead of the law. The escape was big news and stories of his whereabouts flooded the East End: he was reliably reported to be in the Bahamas, New York, Malta, the Cote d'Azur, Southern Spain and goodness knows where else. In fact, he never strayed further north than Finchley or further west than Fulham. He took a few chances to visit Mum in Vallance Road, and the first visit proved very traumatic for him. While he was there, he wanted to see Aunt Rose. But she had died while he was in Winchester and Mum had decided not to tell him until he was better. When she did break the news, Ronnie got up and went into the yard. He stood there, looking up at the railway arch. The death of his Aunt Rose was the biggest blow of his life then. He stood out there, looking up, trying to take it in.

Ronnie didn't want to be on the trot for the rest of his life. But he didn't want to go back to a mental hospital either. While he had been in Wandsworth, he had heard about people who had been in and out of mental institutions for years and was terrified of ending up like them. One had actually been certified insane and was being detained without a firm date for release. Ronnie dreaded the same thing happening to him.

To solve the problem, we had to prove that Ronnie was, in fact, sane. So we booked an appointment with a Harley Street psychiatrist under an assumed name and asked him to give an opinion on Ronnie's mental state. Ronnie made it sound plausible with a cock-and-bull story about getting married and being worried about insanity way back in the family. The psychiatrist was highly amused and, after asking a few questions, sent Ronnie on his way with a document stating that he was, indeed, in possession of all his marbles.

The effect on Ronnie was startling, and very worrying.

Relieved that the dark shadow of madness was lifted, he started taking even more risks. He would have a few drinks here, a few drinks there, and once he strolled all the way along Bethnal Green Road, cheerfully returning the greetings of people who thought he was Reggie.

But after five months the strain of being on the trot began to take its toll. He'd put on a lot of weight through heavy drinking, his face was drawn and haggard, and he'd become morose and anti-social, preferring to stay in and read or sleep. None of us knew what to do for the best. I was told Ronnie was suffering from the after-effects of the drugs pumped into him. He needed medical treatment very quickly, but to get it would mean revealing his identity and recent history.

In the end, the problem was solved for us. Ronnie took one risk too many and was recaptured. He suspected police would be waiting for him to turn up at Vallance Road to celebrate his twenty-fifth birthday, so he waited until the day after and arrived after dark. But the police were still waiting and let themselves in quietly at three in the morning as one of the party guests left.

A few days before, Ronnie had been acting very strangely; sometimes he didn't even recognize Reggie or myself. But when those two uniformed policemen and two male nurses walked into the house that night Ronnie was perfectly normal. He said he knew they had to take him back, and went to get his coat. I think he was relieved it was all over.

The police said they would take Ronnie to Long Grove for a formal discharge, then return him to Wandsworth where he would finish his sentence. But first he would stay overnight in Bethnal Green nick. Alarm bells rang loudly in my mind and Reggie's: we had not forgotten the PC Baynton affair. And although it was now nearly four in the morning, we rang our solicitor, a doctor and a national newspaper reporter.

Two hours later, Reggie and I walked into the police station with the lawyer and the doctor. We were not welcome. A high-ranking officer refused to let us see Ronnie and, in spite of the lawyer's protests, ordered us out of the building.

If someone had talked to us civilly, assuring us that Ronnie was all right and would get the proper treatment, I'm sure that would have been the end of it. But when Ronnie eventually came out, the police laid on a security pantomime that got everyone's back up. He was in a taxi – with a police escort – and they roared past us as though Scotland Yard was on fire. Angry now, as well as concerned, Reggie and I gave chase in our car, with the doctor and lawyer behind in theirs and the reporter behind them. It was like something out of a Keystone Kops movie. And it got even crazier near the Oval cricket ground in Kennington, South London, when a second police car, probably called on the radio, cut in front of Reggie, forcing him to swerve on to the pavement. It was all so stupid and irresponsible.

The security farce continued even when we reached Long Grove. The police escort let the taxi into the hospital grounds, then parked across the drive, blocking the entrance. We simply got out and walked. But then the second police car was allowed through and it crawled behind us as we walked to Reception. What on earth did they think we were going to do? Hurl hand grenades and rush Ronnie to freedom under cover of machine-gun fire?

At Reception, we asked to see Ronnie. The request was turned down. Instead we were shown into the Superintendent's office. He was as charming as before, but repeated that we'd done Ronnie no favours by helping him escape: he was very sick. We agreed, but argued very strongly that he wasn't insane. The Superintendent listened politely, promised to consider Ronnie's case carefully, then arranged for us to see him there and then.

That Superintendent didn't have long to consider the case. Within a couple of days Ronnie was taken back to Wandsworth. He was *not* re-certified, but he was put on tranquillizers. He hated this, but he finished his sentence without further trouble and walked out a free man about seven months later, in May 1959.

The release date surprised us. Ronnie, sentenced to three-years, had belted a prison officer, caused a certain amount of damage to others, then escaped from captivity for five months. Yet he still earned full remission and served just two years.

Did someone blunder, I wonder? Was Ronnie diagnosed wrongly? Did a doctor or psychiatrist prescribe the wrong treatment? Was Ronnie allowed out earlier than he should have been just to keep him happy?

And to keep us quiet?

Chapter Five

The weight Ronnie had put on before he went back to prison had dropped by the time he came out. He looked awful: he was very pale and drawn, and his eyes had no life in them. He would spend much of the time staring into space, unaware of what was happening around him. He recognized Mum and the old man, and he trusted them, but he looked blankly at Reggie and me, refusing to believe we were his brothers.

We'd laid on this big party at The Double R. Dozens of old friends were looking forward to seeing Ronnie again. But he refused to go and I had to apologize to everyone and make up an excuse. All Ronnie wanted to do was sit in the kitchen at Vallance Road and drink tea and smoke. Reggie would sit with him for hours and then ring me to say he couldn't handle it any more. Then I'd go and sit with him. Poor Mum! She didn't know what to make of it all. She didn't understand when Ronnie would suddenly look at me strangely and say, 'You're not Charlie. Why do you keep coming here?' It got worse and worse and he got more and more suspicious, even of Reggie.

And then, inevitably, Ronnie exploded.

We had taken him to a pub to try and cheer him up. Throughout the evening he was very strange, talking funny and making no sense at all. And if he caught Reggie or me looking at him, he'd snap, 'Who you looking at?'

Mum or the old man would say gently, 'Ronnie, that's Charlie, your brother.'

'Yeah,' Ronnie would scoff. 'That's what he tells you.'

It was frightening for all of us.

At about ten o'clock, Ronnie slammed his glass on the table and dashed out of the pub. We all looked at each other, not knowing what to do. Then Reggie and I jumped up and ran after him. We found him trying to smash a shop window with his hands.

'What the hell are you doing?' we yelled.

But all Ronnie said was, 'Go away. I don't know you.'

Luckily for us, a chap we knew – Curly King – pulled up in a car. He seemed to sense a problem. He said hello to Ronnie. Ronnie recognized him and stopped bashing the window.

'Come on, Ron, take me down the billiard hall,' Curly said.

It saved the situation. Ronnie liked the idea and I went back into the pub for Mum and the old man and we all went to the billiard hall. What happened there was one of the most terrifying experiences of my life.

While the rest of us chatted amiably, Ronnie was restless, prowling up and down all the time like a caged tiger. We all tried to calm him down but it was no good: Ronnie was in a world of his own and no one, it seemed, could get in. None of us could relax. Everyone kept looking at me to do something. But every time I tried to talk to him, he kept telling me he didn't know who I was. He just kept prowling up and down . . . up and down . . . up and down . . .

It seemed to go on for ages. And then suddenly Ronnie stopped. He looked all around him, a strange look on his face, staring at us all as if trying to remember us or recognize somebody. Then he turned and walked quickly to the middle of the room where he stood deep in thought, as though he had some major decision to make and he didn't know what to do. His whole body suddenly stiffened as if someone had given him an electric shock. We all stared at him, transfixed. We'd never seen anything like it in our lives and we didn't know what to do. Gradually, Ronnie's stiff, straight body lost its tenseness. The electric shock had been switched off. Slowly, he sank to his knees as if he was praying. He stayed like that for several seconds.

We were all staring. Then I heard someone shouting, 'Charlie, for God's sake, do something!' I don't know who it was but it snapped me out of my shock. I ran over to Ronnie and put my arm round his shoulder, but he shrugged it off and pushed me away. 'Go away!' he shouted. 'Go away from me, I don't know you.'

He stayed like that for a few more seconds, then slowly got to his feet. I told Reggie we had to get him to hospital and he shouted to someone to call an ambulance. When it arrived, Ronnie refused to get in. Then the police came and we all coaxed Ronnie gently, telling him it was for the best, that he was unwell and we needed to make him better. Finally he agreed to get in.

They put Ronnie in a bed with curtains round it and then, at about midnight, a doctor told us there was nothing wrong with him.

We were shell-shocked. I told the doctor what had happened in the billiard hall.

'We're not trying to get him certified, you know,' I said. 'We think the world of him. We brought him here because there's something badly wrong.'

The doctor wouldn't have it.

'He must be developing a cunning mind,' I said. 'Because you're a doctor, he's behaving differently.'

The doctor wasn't impressed. But the situation was too critical for us to be fobbed off and I persisted. 'Ronnie doesn't even believe we're his brothers. Just stand outside that curtain and listen.'

Somewhat reluctantly, the doctor agreed. Reggie and I went in. 'How are you, Ron?' I asked.

Ronnie reacted as we expected. 'What are you two doing here?' he said. 'Get out!'

We pointed to small scars on our faces as proof of our identities but Ronnie said, 'You've had them put on. How clever. Go on, get out – you imposters!'

Ronnie's behaviour didn't please us, but it did convince the listening doctor and he apologized for doubting us. He arranged for Ronnie to be admitted to St Clement's Hospital in Mile End immediately.

For the next two weeks Ronnie was given tests and more drugs to stabilize him. The family visited him every day. He always knew Mum and half-knew the old man, but for the first week neither Reg nor I had a chance: we were still imposters. And then one day I walked in and I could tell straight away that he was all right again.

For the first time Ronnie talked about what he had been going through. It was weird: some of the time he realized the stupid things he was doing but he couldn't stop himself; most of the time he knew I was Charlie but couldn't help denying it.

The doctors told me that the terrifying experience in the billiard hall was a seizure and Ronnie could have gone one way or the other. If he had gone the wrong way he would never have come out of it; he would have gone mad. But he fought it and because his will-power was so strong he came through it.

The price he had to pay was immense. Drugs would be part of his life for ever: four different tablets a day, an injection once a month. Ronnie accepted it without complaint; he realized how unwell he was and he knew that the drugs kept away the paranoia and the eventual distrust that led to extreme violence.

The Ronnie Kray who came back into the world to join

us in the enterprises we had built in his absence not only looked different from the one who had picked up that gun two years before. His movements were more ponderous, his speech slower, his mind numbed. He wasn't the Ronnie we had known.

Things changed when Ronnie got involved in The Double R. He had always been the dominant twin and immediately took over. While he was away, Reggie had more or less had a free hand and made his own decisions, but now Ronnie insisted that everything had to be discussed. And even then he would always have to be right. They would argue, as they had always done, but if it came to the crunch, Ronnie would keep on and on until he got his own way. This had a bad effect on all our finances because it was Reggie who had the better business brain. Ronnie, as generous and kind-hearted as ever, preferred to give money away.

In those late fifties, lots of people were coming out of prison and word soon got around that Ronnie Kray was a soft touch. People I'd never seen before would come into the club and Ronnie would give them fifty quid out of the till. The next day it would be someone else. It never seemed to stop.

Reggie and I would get very uptight about it. We said we didn't mind helping people, but we had to draw the line somewhere. It didn't cut much ice with Ronnie.

'What do you want to do – show ourselves up?' he said. 'People come home expecting to be given something. Do you want us to get a bad name? Do you want people to think we're tight?'

Reggie said, 'We'd better slow down, that's all. We're overdoing it.'

Ronnie wouldn't have it. 'You may think we are, but I

don't. It's not going to change. That's how it's going to be.'

It was frustrating not being able to reason with Ronnie. I'm sure he thought there was a bottomless well of money he could dip into when he liked. And when there wasn't any there, he'd moan about it.

One day he came in for some for himself. The till was empty. 'Where's the money?' he said, all surprised.

'You've given it all away,' I told him.

'We have to do something,' he said impatiently. 'We've got to earn some money.'

'How can we?' I asked, pleased to make the point. 'You give it away as fast as we can earn it.'

But it didn't make the slightest difference. In those days, when the average weekly wage was less than £10, our combined enterprises were bringing in around £200 a week. Ronnie continued to give away twenty, thirty and fifty pounds if he felt people needed it. Children, old people, families who were skint – Ronnie would help them all. But as usual he did it all quietly, without fuss; he didn't want people to know. One day, however, his generosity was made public, much to Ronnie's embarrassment.

Every Wednesday a show was put on for old people at Oxford House in Hackney. Ronnie took great delight in arranging for boxes of apples and pears to be sent over to them. This went on for several months, then one night Ronnie delivered the boxes himself. The owner of the little theatre called out, 'I'm on the stage.' As Ronnie walked out, the man quickly pulled back the curtains, revealing scores of old ladies and gentlemen waiting for the show to start.

He pointed to Ronnie and said, 'I thought you'd like to know that this is the gentleman who sends the fruit.'

Then, to Ronnie's horror, he said, 'Let's have three cheers for Ron!'

Ronnie blushed. He couldn't wait to get off that stage.

If we had to pay a bill for, say, a hundred pounds, Reggie or I would put the money away. But if someone came in and Ronnie felt they needed the money, he'd give it to them without thinking about it. Then later, he'd start worrying about how the bill was going to be paid. If several people wanted help, Ronnie would go out of his way to help them all. Reggie was generous, too, but he was sensible; he wouldn't leave us with no money for the bills. Money meant everything to Ronnie – but it also meant nothing. If he had a million pounds, he wouldn't be happy until he'd given it all away.

His charity didn't stop at cash handouts either. If a kid came into the billiard hall looking for a job, Ronnie would take him on, helping our old man behind the bar or cleaning the tables. We had all the staff we required but Ronnie found it hard not to help someone if he felt they needed it.

With him around, business was like a benevolent fund or welfare office and one day I told Ronnie he'd missed his vocation in life: he'd have made a fantastic welfare officer. In one respect it was true: he was capable of so much patience with people. One of our customers had a sister who was very ill in a mental hospital, and Ronnie visited her a few times. He just sat talking and listening, trying to help her.

Another customer had a sister who had become a drug addict and changed from a lovely girl into an old hag. Ronnie paid doctors a lot of money to try to help her, then bought her a hairdressing salon to give her an interest. Sadly, the girl was hooked for life and became a registered addict. But she appreciated Ronnie's help and wrote to a newspaper explaining what he'd done. When

Ronnie learned that a certain bloke had ruined her life by forcing her to have drugs at a party, he smashed in the door of his home and gave him a hiding.

Ronnie had this thing about the underdog – anyone underprivileged, weak or in trouble. He loathed bullies and flamboyant, overpowering people who thought they were God's gift; and he couldn't stand blokes who took liberties, either. Once, I was with him in a crowded pub when a cocky Irishman came in and ordered drinks all round. When he was asked for the money, he said he would pay the next day because he had none on him. Ronnie was fuming and laid the big Irishman out with a right to the jaw. I picked the guy up and took him outside. When I got back, Ronnie was still seething. 'What a liberty!' he said. 'Walking in like that, then saying he'll pay when he feels like it!'

The irony is that if that arrogant Irishman had gone up to Ronnie and asked to borrow some money to buy a round, Ronnie would no doubt have given him some.

Most of us in a situation like that would have felt like saying something to put the man in his place. But Ronnie had an abnormally quick temper. If someone did something he didn't like, he would see red and lash out.

One night there were about twenty of us having a quiet drink in a pub when two guys came in and started staring at us. I asked the group if anyone knew who they were. No one did. I said that when I bought the next round I'd go over and see if they said anything. A little while later I strolled over, unaware that Ronnie had followed me. I was ordering the drinks, waiting for the two blokes to say something, when there was a scuffle and they both ended up spark out on the floor.

The governor looked at me, stunned. 'I don't know if I saw that, or I didn't.'

Ronnie got the two guys to their feet and took them

outside. When he came back, he said to the governor, 'I didn't want you to have any bother in your pub.'

I told Ronnie I had gone over to see what was happening, but he said he knew what they were up to, and didn't want any part of it.

Strangers who took liberties were always in danger with Ronnie. People he knew were not. He'd bawl and shout at them perhaps, but knock them up in the air? Never.

For the next six months, money continued to flow in, despite Ronnie's philanthropy, and we lived well. We didn't have a lot of staff as such, but we did gather around us a number of loyal and trusted allies who looked after us and who, in turn, expected to be looked after.

There was 'Big' Pat Connolly, a huge, happy man, who was doorman at The Double R; Alf 'Limehouse' Willey, who had a brain like a computer when it came to calculating gambling odds; Tommy Brown, a quiet, withdrawn, but immensely strong young man, nicknamed The Bear of Tottenham; Billy Donovan, one of the hardest men I'd ever met; and two lifelong close friends of the twins, Ian Barrie and George Osborne. We had premises, clients and large sums of cash to protect, and these men helped us protect them. In the East End in those days there were 'firms' and 'mobs'. The mobs consisted of villains and thieves, who specialized in robbery with violence. A firm was a group of people who ran an enterprise which dealt in cash – readies – didn't keep books or records and handled their own social security. We were not the only firm operating in Bethnal Green but we were the best organized and most successful – and, because of that, the best known.

Just as the twins had said they would not tolerate trouble in their clubs, they also made it plain they did not approve of rival spielers opening in their manor. If anyone did open one, the twins went along, said they felt it was a liberty, and asked for a percentage of the takings. It was not so much the money they wanted – they had enough interests of their own – it was the principle. They hated the idea of someone taking a liberty. Such was their reputation that they always got a share. But it wasn't always like that. Because there was rarely any trouble in Kray premises, spieler owners came to the twins asking them to be involved. It was a sensible, practical arrangement and, in most cases, they accepted the offers. But not always. Danny Green, who owned The Grange in Stoke Newington, for example, came to us, saying he was having a lot of bother with local tearaways. With tears in his eyes he begged the twins to give him protection in return for a share in his business. The twins were sorry about Danny's problems but declined his offer. Stoke Newington was outside our manor and we had enough on our own plates.

I understood the principle of discouraging a rival operation starting up in the same area, but I did not approve of the twins leaning on people. If I was around and saw or heard anything I did not like, I would say something about it and we'd have an argument. But the twins rarely listened to what I had to say, so it was really a waste of time saying anything. Ironically, they would ask my advice on many things. They would listen for five minutes, then start arguing with me. Finally I would blow up and say, 'Why ask my bloody advice when you never agree with me?' In the end, I started looking around for other interests, because they got on my nerves.

I could not be with the twins twenty-four hours a day, so I don't know everything that went on. But they only ever approached spielers for money, not shops or pubs.

People on our payroll were well paid and well looked after if they were totally loyal and honest; if there was one thing none of us – particularly Ronnie – could bear, it was dishonesty. One of our most trusted and valuable employees was Barry Clare. We were all devastated to learn that he'd gone home one night and stuck his head in the gas oven. Determined to find out why, we put the word out and soon discovered that Barry was being blackmailed.

I discovered the blackmailer by chance because, from a distance I resembled Barry and was mistaken for him in the doorway of the club. A car pulled up and a bloke in the passenger seat called out, 'Hello, Barry, got it for me?'

I sensed immediately it was the blackmailer. But I resisted the temptation to grab him by the throat. Instead, I said, 'Sorry, mate, I'm not Barry. He's round the billiard hall.'

I knew Reggie was at the hall. And as the car pulled away, I rang and told him what had happened. When the guy arrived for his 'pick-up' Reggie was waiting. The man was given such a hiding it's unlikely he ever put the squeeze on anyone again.

Reggie, like Ronnie, never forgot a favour. And someone who had been very helpful while Ronnie was staying in Finchley when he was on the trot from Long Grove, was a car dealer and gambler called Danny Shay. One day, towards the end of 1959, he came to the billiard hall and asked Reggie to help him collect a hundred-pound gambling debt. The man who owed it, he said, was a Pole called Podro, who owned a small shop in Finchley Road. He was a notorious welsher, it seemed.

The task didn't seem too difficult and Reggie said he was happy to try to persuade Mr Podro to pay up. As an afterthought, he asked George Osborne if he'd mind driving them to Podro's shop. Georgie didn't mind, and off they went.

What the three of them didn't know was that Podro, who obviously expected a visit, had told the police. Three of them were hiding in the back of the shop listening to Reggie's own brand of persuasion, and when Reggie finally hung a right-hander on Mr Podro's chin they ran out and nicked him, Shay and Georgie.

The next day the newspaper headlines screamed: 'Chicago-style gangsters' methods!' And later, at the Old Bailey, Shay got three years and Reggie and Georgie eighteen months each for demanding money with menaces.

It was all so stupid. Reggie didn't need money, he was doing someone a favour. And poor Georgie Osborne had just gone for the ride.

'Demanding money with menaces.' It was a phrase that would plague the twins for ever.

Just before Reggie was jailed, a Leyton car dealer named Johnny Hutton introduced him to Leslie Payne, a big man with a quiet chuckling laugh and great charm. Payne, a year older than me, was talented and knowledgeable and could have made a lot of money honestly, but for some reason he seemed to prefer bending the law. He and a financial wizard named Freddie Gore were operating a second-hand car racket in the East End – at the expense of the finance companies – and after Reggie went away they often turned up with ideas and propositions for us to consider. Although we did a couple of deals with them through a second-hand car business of our own, other projects rarely got beyond the discussion stage.

But then they suggested something that was right up our street.

There was a lot of talk in the early part of 1960 about the Government legalizing gambling, and Payne had been tipped off that a first-class West End club was coming on the market. We had a great opportunity to get in on the ground floor of what promised to be a bonanza.

A meeting to sort out the details of the takeover was held in a flat over the Scotch House, in Knightsbridge: it was the home of Commander Drummond, a retired naval officer with blue eyes and a small moustache. Apart from him, Ronnie and myself, there were four others present: Payne, who just sat and smiled, Gore, who scribbled figures on a piece of paper, and the major shareholders in the club, two gentlemen called Faye and Burns. Why the commander was involved I didn't know, but he did most of the talking. After a pleasant enough chat, a price was agreed, a deal struck and Ronnie and I went home to celebrate. The Kray brothers from the backstreets of Bethnal Green now had a club in Wilton Street, Belgravia, one of the wealthiest parts of London.

It was called Esmeralda's Barn. And it turned out to be a gold mine which was to open up a new life for the three of us, our mother and the old man.

The twins particularly were well suited to the West End club circuit and popular among the expensively dressed pleasure-seekers who frequented it. They loved mixing with the aristocracy, showbusiness stars and millionaire businessmen; they rarely missed out on having their photographs taken at social and theatrical gatherings. In their identical, well-cut, midnight-blue dinner jackets, they certainly looked the part. And their behaviour was always respectful and proper.

Although I was on the spot when it mattered, I preferred to keep in the background. Most of my work was done behind the scenes, keeping a close eye on day-to-day events in a business empire that was rapidly expanding. I had been granted a licence to operate a theatrical agency, which meant I booked all cabaret acts for our own clubs, and others, instead of going through other agencies.

It also meant I could spend more time at home, which was important since Dolly had made it clear that she was being neglected and was bored and frustrated at spending so much time on her own. Something happened, however, that made me wonder whether Dolly had, in fact, been neglected or bored in my long absences.

There was a big group of us in a pub called The Green Dragon. I was standing at the bar talking to a couple of friends and Dolly was sitting at a table talking to George Ince. Dolly's two brothers and the twins were also there.

Suddenly Reggie came over to me, looking tense. He told me to get Ince out of the place or there would be trouble. I was confused but I knew the look in Reggie's eyes; it wasn't time to argue.

I went over to the table and took Ince out of Dolly's earshot. I told him I didn't know what it was about, but he should make himself scarce. He did – quickly. Then I rejoined the twins, who proceeded to tell what everybody, it seemed, knew except me.

George Ince and Dolly had been having an affair for some time.

Boiling with rage, I dashed into the street looking for Ince. It was probably just as well for both of us that he was nowhere to be seen. I went back and confronted Dolly, and we agreed to discuss it when I was calmer and more rational. When we did, she denied the affair. But I was not convinced. I had to make a decision: let sleeping dogs lie, or walk out and let her get on with it. In the end I decided to stay, because Gary was at an impressionable age and I couldn't bear him to suffer the trauma of his parents splitting up.

But something in me died that night in The Green Dragon. And when just a few months later I was attracted to a young lady, I threw myself into a full-blooded affair, which, ironically, nearly destroyed the family unit I so wanted to save.

The young woman was beautiful, bubbly and also blonde. Her name was Barbara Windsor and she was an actress.

Our relationship started when she was appearing in the hit show *Fings Ain't Wot They Used To be* in the West End. An actor friend of mine, George Sewell, was in the show too, and arranged front-row seats for myself and Dolly's brother Ray.

I had met Barbara only once before, with other people, but as the cast took their bows at the end of the performance she kept motioning to me to go backstage for a drink. The audience must have wondered who I was! Ray and I enjoyed a drink with the whole cast, then I asked Barbara to come to a club with me on her own. She agreed, and afterwards I took her home to Harringay, where she lived with her parents. Apart from being a beautiful young woman, with a sexy, shapely body, Barbara was a joy to be with – everything, in fact, that Dolly was not. We agreed to see each other the next night and, making my way home to Wapping, savouring the sweetness of her good-night kiss, I could hardly wait.

Being unfaithful to Dolly did not bother me unduly and I met Barbara as often as I could. I saw several sides of her, but one that surprised me was her kindness and generosity. As we all know, showbusiness people are not known for putting their hands in their pockets, but Barbara found it hard to say no if someone said they were in trouble. She was becoming quite a big name then and people – mostly men – were always tapping her for a few quid. I told her she was too kind for her own good and people were taking advantage. Unless she toughened up, I said, she would never have any money for herself when she needed it. But Barbara said she could not help herself, and in a way I loved her all the more for that.

She worked hard and played hard, and was always lively and happy. Most of the time we were together there was a lot of laughter – something there wasn't at my home.

Once, early in our relationship, Barbara and I were having a drink in a Wardour Street club with some of the cast of *Fings* when a row broke out and someone went tumbling down the stairs. Barbara and the others, worried about their reputations, wanted to get out quickly, but one of the guys in the fight warned everyone to stay where they were: nobody, he said, was leaving the club that night; anyone who tried to would be in trouble. That suited us all fine: we ordered more drinks and carried on enjoying ourselves.

After an hour or so, however, the cast started getting worried, so I decided to take matters into my own hands. I went to the top of the stairs and shouted out that whoever was barricading us in had better get out of the way because we were all coming down. With a friend called Harry, I bounded down the stairs and charged down the door leading to the reception foyer. It opened very easily . . . because it wasn't locked! No one was there. Our captors had probably left hours before. We never did find out what the row was about, but Barbara found it very amusing that we'd waited all that time and I'd charged down that door for nothing.

In her early twenties, Barbara had one of those eye-catching figures that was quite dangerous: how many young men, I wonder, walked into lamp-posts or trees because their heads had been turned by that pert little bottom, tiny waist and big boobs? Even today, Barbara and I still laugh at the time a railway porter at Eastbourne thought he was seeing things when the famous Windsor bustline turned up at his station at the unlikely hour of six in the morning. Barbara and I had been in the Astor Club. Remembering that I had an appointment in Eastbourne later that day, I asked Barbara if she fancied riding down there with me. She phoned her mum to tell her where she was going and we got a train. At the other end, Barbara was clip-clopping along the platform in monstrously high-heeled boots, short skirt and clinging white jumper when the porter, eyes out on stalks, mouth open, stumbled over his trolley. Barbara, used to such attention, just giggled. ''Ere Charlie, look, that bloke's fallen off his barrer!'

The laughing could not last, of course. All the time I was married, I could not devote as much time to Barbara as I wanted. And although she never put any pressure on me, I knew I had to decide whether to leave home for her. If it had been a straight choice between Dolly and Barbara I would have walked out of my Wapping flat without a second thought, but Gary was still my main consideration. I would not do anything to hurt him.

It was a hard decision to make because I loved Barbara and really cared for her. I agonized over it for months, but in the end I said we had to finish because I couldn't bear to put Gary through all the upset of a divorce. I told Barbara she needed a fella who could take care of her, and I was so happy when she told me some time later that she had met someone she loved and was getting married. His name, she said, was Ronnie Knight, and she was sure she was making the right decision.

85

Chapter Six

Mum, as always, was the centre of our lives. And when Esmeralda's Barn started lining our pockets, the twins and I were keen to give her everything she had ever wanted. She wanted very little, however; she certainly didn't want to leave Vallance Road for a bigger house in a posher street. But she and the old man did not say no to holidays. They had never been further than Southend in Essex, and now there was some money around they seized the chance to be more adventurous. Mum had had nothing for herself all her life and I was thrilled to be able to give her a taste of the 'jet-set' life. We went to Tangier, Italy, the South of France, and even lashed out on a wonderfully expensive cruise. It was lovely to see someone who had been nowhere suddenly going everywhere, and enjoying every sun-soaked minute.

Exotic places abroad were all very well for a couple of times a year. But we wanted to enjoy Steeple Bay, a nice little spot I had discovered near Burnham-on-Crouch, Essex, so I bought a caravan and a little motor cruiser and I'd pop down there with Mum and the old man every weekend. They were blissfully happy times. The twins were very funny about me going away at weekends. They would say: 'Going away *again*! Leaving us to do all the work!' We'd argue every weekend. They would call me a playboy and it really got on my nerves. Then they would suddenly turn up in Steeple Bay with their mates. They always had loads of people with them; they attracted people all the time.

Mum lapped up the good life at home, too. Two good

friends of ours, Alex Steene and his wife, Anna, made a point of taking Mum to the Royal Command Performance at the London Palladium every year, followed by a slap-up meal in a top restaurant. Mum always looked forward to that.

It was all a dramatic change from the modest lifestyle Mum had previously enjoyed. But the money that was suddenly available did not change her one bit: although she now mixed with dukes and duchesses, lords and ladies, she was always herself. She wasn't one for intellectual conversation, but what she had to say was said with a simple honesty that endeared her to everyone she met. The twins and I were proud of her.

Ronnie and Reggie never put on airs and graces either. Far from being ashamed of where they came from they were proud, and took a delight in taking friends and business acquaintances home to meet Mum over a cup of tea in the upstairs sitting room.

I was sitting in that room talking to Ronnie one day when the phone rang: it was Lord Effingham, whom we paid to sit on the board of The Barn for prestige. When Ronnie put the phone down he said the friendly peer had told him he needed two hundred pounds immediately; if he couldn't get it, he was going to kill himself. When Ronnie told me he was arranging for someone to deliver the money within an hour I went spare. I said it was an obvious ploy to get money, and Ronnie was mad if he fell for it. But he would have none of it; he said he wouldn't be able to live with himself if something happened to Effingham. I suppose I should not have been surprised. Nothing had changed; Ronnie had been a soft touch when he didn't have much money and now that he had it coming out of his ears he was even more charitable. I'm sure that the word went round London that if you were plausible you could get anything out of Ronnie Kray.

Lucien Freud, a heavy gambler, owed the club £1,400 and I told Ronnie that someone should speak to him about it. A few days later he came up to me and said triumphantly, 'It's all sorted out.'

Relieved, I asked, 'He's going to pay up?'

'No,' Ronnie replied. 'I told him to forget it.'

'What?'

'I said we wanted to see him back in the club,' said Ronnie casually. 'It's better for us to have his custom.'

I tried telling him he had made a bad mistake but Ronnie just said, 'Don't go on about it. I've done it now.'

My dismay at his misguided generosity deepened a few days later when I learned that Freud had offered a very valuable painting as collateral for his debt and Ronnie had turned it down.

One of our customers was Pauline Wallace, a lovely, well-dressed, well-spoken Irish lady. What she didn't know about gambling was not worth knowing, so when she hit hard times we gave her a job supervising the croupiers. A month or so later she told Ronnie she was being evicted from her Knightsbridge flat unless she paid £800 rent arrears. Quick as you like, Ronnie took the cash from the club coffers and gave it to her. When I had a go at him he said, 'It's all right. I can use the flat whenever I like.'

When Pauline got on her feet she never forgot what we had done for her. She would visit Mum in Vallance Road, always with some beautiful flowers. Then one day she told the twins she wanted to give them some money every week to repay them for helping her when she needed it most. The twins refused, so Pauline said she would give it to Mum. They told her it was not necessary, but she insisted. Every week Billy Exley went to Knightsbridge and collected some cash. It was something Pauline wanted to do; she was that kind of woman.

A couple of years later she married a multi-millionaire in Texas and the last I heard of her she was running all the greyhound racing in Miami.

Ronnie did not spend all his time playing the nice guy, however. If someone stepped out of line he'd be swift to crack down on them. Lord Effingham was given a fee, plus all he wanted to eat and drink, but that was not enough for him. One of our senior employees complained that the noble lord was interfering in the running of the club, so Ronnie asked to see him.

'Yes, Ronald?' Effingham said.

'Mowbray,' Ronnie said quietly, using the peer's Christian name. 'You're getting above yourself. You're getting paid for nothing, so you can shut your mouth or leave.'

Effingham knew what side his bread was buttered. 'You're so right, Ronald,' he said. 'I do apologize.'

The people who flocked to The Barn in 1960 seemingly had money to burn; it would shake me when I watched thousands of pounds being risked on the turn of a card at the chemin de fer tables.

Neither the twins nor I were gamblers, but I do remember one night I tried my hand at chemmy and won £350. Well pleased, I told Reggie, who immediately thought he'd have a go. I saw him about two hours later and he was falling about laughing.

'How much did you win?' I asked.

'Nothing,' said Reggie, highly amused. 'I did £750 in an hour.'

Reggie was not as careless with money as Ronnie, but when he had it he was not afraid to spend it.

It was during the early days of The Barn that Reggie developed an outside interest that in time was to change his personality and, eventually, his life.

She was a sixteen-year-old girl and her name was Frances Shea. Like us, she was from the East End and

Reggie had watched her grow from a child to a beautiful young woman. When he fell in love with her it was with the same intensity, commitment and passion he showed in everything he did. Although eleven years younger, she was everything he wanted in a woman; it was as if even then he knew that this was the girl he wanted to marry, and he courted her in the old-fashioned sense, with roses and chocolates, the deepest respect and impeccable manners. Reggie put Frances Shea on a pedestal that would eventually destroy him.

Early in 1961 we got our first warning that the police were not impressed with the Kray success story and that someone somewhere had decided a couple of East End tearaways and their elder brother had no right making a few bob and mixing with wealthy folk far above their station.

Ronnie and I were at Vallance Road when Big Pat Connolly's wife phoned from a call box saying Pat had been taken to hospital. A friend of ours, Jimmy Kensit, ran us to the Connolly home to see if there was anything we could do. When we arrived, we discovered Pat had suspected polio: since we had all been in recent contact with him my first thought was to tell Dolly and Gary to go to the hospital for an anti-polio injection. I made a call from a kiosk in Queensbridge Road, then we all headed back to Mum's house where we could phone everyone who had been in contact with Pat.

We did not get there until several hours later – after a spell in Dalston police station.

Jimmy Kensit had decided to call in for something at his flat in Pritchards Row, in Dalston. Ronnie and I were sitting in Jimmy's banger when a squad car roared up. We thought there must have been some big robbery – a murder perhaps – but in fact we were the lucky ones to be under investigation. A detective constable called Bartlett started asking Ronnie and me who we were, where we were going, etc, while two uniformed constables inspected Jimmy's car.

Fortunately, just as Bartlett was preparing to take us to Dalston nick for further questioning, a friend of ours named Billy Gripp walked by. Billy, who trained for judo at the gym above The Double R, was a respected citizen of Bethnal Green and I admitted to him I was worried about a frame-up: would he mind searching Ronnie, Jimmy and myself, and the car, to satisfy the police and a gathering crowd that we didn't have anything we should not have? Bartlett objected, but Billy went ahead anyway. Then we were taken to the police station. While Bartlett strutted around, warning us that we'd be inside soon, our homes were searched – without warrants – and later we were charged with . . . loitering with intent to commit a felony!

Poor Pat Connolly had to take a back seat for a while, as did all the people we were keen to warn to have anti-polio jabs.

The case actually went to court but, happily, did not last too long. Bartlett told the Marylebone magistrate under oath that Ronnie and I had been seen in Queensbridge Road trying the door handles of parked cars, and that we fled after Kensit hooted his horn to warn us we were being watched.

Jimmy's car horn was found to be out of action, and we proved we were somewhere else at the time of the alleged offences. But we were far from happy walking out of Marylebone Court that day. It was obvious we were marked men.

Bartlett – a pervert later convicted of molesting young girls – was merely a pawn in a game controlled by far more senior and influential officers.

91

A few days later I arrived at Vallance Road to find Mum comforting Frances, who was crying: some police-man had turned up and arrested Reggie for breaking and entering an East End house. Seething, I raced round to Bethnal Green nick and told them I knew it was a 'get up'; that they were framing Reggie for something he didn't do.

The police said they had a witness – a Jewish woman in her seventies called Lilia Hertzberg who claimed to have seen Reggie and another man running out of her hus-band's Stepney home with jewellery and cash valued at £500.

The case was a laugh throughout the East End, for most people knew that Reggie would rather give an old couple £500 than steal it from them. But Reggie was still sent for trial at Inner London Sessions. We were not sure if there had actually been a robbery or if Mrs Hertzberg was being paid by the police to invent one. But we knew she had not seen Reggie so we offered her £500 to encourage her to tell the truth in court. Since she and her husband were due to leave to begin a new life in Australia shortly, they both jumped at the idea.

It was decided that on the day of the hearing someone would go to the old man's house with the £500. As soon as Reggie was released, the husband would receive a phone call from the court and the money would be handed over.

That's exactly what happened – except that the old man never got the £500. When the phone call came through and he asked for it, our friend said, 'You've got to be joking. You're lucky you're not younger – I'd knock you up in the air for what you've tried to do.'

Since we had discovered he was a paid police informer, none of us had any qualms about not giving him the £500.

As for Reggie, he was awarded costs against the police

– satisfying in a way, but hardly compensation for the seven weeks he had been held in custody.

Later, Reggie admitted to me that he'd panicked when the police arrived at Vallance Road. I was amazed because Reggie had never been intimidated by the law. But it was all to do with Frances. Reggie knew the robbery allegation was a joke and he felt they might go the whole hog and claim the woman had been assaulted. The thought of Frances thinking for a second that he had touched another woman sent him into a cold sweat; and when the police said it was only robbery he was relieved, and went quickly and quietly – even though he hadn't been anywhere near the scene of the alleged crime.

The warnings were there for the future: the police had played two tough games against the Krays and lost badly each time. But there was bound to be another time. We had bought cars, clothes, jewellery, exotic holidays, and other luxuries that make life sweeter. But we had not bought any policemen.

When the police moved in and closed The Double R, the twins got the hump. Why did the Old Bill have it in for them? they wanted to know. One minute they were millionaires, demanding with menaces all over London, the next they – and I – were supposed to be pilfering from cars. Now a harmless club was shut down. It did not make sense.

Around this time Billy Hill gave the twins some advice, which he urged them to take and never forget. Over drinks at his sumptuous flat in Moscow Road, Bayswater, the notorious gangland figure of the fifties told Ronnie and Reggie that they were fortunate in having a brother who was straight, who had no criminal convictions and was not involved in villainy of any kind. It was vital to keep it that way, he said, because I would always be an ally; an important weapon they could use to set legal machinery in motion if things went badly with the law. 'Never involve Charlie in anything crooked,' he said.

And he begged them to remember that advice.

Billy's remarks gave the twins an idea. Since I was trusted one hundred per cent by the Old Bill, could I not have a word with someone to find out just why they appeared to be marked men. I said I'd speak to someone in the know, which is how I came to be talking to two plain-clothes coppers in an out-of-the-way pub in Walworth, South London.

The men arrived with a load of papers. And what they contained blew my mind. To me, the twins were just two ordinary cockneys from the back streets of Bethnal Green: tough, certainly, but likeable and respectful unless their feathers were ruffled by idiots. But to Scotland Yard, it seemed, the twins were a highly important duo, worth watching closely. I was shown telexes to Scotland Yard from forces in other countries, giving details of where the twins had gone and who they had met. There was a lot of stuff on Tangier and Ronnie's meetings with Billy Hill, who had a house there.

I told the two coppers that I couldn't dispute that the twins had had a few rows. But they were not robbing people; they were just club owners who wanted to make a few bob. Why, I asked, was the Yard going to such lengths to find out what they were up to?

The coppers told me that, quite simply, the twins had become too powerful. They may have started out as two ambitious, but insignificant, East Enders of modest intelligence, but now they were powerful; too powerful. They had money, and friends in high places with a lot of influence. The mixture was too dangerous.

I said I couldn't understand it. How could the twins be

a danger? All they wanted to do was to run a few clubs, have no money worries and be able to count the rich and famous – particularly sporting and showbusiness celebrities – among their friends.

Top political figures, it seemed, believed the twins could get 1,000 men behind them from all over the country, with a few phone calls.

The twins knew a lot of people, I agreed. But if they could get 1,000 people, what would they want them for? What would they all do?

The coppers didn't have an answer to that. They just said that the people who ran the country considered them too powerful and were thinking of ways to control them. But I could be sure of one thing, they told me, and the twins ought to be aware of it: they would not be allowed, under any circumstances, to become more powerful.

I paid the coppers the agreed £100 for their information and went home, my head swimming with the implications of what I had been told.

Surprisingly, the twins were not at all bothered. Ronnie, particularly, thought it a big joke.

'What do they think we're going to do?' he quipped. 'Take over the bleeding country?'

Chapter Seven

With Esmeralda's – and other projects dreamed up by Leslie Payne – bringing in hundreds every week, it wasn't long before we decided to open another club in the East End to replace the much-missed Double R. We called it The Kentucky and it was packed every night after it opened early in 1962.

I must admit the way the twins chucked money around worried me and, since the Betting and Gaming Act had made gambling legal, I suggested investing some of our profits in betting shops, which were springing up all over the country. But Ronnie and Reggie did not fancy the idea.

What we did agree on, however, was using some of our money and growing business and showbusiness contacts for charity work. The three of us had always been eager to help old people and children and now we took huge pleasure in organizing fund-raising activities for Mile End Hospital, the Queen Elizabeth Hospital for children, the Repton Boys' Club and various other organizations.

One of Reggie's promotions at the York Hall in Bethnal Green was unique. He matched Bobby Ramsey – who had been responsible for the ill-fated bayonet attack in 1956 – as a properly gloved boxer against a judo and karate expert called Ray Levacq. Although the 'anything-goes' bout lasted only a few minutes – Ramsey winning by a second-round knockout – the star-studded audience loved it, and local charities benefited by several hundred pounds.

The Kentucky had a colourful, if short, life. A number

of international stars – including Billy 'That Ol' Black Magic' Daniels – came there for a few drinks after their shows and the club even provided the setting for a film, *Sparrows Can't Sing*. The mayor of Bethnal Green, Mr Hare, asked if we could help him by selling tickets for the charity première at the Empire Cinema opposite The Kentucky. We bought £500 worth – and sold the lot. Later, people would say this was 'demanding', but it wasn't. East Enders were keen to support charities, always had been. And anyway, people liked a good night out. After the première we threw a party for the whole cast that was talked about for months. Throughout 1962 and early 1963 the East End in general, and The Kentucky in particular, was the place to be.

You could never be quite sure what was going to happen. One night, for instance, a midget singer called Little Hank took the stage for a cabaret spot when Ronnie suddenly emerged from the wings, holding a donkey on a leash. Little Hank – no doubt as surprised as the rest of us – gravely climbed on it and sang his opening number as Ronnie stood alongside with a straight face. After Hank's performance, Ronnie led the donkey down to the bar and it waited next to him patiently while he had a few drinks. Later he gave the donkey to a club member for one of his children.

At around three in the morning, Ronnie was woken up by a knock at the door in Vallance Road. The recipient of Ronnie's thoughtful gift was extremely grateful, but wanted to know what to do to stop the blessed animal's deafening hee-haws, which were keeping everyone awake.

'Put its bloody head in a sack,' Ronnie offered, and went back to bed.

Charitable Ronnie even gave some local buskers a chance to take the Kentucky stage. We were walking

97

along Bethnal Green Road one day when Ronnie pointed at four or five blokes playing trumpets and various other instruments on the pavement.

'They're terrific,' said Ronnie. 'I always give 'em a few quid.'

I nodded. A few quid probably meant ten.

'Oh, by the way,' he added, 'I've told a couple of them to come to the club tonight and play us a tune. I said we'd give 'em a few quid.'

'Do me a favour, Ron,' I said. 'They're amateurs.'

'They're very good, let me tell you,' Ronnie said indignantly.

'You can't have them in the club,' I told him.

But, of course, he did. They played a tune and Ronnie paid them. That's how he was.

Both the twins had a lot of will-power, but Ronnie's was phenomenal. He had a sort of obsession about it: if you really wanted to do something, he'd say, nothing should be able to stop you.

One night in The Kentucky, Ronnie was at the bar, having a heated discussion about will-power with a much younger guy.

'I'll prove you can do anything you want,' Ronnie was saying. And he took a knife out of his pocket and plunged it into his left hand. Blood spurted everywhere. Reggie and I looked at each other, not believing what we had seen. We ran behind the bar and got a towel and wrapped it round Ronnie's hand, which seemed nearly cut in half.

'What were you doing?' Reggie yelled. 'Are you mad?'

Ronnie just said he was trying to prove a point.

'Fantastic!' I said. 'You're so bright.'

We took him to The London Hospital at Whitechapel and a doctor told him he had come within a fraction of an inch of losing the use of the hand.

Ronnie said he had put his hand through a window, but

the doctor did not believe him. When we got home, Mum broke her heart. She kept asking Ronnie why he had done it, but all he would say was, 'To prove a point.'

When I told him I thought he was barmy trying to prove a point to some idiot, Ronnie said, 'Shut your mouth. It's done now. It's finished.'

You could never tell Ronnie anything.

Both he and Reggie could not bear anyone who took liberties, particularly where women were involved. One afternoon, some girls from a dress-making factory hired The Kentucky for a firm's party. The twins and I greeted them, then left them to enjoy themselves. Later we learned that two brothers named Jordan had gone to the club and made themselves busy with the girls, grabbing them and generally trying it on. The bloke in charge of the club had not tried to stop the brothers because he feared they would smash the place up.

We hit the roof. I was happy to find the brothers and warn them verbally but the twins didn't think that was enough. The next morning Ronnie got up at five o'clock to go to Smithfield market where one of the brothers worked; he told Reggie and me to go to a local glass factory to find the other one.

When we got there, Reggie told me to leave everything to him because two on to one wasn't fair. One massive punch to the jaw did it: Jack the Lad Jordan didn't know what hit him. But, as usual, Ronnie was not able to throw just one and walk away. Apparently, he charged around Smithfield and when he found his Jordan, knocked him all over the place, leaving him in a right mess. The brothers never came into The Kentucky again.

Sadly, it was only a few months later that no one came to the club at all. Mysteriously, our request to have our licence renewed was turned down by the local justices. The club had been run properly, with no complaints from anyone, and applications for extensions had always been granted. But our renewal application was thrown out anyway. The local justices were not obliged to say why, and they didn't.

It did not need an Einstein to work out the reason. Because we refused to give the police back-handers to leave us alone we were still marked men. The daft charges of fiddling with car doors and robbing defenceless old-age pensioners had blown up in the police faces, so other tactics had to be used. They had easily closed The Double R without good reason, and they did the same with The Kentucky.

The closure had a bad effect on all of us, but particularly Ronnie. He hated the police aggravation and the violence. He would often say to Mum, 'I'm going to move. I can't stand it any more.' He wanted to get away from an area that bred violence and people who revelled in it. Ronnie, of course, was violent himself. But afterwards he would hate what he had done. I remember once he got extremely depressed and said, 'That's it. I've had enough.'

Leslie Payne had come running to the twins asking for help because Bobby Ramsey had taken a pop at him. Ronnie and Reggie were going to see Ramsey at a garage in Stratford and they asked me to go with them; why, I can't remember.

Ramsey came out into the courtyard. Ronnie told him not to take liberties with Payne, then laid him out with a right to the jaw. As Ramsey went to get up, Ronnie picked up a shovel and raised it menacingly. Reggie and I were convinced he was going to kill Ramsey before our eyes, but he calmed down and later went into the office to apologize. But he told Ramsey he had been wrong to hit Payne.

In the car going home, Ronnie was extremely

100

depressed. 'I'm sick of all this,' he said. 'I had to go and hit Ramsey on the chin because of Payne. I'm sick of the whole life. I want to get out. I've had enough.'

When he got like this he would go to Turkey or some other sunny place to get away from it all. But he badly wanted to move away for good.

Eventually he was to buy a place in that part of England he had loved so much as a war-time child. But by then it was too late.

We were sorry to see The Kentucky go: it was well liked and well used by respectable local people, and enhanced the area. But if the police thought the closure would put the Kray brothers out of business they couldn't have been more wrong. Esmeralda's Barn, which now had a basement disco, had enabled us to buy into other, smaller West End clubs. The twins also bought a small hotel, The Glenrae, in Seven Sisters Road, North London. And Leslie Payne, who was buying a controlling interest in The Cambridge Rooms on the Kingston bypass, was about to launch a legitimate company, The Carston Group, with a posh Mayfair office.

The police may have hit our East End connection. But up West, the money was rolling in.

To three East End blokes in the nightclub business, Leslie Payne's scheme sounded senseless. He had returned from the Eastern Nigeria city of Enugu and partly committed us to building a new township in the bush. It was a project more suited to merchant bank investment, but the more Payne explained the financial possibilities the more excited we all got. Ronnie and Reggie flew to Enugu with Payne and Gore to see the development site and when they returned plans were made to approach wealthy and influential people for investment. One of these gentlemen was Lord Boothby; another was Hew McCowan, son of a rich Scottish baronet and landowner.

What we did not know at the time was that Ernest Shinwell, son of the late, much-respected Labour MP, had hawked the proposition round for a long time without finding any takers. He must have gone to Payne as a last resort. Blissfully unaware of this, we happily poured money from our various London enterprises into the Great African Safari – GAS for short – confident that Payne knew what he was doing. As 1964 wore on, however, we became worried: not only was more and more money being swallowed up by GAS, we also got word that the police were taking an even closer interest in our activities. So it was with some relief that we greeted Payne's assurances in October that it was pay-off time and we would soon all be rolling in money again. Four of us – Payne, Gore, a well-connected Canadian called Gordon Anderson and myself – flew to Enugu full of hope.

It took me just three days to sense that all was not well.

Payne, as usual, strutted around like a Great White Chief – the faithful Gore forever in his wake – but I could not fail to notice he was always avoiding a native building contractor who, I knew, had paid us a £5,000 introductory fee months before. The man wanted to get on with the building work and was always in the foyer of the Presidential Hotel looking for Payne who, in turn, was forever dodging him. I talked to Payne about it but he told me not to worry.

Payne gave the impression he knew what he was doing. But he didn't. That contractor got fed up and opted out of the scheme. He managed to track Payne down and demanded his £5,000 back. After a blazing row in which Payne said he didn't have the money, the man went to the police. Payne and Gore were arrested and thrown into jail.

Overnight the warm, friendly atmosphere became cold and frosty: no more smiles, polite bows and handshakes from Government officials; no more smart cars with motorcycle escorts at our disposal.

Payne was still playing the Great White Chief in his prison cell, vehemently insisting that he and Gore would join us at the airport as soon as he'd put the local police chief in his place. When they didn't show up, I told Anderson to go on to Lagos while I dealt with the matter. The only way to sort it out was to pay back the £5,000, so I rang the twins and told them to wire the money at once. I sat by the phone for the next twenty-four hours until I had absolute confirmation that the cash was on its way. Then a solicitor I'd met on previous visits found a judge who would sign the necessary bail forms if I arranged for £5,000 to be paid.

The journey to that judge was a nightmare. The solicitor and another black guy drove me off into the jungle, along a narrow road that looked as if it didn't lead anywhere. The solicitor assured me we were going to the judge's house but the way Payne had behaved made me fear for my life. As we drove deeper into the jungle I had visions of being bumped off and dumped – just another mysterious disappearance. But after the longest fifteen minutes of my life, the jungle opened up and there was the judge's bungalow, set in beautiful gardens. I showed the relevant documents, signed some forms, tingling with relief, then went back to get Payne and Gore out of the nick.

They were filthy, thirsty, hungry and exhausted. Gore was demoralized; Payne on the brink of a breakdown. I didn't give either of them any time to say much: I spelled out the seriousness of our predicament and told them we were leaving – right then. It was not until the plane had left the runway at Lagos Airport that I was able to relax for the first time in three days.

The GAS had blown up in our faces and, once back in England, the twins and I gave Leslie Payne the elbow.

Towards the end of the Nigerian affair, the Boothby Photograph 'Scandal' hit the headlines. What a storm in a teacup that was! The whole nation, it seemed, was led to believe that Ronnie and the charming, multi-talented peer were having a homosexual affair. But nothing was further from the truth.

Ronnie went to Lord Boothby's home in Eaton Square just twice – on business. Boothby seemed keen to invest some money in the Nigerian project, but ultimately wrote to Ronnie saying he did not have the time to devote to it. That's where the matter should have ended. But Ronnie's passion for having his photograph taken with famous people set off a dramatic chain of events that ended with Boothby being paid £40,000 libel damages by the *Sunday Mirror*.

The photograph in question – one of twenty or so taken during Ronnie's second visit to Boothby's flat – was an innocuous one, showing the two men sitting side by side on a settee. They were both dressed in suits and, since they had been discussing a multi-million pound business proposition, they looked fairly serious. Keen to make a few bob, the photographer showed a print to the *Sunday Mirror* and on 12 July the paper ran a sensational front-page story – under the headline PEER AND A GANGSTER: YARD PROBE – alleging 'a homosexual relationship between a prominent peer and a leading thug in the London underworld'.

The story did not name Boothby or Ronnie, but claimed that a peer and a thug had attended Mayfair parties, that the peer and prominent public men had indulged in questionable activities during weekends in Brighton, that the peer was involved in relationships with clergymen, and that people who could give evidence on these matters had been threatened.

Not surprisingly, the *Sunday Mirror* story – based on little fact – blew up into a major scandal. The questions on the lips of the nation, it seemed, were: Who is the peer? And who is the gangster?

Well, the satirical magazine *Private Eye* did its best to put people out of their misery by naming Ronnie as the thug. And then Boothby himself brought the whole thing into the open in a frank letter to *The Times*, in which he referred to the *Sunday Mirror* story as 'a tissue of atrocious lies'.

On 4 August, both Ronnie and Boothby agreed for The Photograph to appear in the *Daily Express*, and the next day the International Publishing Corporation, which owned the *Sunday Mirror*, paid Boothby £40,000 compensation for the paper's unfounded and libellous story. IPC chairman, Cecil King, also made an unqualified apology. Ronnie was given no cash compensation but on 19 and 20 September the *Daily Mirror* and *Sunday Mirror* did allow four column inches to apologize to him.

To celebrate the end of the affair, Ronnie threw a party at a Bethnal Green pub. Boothby didn't come; nor did Reginald Payne, who was fired as editor of the *Sunday Mirror* on 14 August. But many celebrities *were* there. And among those who showed no fear at being photographed with the so-called thug, Ronnie Kray, was someone who was to become a dear, dear friend. Her name was Judy Garland.

The spider spinning a web to trap the twins made his first move in January 1965. Detective Inspector Leonard Read

– known as 'Nipper' in criminal circles – walked into the basement bar of the Glenrae Hotel and charged Ronnie and Reggie with demanding money with menaces from a Soho club owner. They were said to have threatened Hew Cargill McCowan with violence unless he gave them a percentage of the takings of the Hideaway Club in Gerrard Street. When McCowan refused the twins' offer, the prosecution alleged, a drunken writer called Teddy Smith smashed some bottles and glasses at the club, causing twenty pounds' worth of damage.

The evidence was wafer-thin and, thankfully, Ronnie and Reggie were acquitted. But they were subjected to two Old Bailey trials and three months on remand in Brixton before being cleared. Police objected to bail four times because they feared Ronnie and Reggie would not turn up to stand trial. But the twins offered to give up their passports, report to the police twice a day and undertake not to interfere with witnesses – all this in addition to sureties of a staggering £18,000. The court's refusal to allow bail caused widespread controversy and Lord Boothby was so incensed he asked the Government in the House of Lords whether 'it is their intention to imprison the Kray brothers indefinitely without trial'.

The trial took place at the Old Bailey in March 1965, but after a nine-day hearing the jury failed to agree. The retrial started on 30 March, and I was spending money and time trying to find witnesses who could help the twins. I went to the solicitors' at 9 A.M. every morning to tell them what I was doing. I had a private detective running around all over the place. And I had a tape on my phone, to cover every call.

The police had the hump with me for trying to help the twins and tried to fit me up one night.

I arrived home and Dolly told me a man had just phoned from Finchley saying he had some information that would interest me; he was going to ring back. About fifteen minutes later, the phone went. The guy was at Aldgate; could I meet him there? And would I be in my white Mini? I smelled a rat. How did he know what car I drove? And if he had rung from Finchley the first time, how had he got to Aldgate in fifteen minutes? I pulled him on this and he gave me some story, but I wasn't fooled. I told him I knew he was a copper and if he thought he was going to fit me up he had another thought coming. Both conversations had been taped, I said, then I put the phone down. I did not keep the appointment. And I never heard from the guy again.

I was spending so much time on the case – chasing witnesses, helping the private detective or attending court – that I had no time for my work as a theatrical agent. No work meant no bookings. And no bookings meant no money. But money was what was needed if the twins were to get off; for lawyers want paying, no matter which way the verdict goes.

I had been dipping into my savings and was absolutely boracic when I got a call from the solicitor representing the twins. The legal costs had been paid up front, but they had run out, the solicitor said. He wanted £1,500 for the next day's hearing, or he and the barrister were pulling out of the case.

I was owed money that would have more than covered the required amount, but I would not get it until the end of the week. I needed the £1,500 urgently and racked my brains for someone who had that sort of money at the drop of a hat.

I could think of only one person: Lord Boothby.

I rang his Eaton Square house and Boothby's charming butler arranged for me to see the noble lord that afternoon. Boothby was very pleasant: he offered me a drink and allowed me to say my piece. I explained why I needed

107

the money so quickly and stressed that I wasn't broke, just in a tight financial corner.

I honestly felt Boothby would agree to a loan: he'd just been awarded £40,000, and he knew the 'menaces' charge against the twins was nonsense. So I was shell-shocked when he said, 'I'm sorry, my dear boy. The forty thousand's all gone. I owed so much.'

I was choked. I didn't know what to say; there wasn't anything I could say. I'd blown out. I needed to get out of there quickly and try someone else, or else the twins would find themselves with no legal brief the next day – which would almost certainly mean a verdict of guilty and a prison sentence.

I left Eaton Square a very worried man, and not a little disappointed in Lord Boothby who, I'm sure, could have found £1,500 if he had really wanted to.

Of course, I got the money in the end; you always find a way when it's critical, don't you? And then I got on with the business of tracking down witnesses willing to tell the truth and get the case against the twins kicked out once and for all.

They *did* get off. But, sadly, I wasn't there to hear the Not Guilty verdicts.

On the sixth day of the retrial I went to see a possible witness instead of going to the solicitor's office first. When I finally turned up an hour or so later to tell them I'd found someone willing to give evidence, one of the clerks said, 'That was good, wasn't it, Charlie?' I didn't know what he meant. A minute later, in an upstairs office, a solicitor said, 'Congratulations.'

'What for?' I asked.

'Your case,' he said. 'It was thrown out this morning. Your brothers have been cleared.'

I was pleased, of course. But also cheesed off. It was the first day of the case I hadn't been in court, and I'd missed the best moment. By the time I got home to Vallance Road, the Fleet Street hounds were outside the house and the twins were having cups of tea – free men for the first time since their arrest three months to the day before.

That homecoming made even bigger headlines than the trial itself and when all the reporters and photographers and well-wishers had left Vallance Road, I took the twins in the front room and gave them some strong advice that, had they heeded it, could have changed the tragic course their lives were to take. They had proved their point, I said. Once again, the police had tried to put them away on trumped-up charges – and failed. But Nipper Read and his men would not give up; if anything, they would take the latest setback to heart and try even harder next time. Whatever the twins had in mind, I said, they should stop and think and be very careful. If they stopped now we could go on for ever and be looked on as respectable businessmen; we could have everything we ever wanted, with no villainy, no worries, no police harassment. Having won a few battles, we could go on and win the war.

Ronnie and Reggie nodded. What I said was right, they agreed. They had indeed proved their point to the police. It was time to quieten down and become respectable businessmen. Reggie even admitted that he and Frances were getting married.

But already it was too late. Reggie's marriage was tragically doomed. And in Westminster's corridors of power, one of the top men in the country was preparing a Top Secret document that was to lure the twins into the spider's web and trap them for ever.

Chapter Eight

Reggie could have married Judy Garland. She truly loved him, fawned all over him and was always trying to persuade him to stay at her house in Hawaii. But Reggie only had eyes for Frances Shea. She was all he had ever wanted in his life and could ever hope to want: the beginning and the end of everything. Reggie was very old-fashioned in his attitude to women and he courted Frances in an old-fashioned way. He took her to the top clubs and restaurants, always making sure she had the best of everything, but he liked the less flamboyant touches, too. If they were walking down a street together, Reggie would think nothing of stopping at a florist's to buy her a bunch of roses. It was a beautiful love affair, and the flower of their love grew and grew until it blossomed into marriage on 19 April 1965.

The wedding took place at St James the Great in Bethnal Green Road, and photographs of the happy event were taken – as a wedding present – by David Bailey, himself an Eastender, and the most famous photographer on the scene at the time. Hundreds of Cockneys turned out that sunny spring afternoon to wish the newlyweds good luck. But good luck, it seemed, was a luxury Reggie and Frances did not need. Fate had dealt them a kind hand. Although Reggie was eleven years older than his bride they were well-matched, joyously in love, and looking forward to spending their lives together. Reggie was already confiding his excitement at the prospect of becoming a father.

On the business side, too, he and Ronnie had fallen on

their feet after the nightmare of the two Old Bailey trials. Gilbert France, who had rented the Hideaway club to McCowan, had told the jury the twins did not need to demand from anyone; because they were so successful with clubs he would have been happy to give them a share. And when the twins were acquitted this is precisely what he did.

While solicitors prepared the paperwork for the partnership, Reggie and Frances flew off to the Greek sunshine. Their new-found good fortune quickly brought them into contact with high-ranking officers from the *Saratoga*, the renowned US aircraft carrier, who took a liking to the honeymooners and invited them on board. For two impressionable Cockneys it was a rare honour, and for years afterwards Reggie treasured a specially engraved lighter, given to them as a memento of their visit.

Back in London, it was decided to give the Hideaway a new name – El Morocco. When a star-studded party was arranged to mark its opening on 29 April Reggie and Frances cut short their honeymoon to be there, with a host of current celebrities – and 'Nipper' Read who, for some reason, popped in for a glass of champagne. One of the celebrities was Edmund Purdom, a very well-known film star who was living in Italy. Like most of the celebrities we encountered, Edmund took to the twins, particularly Ronnie, and he would always make sure he spent some time at El Morocco when he was in London.

One night Edmund came up to Ronnie and said he desperately needed to borrow two hundred pounds. Ronnie agreed to lend it to him, but said he would have to go to Vallance Road in the morning to collect it. Ronnie always preferred the house as a meeting place, feeling that if it was not grand enough for anyone they probably were not worth knowing anyway. It was perfectly acceptable to Edmund and he arrived on time the next morning, much to Mum's delight.

Always ready for a giggle, she asked me not to mention Edmund's presence to a neighbour, Rosie Looker, who came in every morning to help Mum around the house. When Rosie arrived she went into the kitchen at the back of the house while the twins and I talked to Edmund in the front room. After a while I went out there and asked Rosie if she would take some tea in to the twins and their guest. I stayed in the kitchen with Mum, waiting for Rosie's reaction. She did not disappoint us: she came running out, her face flushed with embarrassment, saying, 'Oh, Charlie, you should have told me. I'd have put something different on.' Mum and I laughed. It was the equivalent of coming face to face with Paul Newman today.

On 19 June that year Dolly had a baby. It was a posh affair in the exclusive London Clinic and the baby girl was wheeled into her ward in a cot fringed with lace. She was blonde and beautiful, and as I held her in my arms I knew what love was. She had marvellous laughing eyes and we called her Nancy.

Ronnie, thankfully, was anxious for violence to play no part in the new operation. One night, for instance, he took care of two massively built bodybuilders – one black, the other white – with little more than a tug of the sleeve. I wasn't in the club at the time, but I gather the two blokes started shouting and swearing and generally making a nuisance of themselves shortly after coming into the club late one night. Ronnie, who was sitting at a nearby table quietly talking with a friend, did not like their behaviour at all. After tolerating it for a few minutes he got up and walked over to the musclemen who were standing at the bar.

'Excuse me,' he said softly and pleasantly. 'Could you be quiet, please? There are ladies present. They don't like your language. Nor do I.'

Ronnie never gave anyone the chance to argue with him. He always said what he had to say and that was it. So, having said his piece, he turned and walked back to his table. His request did not cut any ice with the two unwanted customers: no sooner had Ronnie sat down than they started mouthing off again. Ronnie's face, I was told later, was a picture: it tensed in irritation then, as the swearing got louder, it tightened and went white with anger. I had seen that look many times and, to strangers, it must have been quite frightening. Finally, unable to stand it any longer, Ronnie got up again and walked over to the two hulking giants. Grabbing each by the arm, he said quietly but convincingly, 'You're leaving.' And he started walking them to the door. As he bundled them into the street he said, 'Don't come back. You're not welcome here.' Then he returned to his seat and calmly carried on talking to his friend as though nothing had happened.

For Ronnie to restrain himself when so angry was remarkable. I would not have been surprised to have been told he'd laid them both out at the bar. I was pleased when I heard the story. Maybe for once he was heeding my advice.

From the early days of their club life the twins had always liked to rub shoulders with famous people and now, in 1965, they were given an opportunity to meet legendary American stars, not only from the showbusiness world but boxing too. The chance came when they were introduced to a genial, nineteen-stone former American football star named Eddie Pucci, while he was in England as bodyguard to Frank Sinatra's son.

Eddie, who had been connected with Sinatra for five years, was getting involved in arranging for American showbusiness stars to perform in England. As the twins knew the club scene backwards, he asked them if they would entertain the stars and generally make them feel at home. It was through Eddie we met the actor, George Raft, singers Tony Bennett and Billy Daniels, and goodness knows how many other celebrities who were household names in Britain then. The twins persuaded several to come to meet Mum at Vallance Road but none made more impact than the unforgettable Judy Garland. She was very warm and friendly and Mum adored making her feel at home. Once, we amazed the regulars at the Crown pub – just around the corner from the house – by taking Judy to a party there. The pub was packed and people were standing on chairs trying to get a glimpse of her. We were besieged by people wanting us to ask her to sing, but we told them we had brought her as a friend, not as a star. We said Judy just wanted to relax and be herself and, thankfully, everyone understood and respected her wishes. All our relatives and friends were there, and for several hours Judy sat in an armchair, drinking and chatting away about life in general and the East End in particular. We had records on all the time and some of them were Judy's but no one asked her to sing. When we left she said it was one of the most pleasant nights she had spent anywhere because she had been allowed to be herself. I like to think she meant it.

Life in 1965 seemed to be one long, glittering merry-go-round of star-studded events and Reggie delighted in taking Frances to all of them. He had put her on a pedestal high, high above any other female, and he seemed to live in constant fear of looking less than perfect in her eyes. When she was with him he seemed to be on a knife-edge, always worried about whether she was all right. Once we all went backstage at the London Palladium to see Judy Garland after one of her performances. The dressing-room door suddenly opened and Judy rushed out and threw open her arms to give Reggie a hug. But Reggie backed away nervously, and Judy almost fell over. Frances was not in the least concerned or worried by Judy Garland, but Reggie was terrified to get in a clinch with her in case Frances thought something was going on. That's how he was all the time. He even took her to the opera and was invited backstage to meet the fabulous Australian singer Joan Sutherland. Nothing seemed out of reach. Mum, for instance, always dreamt of meeting the French film heart-throb Charles Boyer and, of course, the twins set it up. As they prepared to escort her to the rendezvous, Ronnie kept winding up the old man that he was about to lose her to the most romantic, charming celebrity of the day. The next day I asked Mum how it had gone and she just said, 'Amazing.' It was a dream come true, and the twins were delighted to have made it possible.

Not all their thoughtfulness had such pleasing results, however. The time they extended a helping hand to American boxing hero Joe Louis, for example, rebounded on them nastily and showed how much they were marked men. Eddie Pucci told us that the former world heavyweight champion was coming to England and, as he was down on his luck, could do with some work. Joe was no song-and-dance man like Sugar Ray Robinson, but he was a gilt-edged celebrity who was still a big-name attraction and the twins – particularly Ronnie – wanted to help him. They knew some club and restaurant owners in Newcastle who would pay Louis to promote their premises and so they took the train up there, planning to spend some days trying to earn the genial giant a few bob. They had not been in the city two days when a posse of police pounced on them in their hotel room. Ronnie told them why they were there but an inspector would have none of it: the twins were the 'London mob' and were now trying to take over Newcastle; he wasn't going to stand for it and he wanted them on the next train back to London. It was like something out of a western, with the sheriff giving the bad boys an ultimatum to get out of town. Ronnie said if the stories about them taking over London were true, why did they need to bother with a smaller city nearly four hundred miles away? But that argument didn't impress the inspector. Frustrated by it all, the twins called Louis in his room and told him what was happening. Dear old Joe was bewildered. He told the police the truth, that the twins were friends trying to help him, but the inspector didn't want to know. He handled the Brown Bomber very carefully but told him he was just an excuse; he'd heard all about the Kray twins and they were not going to bring trouble to Newcastle like they had to London. There was a train to London very soon – and the twins would have a police escort to see they caught it.

In the end, the twins had no choice.

They asked Louis to stay on with some friends, then phoned me with the full story. Convinced the police would try to frame them in some way, they asked me to arrange for our solicitor, Ralph Hyams, to be waiting for them.

When the train arrived at Euston, I was surprised to see Reggie in shirtsleeves. He told me he had held his jacket the whole journey because some Newcastle police had travelled with them and he wasn't risking anything being planted.

When Louis returned to London he apologized to the twins for inadvertently getting them into trouble, but they

116

told him not to worry about it. Many of the worthwhile things they did were misconstrued, they said, and they had grown used to it. Later, Eddie Pucci told us that the much-loved American hero really appreciated what the twins had done for him. But they thought nothing of it; Joe Louis had the same courage and dignity when his luck was low as he had when he was riding high as one of the greatest boxing champions ever. Ronnie and Reggie considered it an honour and privilege to help him in some small way.

Around that time, Reggie did a favour for another world boxing champion. But this time it did not go down well at all.

Sonny Liston, who held the heavyweight crown from 1963 until he was beaten by the then Cassius Clay in 1966, visited the twins at the Cambridge Rooms one night. After a pleasant evening drinking and chatting to various friends and acquaintances, he accepted Reggie's offer to drive him back to the May Fair Hotel in Stratton Street. As they pulled away, Reggie drove the wrong side of some bollards in the road. I thought, 'Good luck, Sonny, you're going to enjoy that drive.'

A friend of ours, John Davis, who was in the front passenger seat, told me it was a wild ride, even by Reggie's hair-raising standards: they went through red lights, screeched round corners, narrowly missed other cars and clipped a couple of kerbs before shuddering to a halt outside the May Fair.

Jauntily, Reggie climbed out and opened a back door for Sonny and his manager, then he pumped Sonny's hand cheerily and said, 'I'll see you tomorrow, Sonny.'

The world champion returned the handshake but then looked seriously into Reggie's face. 'Reggie, I'm going to tell you something,' he said. 'There's no man in this world I'm afraid of . . .'

117

Reggie nodded knowingly: it was the sort of comment you'd expect from a huge, hulking bear of a man who was heavyweight champion of the world.

'. . . except one,' Sonny added.

Reggie frowned, mystified.

'Who's that?' he asked.

'You,' said Sonny. 'I've never been so terrified in my life. You'll never drive me again. Ever.'

Reggie laughed. And no doubt zoomed off through the Mayfair traffic in precisely the same reckless manner. He simply didn't appreciate what it was like for his passengers. His adrenalin was always running fast; he was always in a hurry. In his life, as in his boxing, he was always lightning quick, but his brain was one step ahead. Behind the wheel of a car, though, he was a menace. A lot of it was to do with his short-sightedness.

One night, driving me from his house in Casenove Road, he suddenly said, 'Is that a bus coming up here?'

'You *are* joking!' I said, staring at the huge red monster bearing down on us.

'Well, I haven't got my glasses,' Reggie said, matter-of-factly.

'For Christ's sake, stop then, and let me out!' I roared.

Once I went with him to collect a new Humber from Commercial Road. Driving back along Cambridge Heath Road we approached a badly parked lorry on our side of the road. A bus coming towards us was already alongside the lorry and the space was obviously too small for Reggie to get through. Anybody in their right mind would have stopped but Reggie steamed on through, and duly scraped the side of the car from front wing to the back.

'That's clever,' I said. 'You've ripped a car you've only just bought.'

Reggie shrugged. 'That's all right. I can soon get it done.'

118

A Buick also had an eventful life in Reggie's hands. One night he was driving a load of his mates along Commercial Road when they came to some road works. The area was roped off, with lanterns warning drivers, and Reggie's passengers thought he was larking about as he headed straight towards it; they were convinced he was going to swerve at the last minute. But Reggie drove straight on . . . and the big American car disappeared down a hole. Reggie was lucky the hole wasn't that deep, otherwise some of those passengers – and maybe himself – could have been killed. As it was, they all climbed out unhurt. Reggie merely looked down at the wrecked car and said, 'We'll have to walk home.'

The next day a police inspector called at Vallance Road, asking for Reggie.

'Do you own a Buick, registration number . . .?'

'Yes,' said Reggie.

'Well, I don't know how it got down a hole in Commercial Road but you'd better get a breakdown truck to pull it out.'

Reggie just said, 'Oh.'

He never cared about cars – or any material thing, come to that.

The Cambridge Rooms should have been a profitable venture but Ronnie's generous nature sent it into bankruptcy. He paid the staff too much and gave free drinks to too many people. He even took £1,000 out of the till to buy a racehorse – then gave it away!

The horse, called Solway Cross, never won anything, and a leg injury finally ended an undistinguished racing career. We were wondering what to do with it when Ronnie had a brilliant idea: we would raffle it at a big party we planned to throw at the Cambridge Rooms in aid of an East End charity, the Peter Pan Society for

Handicapped Children. The party was held towards the end of the summer of 1963 and we had a big turnout of East End bookmakers and publicans, showbusiness celebrities including our old mates Barbara Windsor, George Sewell, Victor Spinetti and Ronald Fraser, and boxing stars Ted 'Kid' Lewis, Terry Downes and Terry Spinks. There were a few titled gents too, including Lord Effingham and Vice-Admiral Sir Charles Evans. Guest of honour was Sonny Liston.

The main event of the day was the raffling of Solway Cross at £1 a ticket – the entrance fee – and it was won by a Stepney publican, who said she had not time to enjoy the horse and put it up for an impromptu auction.

Lord Effingham mounted an improvised rostrum and within a couple of minutes Solway Cross had a new owner – Ronnie Fraser. The genial actor had had a couple too many and had got landed with the horse for £200. He couldn't believe it; he'd only joined in the bidding for a giggle. He turned to me and grumbled, 'Apart from getting ratted, I'm going home with a filly I hardly know.'

Fraser may not have been too pleased with that lovely summer afternoon party. But the Peter Pan Society was delighted. Their representatives went away with £1,200 all collected on the day.

Alan Bruce Cooper's name spelt ABC. But he was a trifle more difficult to read than the alphabet. He came on the scene around the time the El Morocco opened and we did not know what to make of him. He was rumoured to be one of the organizers of an international arms smuggling ring, supplying the IRA, Palestinian terrorists and groups of mercenaries. It was also suggested that he had a finger in gold and narcotics smuggling. At one time the twins and I even thought he was part of the Mafia.

Three years later – as the spider's web was closing

around the twins – we discovered that the little man with the moustache and a stutter who lived in great style in Kensington and drove a Rolls Royce was indeed in a sinister line of business.

From the moment they met him the twins were impressed with Cooper: he talked in telephone numbers and had an air of mystery that fascinated them. It was clear he was trying to involve them in some form of international intrigue, but the twins did not seem to mind. When he suggested a trip to New York, Ronnie jumped at it. People with criminal records are not allowed to have a visa for entry into the US but Cooper, who travelled on an American passport, got round this by taking Ronnie to Paris and obtaining a visa from the US Embassy there. Ronnie thought it was great fun, not only because he spent a lively week in New York but also because it was a victory against the Old Bill at home, who seemed to be going round the bend wondering where he was.

Cooper, who was about thirty-five, captured Ronnie's imagination with stories of how he was responsible for several assassinations in which he used highly sophisticated lethal devices, including a hunting crossbow and a briefcase containing a hypodermic syringe full of deadly poison. He was a nondescript character, who could easily have passed for an insurance salesman. But behind that bland exterior there must have been a clever man, for I checked him out and found no trace of a criminal record, either in Britain or the US. He thrived on mystery. One day he would be in his office in Mayfair then he would be off to the States, saying he had to visit a daughter who had meningitis. When he returned, there would immediately be phone calls from Madrid or Paris or Geneva or Brussels; it was difficult keeping track of him. One day he walked into the Carpenter's Arms with a mild-mannered gentleman with glasses who looked like a school-teacher.

121

In a dramatic whispered aside, Cooper informed me he was a hit man for the Mafia.

A friend of ours, Tommy Cowley, said early on that Cooper was a police spy. I laughed it off. He was a harmless Walter Mitty no one should take seriously, I said.

Chapter Nine

The three bullets that shattered my dreams of a quiet, peaceful and successful future were fired in the saloon bar of The Blind Beggar pub in Whitechapel Road, around 7 P.M. on 9 March 1966. The first was shot into the air by a member of the twins' Firm, Ian Barrie. The next two were fired by Ronnie into the head of a man sitting at the bar.

The victim was George Cornell, a member of a gang operating in South London. He was known to the twins as flash and loud-mouthed and was going around town boasting that he was 'going to put that fat poof Kray away'.

On that Wednesday evening, Ronnie and the twins' Firm were drinking in a pub we called The Merry Widows. Suddenly Ronnie got up and said to Barrie and Scotch Jack Dickson: 'Let's go for a drive.' He often suggested this if the mood took him and the other two thought nothing of it. They followed Ronnie out of the pub.

Cornell often spent some weekdays in the East End; that night, Ronnie wanted to have a look in a few pubs to see if he was, in fact, around. There's not much doubt Ronnie hoped he was. For he didn't like what Cornell was saying, and was determined that if anyone was going to be 'put away' it would be the South Londoner, not him.

After the fatal shots, Dickson drove back to The Merry Widows. Ronnie told Reggie and their close friends, 'I've done Cornell.' He suggested they went to a pub away from the scene of the crime and within minutes they were on their way to Walthamstow.

Earlier that day I'd seen Reggie at Vallance Road and he'd asked if I was going drinking that night. 'We'll be in the Merry Widows,' he said.

'I may see you later,' I replied. I never committed myself. If I fancied a drink with the boys I would go; if I didn't, I wouldn't. I liked to be able to please myself.

That night I did fancy a drink. But when I got to the pub it was half empty. 'Where did they all go?' I asked Madge, the missus.

She shook her head. 'They had to see someone. Don't know where.'

I walked round to Vallance Road and asked Mum but she did not know where the twins were either. I nipped back to the Merry Widows in case I'd missed them and no sooner had I walked in than the phone rang. Madge looked at me. 'It's Reggie. For you.'

I took the phone. Reggie quickly gave me the name of a pub in Walthamstow. 'If I was you I'd pop over here and see us.'

When I got there Reggie motioned towards Ronnie and said, 'He's just done Cornell.'

I looked at Ronnie. 'I shot him.' he said.

He spoke so matter-of-factly, I couldn't take it in at first. Then I started asking questions: Where? How? Was it bad? Was he dead?

Ronnie told me what had happened. But he didn't know if the shots were fatal. Just then the news came on the pub radio. Everyone was listening to it: 'A man gunned down in a Stepney pub earlier tonight has died in hospital.'

I looked at the faces of all Ronnie's friends then told Ronnie, 'You're in trouble. Everybody knows.'

But he just said, 'I don't care.'

After a couple of drinks I decided to make a move.

'Better not go home,' Ronnie said.

'Why not?'

'The law will be about.'

'Why should I worry about that?' I asked. 'It's nothing to do with me.'

'You know what they're like. They'll try and involve you.'

'I'll take my chances,' I said.

'Well, we're not going to be around for a few days.'

And they weren't. As the law buzzed around the East End looking for witnesses to the killing, the twins stayed in Walthamstow, out of sight in a friend's flat. About a week later they surfaced and carried on as if nothing had happened. The heat was off. No one was coming forward to say who had shot Cornell. Ronnie, it seemed, was getting away with murder.

If the police were not sure who had killed Cornell there was one person who was in little doubt – the dead man's widow. She came round to Vallance Road and threw a brick through Mum's front window; fortunately she and the old man were out at the time. Cornell's widow stayed outside the house, yelling insults and accusations until Aunt May told her that, no matter what the woman thought the twins had done, it was nothing to do with the parents. Finally, Mrs Cornell left. I can understand her wanting to vent her anger and hate, but her reaction did nobody any good.

The Cornell murder shook me, naturally, but I should not have been too surprised. The twins and I had had our rows about guns. I tried to make Ronnie see that it was daft to walk around London armed to the teeth like some commando but he would reply, 'If they're tooled up, so will I be. They won't have me over.'

'Hold up,' I'd say. 'Think about what is going to happen.'

But of course he wouldn't. 'I'd rather accept the consequences than have my head blown off,' he'd say.

The twins were very disappointed in me for not sharing their views about weapons, and I did not endear myself to them when I put my foot down over a row between two of their Firm – Connie Whitehead and Scotch Jack Dickson. Ronnie had already told them to cool it but Connie and Jack took no notice. Then one night when I went to one of our clubs, The Starlight in Oxford Street, the doorman, Tommy Flanagan, said, 'I'm glad you've come, Charlie. Jack's inside, waiting for Connie. With a gun. He's going to do him.'

'It's not going to happen,' I assured him.

Relieved, Tommy said, 'Tell him, Charlie.'

When I walked through into the club Ronnie came up, wanting to know why I was there. I told him I'd popped in for a drink, then asked what was going on between Connie and Jack.

Ronnie said, 'I could have guessed you'd interfere.'

I went up to Jack and asked him if he had a gun. He admitted he had. 'So you're going to shoot Whitehead.' I said. 'You were pals a little while ago. Now you've had a row, you want to shoot him.' I turned to Ronnie. 'Are you just going to stand there?'

'Let 'em get on with it,' Ronnie said. 'If he wants to shoot him, let him. It's nothing to do with me.'

'You can't just stand by and watch,' I told him.

But Ronnie said, 'Don't interfere. Get on with your own business. I couldn't care less.'

I turned to Jack again. 'The only reason you have a gun and you're standing there like a big guy is because Ronnie is standing with you. You wouldn't have the bottle on your own.'

126

Jack said nothing. Ronnie drew on a cigarette, watching me. We stood there in silence.

'Well, it's not happening,' I said finally. 'I promise you that.'

'What do you mean?' Ronnie asked.

'If Connie comes down here, I'm taking him away. I won't let it happen.'

Ronnie launched a tirade of abuse at me, but I ignored him and I looked at Jack. 'Give me the gun,' I said.

He didn't want to, but after a few minutes he handed it over.

'Happy now?' asked Ronnie.

I continued to ignore him and went upstairs with the gun and told Tommy to dump it.

'Thank God for that,' Tommy said. He was pleased I'd intervened. No one else would have stood a chance of overruling Ronnie.

But Ronnie thought I was an idiot.

For the next five months the East End was alive with rumours: everyone, it seemed, knew who had shot Cornell. People would come up to me and try to pump me, hoping I would confirm what everyone suspected. 'I hear old Ron had Cornell over, then,' they'd say. 'Is that right?'

'News to me,' I'd reply. 'Better ask Ron.'

I was up to my eyes running my theatrical agency, a coat factory and distributing potatoes, and did not see a lot of the twins. When I did see them, neither mentioned the murder. They did not seem the least concerned; it was as if it had never happened. But throughout that spring and summer I was on edge all the time, expecting something to happen – waiting for it, almost.

In August, it did. Detective Chief Superintendent Tommy Butler swooped on a number of East End houses

– including the twins' in Vallance Road – and took in several men he felt might be able to help with his inquiries into the Blind Beggar mystery. Ronnie and Reggie appeared in identity parades at Leyton police station; neither was picked out, but it was clear that if they felt the heat had gone out of the police investigation they were wrong.

I came up with a suggestion that the twins should leave the country for a while, and for once they took the advice. I insisted that only two people, apart from the three of us, should know where they were going – Mum and the old man. The twins loved that idea, too, and a few days later took a private plane from Lydd in Kent to France, where they picked up a scheduled jet to Tangier. To keep the secrecy watertight, I told them never to phone the house but to dial the number of a public call box in Bethnal Green Road. They agreed to phone every Tuesday and Thursday at 8 P.M.; if the phone was engaged they would keep ringing until I picked it up. For the next month I felt like a spy, slipping out quietly just before eight and waiting for the phone to ring, and of course the twins loved the intrigue.

The effect on the East End was startling: the twins' friends were very curious, but not as much as the police were. Soon, rumours started flying around, including one that the twins had been murdered. When I told them, they roared. It wasn't easy keeping the secret for four weeks but somehow we managed it. And it was worth it. It gave the police something to think about and, as far as the twins' so-called friends were concerned, the rumours proved something I'd always suspected: that they couldn't stop bragging that they knew everything about the twins when, in fact, they knew absolutely nothing.

When the twins were due to return, I decided to see how fast the truth travelled by telling just one person where they'd really been. It was all over the East End in minutes.

When they finally arrived home, tanned and rested, Ronnie and Reggie took a great delight in the fuss their sudden absence had caused. A lot of people were glad to see them back, but in Tangier many – chiefly hotel waiters and taxi drivers – had been sorry to see them go.

Ronald Kray was the biggest tipper the city had ever seen.

With the law still buzzing on the Cornell mystery, Ronnie and some pals started spending their evenings at the Baker's Arms, a quiet pub a couple of miles away in Northiam Street, Hackney. One summer night Detective Sergeant Leonard Townsend from Hackney police station walked into the saloon bar with a colleague called Barker. Ronnie and most of his friends walked out.

Townsend looked at one who stayed behind. 'They have got to drink somewhere,' he said. 'And they might as well use this pub. If you see the Kray twins tell them if they want to play ball with us, we'll play ball with them.'

When Ronnie heard this he went spare, but he agreed to meet Townsend in the pub the following night.

They went into a private room at the back of the pub and Townsend quickly came to the point. 'I know you like it here because it's nice and quiet. But if you want to be left alone it's going to cost you a little bit of rent. There are two of us in it – a pony a week each.'

Inwardly Ronnie was boiling. Fifty quid a week to be allowed to drink in a pub! He felt like laying Townsend out on the spot, but he controlled himself – he had had an idea. He asked for a day to talk it over with Reggie and agreed to meet Townsend in the pub again the next night.

When Townsend left, Ronnie told the licensee, Eric Marshall, who exploded. 'I'm going to Scotland Yard,' he said. 'I'm a straight man. You've done nothing. You and your mates spend your money here. You're always treating the old people. The police are driving you away. I'm not having it.'

Ronnie quietened him down. They needed proof, he said, and he knew how to get it. He would meet the greedy copper the next night, as arranged, but this time the conversation would be taped.

When Ronnie asked my opinion of the plan I said it sounded a good idea because it would put a stop to the police corruption we knew had been going on for years. It would do the public good to learn that while the Kray twins had been accused of demanding money from people, the police had been demanding it off them. But I knew Ronnie well and suspected he wouldn't follow it through all the way. 'You'll get them nicked all right,' I told him. 'But when it comes to court, you won't give evidence.'

'Oh, yes I will,' Ronnie said. 'They asked for this trouble. And I'm going to give it to them.'

I shook my head. 'Don't bother wasting your time. You should go through with it, but you won't.'

I suppose Ronnie really believed he would. But I knew him better than he knew himself.

Before the meeting Ronnie contacted a private detective friend who set up two tape recorders in the room – one in an empty tin, the other strapped to Ronnie's chest under his shirt. The trap worked like a dream: Ronnie got Townsend to spill out all the incriminating evidence of corruption, then he took the recording to a solicitor who went to Scotland Yard.

Four days later Eric Marshall kept a rendezvous with Townsend carrying ten £5 notes, the numbers of which had been listed by a Scotland Yard Detective Chief Inspector. Townsend got into Mr Marshall's car at the

Triangle, Mare Street, Hackney, and a microphone hidden under the front seat recorded the conversation as the money was handed over. The hard part of the plan was over: the greedy cop had taken the bribe. But sadly, the watching police made a mess of the next part of the plan. Over-zealous C11 men blew their cover too soon and Townsend made a run for it, throwing the incriminating packet into the road. He was caught after a mild chase, but not with the evidence on him. As it turned out, it didn't matter; the tape recordings were enough to convince the police Townsend was guilty of corruption and he was duly charged.

All that was needed now was for Ronnie to make a statement and go to court and Townsend would be kicked out of the force, possibly jailed.

Surprise! Surprise! Ronnie said he couldn't, and wouldn't do it.

I tried to reason with him. I told him he had gone through all the aggravation so far and it would be easy to follow it through. When Ronnie still refused I said he owed it to other victims of police corruption to try to end it once and for all. No joy there, either. Finally, I told him straight out that he would be totally in the wrong if he turned his back on the case: not only would a bent copper go free on his money-grabbing way but Ronnie would have wasted everyone's time: his own, Eric Marshall's and God knows how many police.

I may as well have been talking to a brick wall. Ronnie said he would never go into a witness box to put somebody away, no matter who they were. Yes, Townsend was a bad copper, but giving evidence against him would make them as bad as each other, Ronnie argued. It was a strange, maddening philosophy and I tried my damnedest to change Ronnie's mind. I should have saved my breath, for when a summons arrived in December ordering

131

Ronnie to attend Old Street Court in North London as a witness, he promptly went into hiding. The case opened, but without Ronnie there it could not get very far and, not surprisingly, Townsend was remanded on bail.

We found Ronnie a flat in Kensington, near Olympia. He took a few chances to come to Vallance Road to see Mum, but generally he stayed in that flat. The police did not make a huge effort to find him and whenever I got the chance I told them they didn't want to. The absence of a key witness was a good excuse for their man to get off, wasn't it? With the case unlikely to be heard for a few months, Ronnie prepared himself, somewhat reluctantly, for a Christmas away from the family.

The case against Townsend started at the Old Bailey in April 1967. He was accused of trying to obtain £50 from Ronnie as an inducement to show favour and of corruptly accepting £50 through Eric Marshall for showing favour to Ronnie.

The jury was out nearly eight hours, but could not agree and a new trial began two months later. The tape recordings were present, but Ronnie wasn't; he was still holed up in Kensington. It didn't matter. Again, the jury could not agree and Mr Justice Waller ordered the detective to be found not guilty and discharged. Townsend was dumbfounded – he knew how lucky he was – but one person who probably was not surprised by the verdict was the prosecution's own counsel, a barrister named John Mathew. As prosecuting counsel his job was to prove Townsend guilty. For some inexplicable reason, however, he gave the jury the impression the twins were on trial. In his opening speech, he said: 'It may well be that some of you have heard of two persons known as the Kray brothers, Ronald and Reginald Kray. They are notorious characters. They are persons of the worst possible character. They have convictions between them

132

for violence, blackmail and bribery. Their activities were always of interest to the police.'

Mr Mathew, one might be interested to learn, was prosecution counsel when the twins were cleared of demanding money from Hew McCowan two years before!

The day after Townsend walked free Ronnie came out of hiding, pale and wan from his self-imposed imprisonment. As we were leaving an outfitter's in Bethnal Green Road next to the police station two policemen saw us. 'All right, Ron?' one of them called out casually, as though Ronnie was a dear friend he saw every day.

'I'm all right now,' Ronnie replied. 'Do you want me?'

The policeman said, 'No. We heard you were in Tangier. You don't look very tanned.'

'No,' Ronnie said. 'I've been here all the time.'

The policemen laughed and walked on. We got in the car and drove to Vallance Road.

That ended one dramatic episode in Ronnie's life. But another was already hitting the headlines and it was to end at the Old Bailey with Ronnie facing a charge of murder. It was The Strange Case of Frank Mitchell, a giant whose brutality had earned him the nickname 'Mad Axeman'.

Mitchell stood over six feet, had enormous muscles and was immensely strong. Yet he was shy and inarticulate, with the mentality of a child. He had had a sketchy education at a school for the sub-normal and turned to crime early in life, quickly progressing from remand homes to Borstal, then to prison. He was four years older than the twins and had spent most of his life in one institution or another.

Reggie met him in Wandsworth Jail in 1960 while serving eighteen months for demanding money from Podro the Pole. Almost from the moment they came into

133

contact Reggie felt compassion for the gentle giant. Mitchell was constantly being beaten up by sadistic prison officers, but he never complained and always came back for more, fighting his persecutors with the power and strength of a bull. At the same time, though, he responded readily to a kind word or gentle gesture, and when Reggie went out of his way to make his life more tolerable, Mitchell developed a bizarre sort of hero-worship for him.

He demonstrated this in a spectacular way that endeared him to Reggie and, with tragic irony, prompted a chain of events that was to lead to his mysterious, and still unexplained, death.

Reggie had just three weeks of his sentence to go when some officers started winding him up, tried to light his notoriously short fuse. It was not difficult. From the moment he had gone into prison he seemed to be the target for officers' bullying and he had never taken it lying down; this occasion was no exception. He was just about to retaliate when Mitchell roared from his cell, 'Leave the bastards to me, Reg. You've only got three weeks. They're only trying to keep you in here.'

For some reason it did the trick and made Reggie see the sense in swallowing it. He didn't lose any remission and left the jail three weeks later. But he never forgot Big Frank and ensured, through various means, that he never went short of comforts. Some time later, Reggie got a chance to prove his friendship in a more profound way. Mitchell was accused of stabbing another prisoner with a knife, and Reggie arranged for him to be defended at Marylebone Magistrates Court by a brilliant young barrister named Nemone Lethbridge.

Thanks to her superb defence Mitchell was acquitted on a charge of causing grievous bodily harm. He returned to Wandsworth, but was later transferred to Her

Majesty's Prison, Princeton, Devon, a massive, dark, forbidding Dickensian building more commonly known as Dartmoor. And although he often worked outside the prison he wanted nothing more than to be free permanently. Reggie had been doing his best to get his case investigated by persuading influential friends to write to the Home Office. But no hope was on the horizon.

Then, one wintry afternoon – while Ronnie was playing Puccini in his Kensington hideaway – Scotch Jack Dickson went to Reggie with a story that Mitchell was threatening to kill one of the prison officers to draw attention to his case. Reggie thought about it carefully, then made one of his swift decisions. He gave Dickson a couple of hundred quid and told him to get Mitchell out of jail for Christmas.

Dickson enlisted the help of a couple of mates – Albert Donaghue and a former boxer named Bill Exley – and planned the escape. It was surprisingly easy: on the morning of 12 December the three of them turned up in a car at a pre-arranged spot and Mitchell, who had slipped away from a group building fences on a military range, was waiting for them. Later that day, radio and TV news reports informed the nation that helicopters and commandos were scouring the moors for 'Mad Axeman' Frank Mitchell. But by then the subject of their search was tucking into a fry-up at a council flat in Barking.

As Londoners packed the shops in the frenetic pre-Christmas shopping build-up, two of the most infamous men in Britain sat it out quietly in their comfortable 'prisons' on opposite sides of the city: Ronnie in upper-crust Kensington in West London, Mitchell on the outskirts of the more modest East End.

I was a virtual 'prisoner', too. I'd developed a throat infection, which confined me to bed at the time of Mitchell's escape and for some days afterwards. I could not get involved in the big man's problems, even if I'd wanted to. For no sooner had I recovered than I had to get busy, tending to Ronnie's needs. I felt like someone from MI5 again when I went over to Kensington to see him: just in case I was being followed, I jumped on and off buses, in and out of taxis and sometimes walked round in circles just to shrug off would-be pursuers. With Ronnie wanted by every policeman in London I couldn't be too careful. It was a bit of a drag sometimes, having to go through all that fuss, but I didn't mind. I couldn't expect Reggie to spend a lot of time with Ronnie: he was having great problems with his in-laws over Frances who, sadly, was suffering from depression.

I quickly discovered that Mitchell had had no intention of killing anyone: Dickson, Donaghue and Exley had dreamt it all up as some sort of exciting escapade. To them, minding a dangerous man on the run was a huge joke. But, tragically, the joke misfired. An attractive nightclub hostess, Lisa Prescott, was hired to satisfy Mitchell's sexual urges, but the poor man – unworldly and naïve as they come – mistook her professional competence for true affection and fell in love with her. Then he got hold of Exley's gun and suddenly what had been a manageable, if troublesome, situation was out of control. Something had to be done.

It was decided that Mitchell would be smuggled out of the country. More money was provided and Donaghue was told to take him to a remote part of Kent, on the first leg of his journey. On Friday night, 23 December, the two men left the Barking flat together. Frank Mitchell was never seen again.

As that 1967 spring turned into summer, tension in the East End mounted. The police were no nearer to bringing Cornell's killer to court and now they had another East

136

End mystery on their hands. However, a far more significant event had been taking place at the Old Bailey which was to have a serious knock-on effect for the twins, their Firm and me. A South London gang, led by one Charles Richardson, had received massive sentences in what had become known as The Torture Trial. The victory had given police chiefs at Scotland Yard a tremendous boost in their war against London's gangland. The spotlight, we quickly discovered, switched from south of the Thames to the East End, and the twins' manor in particular.

I didn't see a lot of the twins but whenever we did meet I got the feeling that they were under scrutiny – in their favourite pubs there always seemed to be somebody in a remote corner, watching points, taking notes.

Ronnie and Reggie had followed the sensational month-long Torture Trial and appreciated the dangers ahead. But they had such a total lack of fear that they took the increasing pressure lightly, particularly Ronnie. In the Grave Morris pub in Whitechapel Road, for example, he would wave a mocking greeting to anyone he detected was a copper, and invite him over for a drink. Once he walked down Vallance Road to find detectives watching the house from a car. He apologized for keeping them waiting, then went in and told Mum to make some tea. He took it out to them in four of her best china cups and told the surprised policemen to make sure they returned them when they had finished.

Always the more dominant, more fearless, more reckless twin, Ronnie was convinced that he was above the law and that the Cornell business proved it. It was over a year since the killing. If the Old Bill were going to nick him, he said, they would have done it by now. The fact that nothing had happened proved they couldn't touch him.

I told him to cool it and warned that both he and

Reggie were heading for serious trouble. But as usual Ronnie didn't listen. With this air of invincibility he started embarking on wild, extravagant plans to make vast fortunes with Alan Bruce Cooper, the moustachioed, stuttering American who was now permanently on the scene. I didn't trust the man; he reminded me too much of Leslie Payne, whose elaborate plans also came to nothing. I was to discover that my intuition was right.

In the spring of that eventful 1967 I went to Spain with Dolly and my daughter Nancy on an all-expenses-paid trip organized by an American friend, Joe Kaufman, who had gambling connections and an antique shop in New York. Shortly after our arrival at the Avienda Palace Hotel in Barcelona, Joe, a keen amateur photographer, told me he'd been taking some long-range pictures from his balcony and seen someone else's telephoto lens focused on him. At the time I was amused: I told Joe he probably wasn't the only photographer in Barcelona. However, the incident was to have sinister implications.

We all went on to the resort of Sitges, further along the Costa Brava, and who should turn up but A. B. Cooper and his wife. He claimed he was in Spain on business and had decided to drop in and say hello. I presumed that Joe had told him and thought no more about it. But we discovered later that Cooper was, in fact, an informer for the CIA or FBI and had provided the police with a comprehensive diary of the twins' movements over the previous couple of years. We tumbled him when he tried to trap the twins into parting with some incriminating evidence in a room bugged by police. Cooper's plan, almost infantile in its conception and execution, began with a spate of phone calls and telegrams to the twins, and culminated with a frantic phone call from a Harley Street nursing home. He was, he claimed, suffering from a duodenal ulcer and wanted the twins to visit him.

Precisely why was not clear. The twins were convinced it was a set-up and sent Tommy Cowley instead.

Tommy told me later that he smelled a rat the moment he walked in; Cooper simply did not look like a man with an ulcer. Then, shortly after they began talking, a nurse burst in, the Old Bill written all over her. She handed Cooper a menu and asked him what he wanted for dinner, which Tommy took to be a cue for Cooper to turn up the volume on the mike, probably hidden under the bedclothes.

As soon as the nurse left the room Cooper started talking about the gelignite Paul Elvey had gone to Scotland to get. Tommy looked suitably puzzled and asked why Elvey had gone there to get gelignite.

'To blow something up, of course,' said Cooper.

Tommy roared with laughter. 'You delirious or something?' he said. 'We're supposed to be the guv'nors in London. If you want any gelignite, I can get you some today.'

It was all too ridiculous for words, and shortly afterwards Tommy made his excuses and left, without giving the listening law one shred of information that could have landed the twins in trouble. That was the last they saw of A. B. Cooper – until he turned up at the Old Bailey to testify against them.

A friend of the twins', Harry Hopwood, called at my flat wanting £2,000. The twins had decided to buy a pub and needed the money. I wasn't very happy about the hurry-up approach and sent Harry back with a message that I'd see them tomorrow. In those days it was quite easy to buy a pub and within a matter of weeks The Carpenter's Arms in Whitechapel Road was ours. We suggested Harry's sister and her husband ran it for us, in return for a weekly wage plus a flat above. The couple had no home of their own at the time and were delighted with the deal. A 'godsend' was the word used.

The pub was to become a regular meeting and drinking place for the twins and their Firm. But for a while a different type of customer made a name for himself. He was a tramp who Ronnie befriended after seeing him looking for dog-ends at the front of the house in Vallance Road.

Most of our family smoked, and the old man used to collect all the dog-ends and put them on the pavement, much to the delight of the local tramps who thought all their birthdays had come at once. The hoard was like gold dust, especially Ronnie's throwaways; he used to take only one or two puffs, leaving virtually a full cigarette. Ronnie, who had no idea the old man looked after the local tramps in this way, came out one morning and was horrified to see a shabby bloke with a beard and unkempt hair rummaging around the dog-ends.

'Throw them away,' Ronnie said. He took a packet of cigarettes from a pocket. 'Have some of these.'

The tramp, a shortish, stocky guy in his mid-forties, could not believe his luck. Later, Ronnie mentioned the incident at home.

'I've always left the dog-ends out there,' the old man said.

Ronnie shook his head. 'You can't expect people to smoke dog-ends, Dad,' he said, horrified.

After that, Ronnie used to wait until the tramp came along then go out and give him some fags. Over the next few days he got to know him quite well and took him to the public baths in Chesley Street for a clean-up and shave. The next thing we knew, he had brought his new-found, fresh-smelling friend a new suit, shirt and tie and wheeled him into the Carpenter's Arms. 'Let's give him a few quid,' he said to Reggie and me. 'And if he wants a drink, don't charge him.'

The mounting police interest did not bother Ronnie. And Reggie had a far, far bigger problem on his mind early that summer – Frances. She was becoming more and more depressed and seemed on the verge of a nervous breakdown. She had always been a highly strung woman; Reggie did not know it when he met her but she had had a couple of minor breakdowns in her teens. In the early days the Shea family had accepted Reggie but gradually as he became more and more successful and Frances was taken to West End shows and one champagne party after another, they grew to resent the relationship. In a strange way, they seemed jealous of their own daughter and this, I'm sure, played on her mind.

For several months, just before Christmas and after, she was very depressed. Reggie suggested it might do her good to stay with her parents for a while but Frances didn't seem too keen. A few days later, however, she suddenly disappeared. Reggie was out of his mind with worry. Nothing was heard of her for three or four days, then Reggie got word that she was in hospital. When he discovered that her family had known where she was he hit the roof, unable to understand why no one had bothered to tell him. He rang me at the time in a terrible state. 'How do you think this makes me feel,' he said, his voice shaking with emotion. 'A wife in hospital and the husband doesn't know!'

I couldn't say it to Reggie but I wasn't too surprised at the Shea family's behaviour. They had never treated Reggie with any respect. Whenever he called round at their house to pick her up – before they were married – the parents never invited him in. They would call down from an upstairs window, 'She'll be out in a minute.' And

141

they would leave him to wait in his car. Sometimes he'd wait an hour. I told him I could not have stood for it, I would have driven off, but Reggie loved Frances enough to put up with anything.

Naturally, he went to see her in hospital and a day or two later she came home. But she did not look well: her eyes were lifeless, her face pale and drawn. All the vitality and effervescence she had displayed on her wedding day two years before had gone, leaving her looking much older then her twenty-three years.

Then she went to stay with her brother, and the next time Reggie saw her she was dead.

It was a Saturday morning in June. I was at home when the phone rang, and the moment I heard Reggie's voice I knew something was wrong. He started breaking his heart. For some time I couldn't make out what he was saying but eventually he got out that Frances had taken an overdose. He had gone round to see her at her brother's house and when he hadn't got a reply he had located the brother and they'd found her in bed. Dead. I couldn't take it in. It didn't seem possible. Reggie was sobbing on the phone and I told him to go to Vallance Road; I'd see him there. I dropped what I was doing and raced round but Reggie was already there and had told Mum. She was as devastated as we were. Reggie just sat in a chair, staring ahead and repeating, 'If she'd been with me it wouldn't have happened . . . it wouldn't have happened . . .'

I told him it was an accident; Frances had surely not meant to kill herself. She was probably feeling neglected and took an overdose to try and get some attention. But Reggie did not even hear me. He just said, 'Why did she do it? Why?'

Reggie's heart was broken. He wanted to see Frances' body after the autopsy at Hackney mortuary, and he

142

asked me to go with him. There is a police station near the mortuary and while we were in a small room waiting to be called two policemen walked in. We couldn't believe it. Reggie started to choke with anger but I begged him to ignore them: they would probably have excused themselves by saying they were checking that Ronnie wasn't around. They just stood there, watching us. I felt like saying, 'Can't you find a better time?' but heeded my own advice to Reggie. Having a row in a place like that would have been dreadful; it would have made us lower than them.

Finally, we were called and went into another room where we could look through a window at the body. The two policemen moved so that they could half-see us in a mirror. Reggie and I stood looking at Frances and then Reggie started to cry, and I walked out of the room, leaving him to release the grief and heartbreak he'd been bottling up since that terrible Saturday morning. The policemen were watching him, and as I passed them I felt like lashing out. But I just sat down and ignored them and waited for Reggie, and when he came out, still choked, I just said, 'Come on, let's go home.' The policemen followed us out and were still watching us as we drove away.

It was then that I began to understand my brothers' rebellious attitude towards the police.

Mum, the old man and I tried to give Reggie support, but more than anything he needed the companionship of his twin, who could understand what he was going through without the need for words. However, the Townsend second trial had still to be heard and Ronnie was holed up in the flat in Kensington. He felt he would make things worse for everyone if he suddenly reappeared.

Reggie wanted Frances to be buried in her wedding dress but the family said no. They blamed him for her death, and their hatred was so deep that they tried to have her maiden name of Shea substituted for her married name on the coffin and memorial stone. But, of course, Reggie resisted that.

The funeral was held at the church where Frances and Reggie had been married just two years before and it caused a personal problem for Father Hetherington, who would conduct the burial service. He was a very Christian man and couldn't come to terms with his resentment towards the Shea family for the appalling manner in which they were treating Reggie: it hurt him to feel so badly towards them. Nevertheless, he refused to be hypocritical and insisted that Mr and Mrs Shea did not travel in the first car with Reggie. He also called me into the vestry and made it clear Ronnie must not turn up at the funeral. He urged me to make him promise not to come, even if he felt he had a duty to be present. Ronnie wanted to pay his last respects to his brother's wife but he thought too much of Father Hetherington and Reggie even to consider breaking his promise.

The police did not know this, of course, and on the day, police cars lined the route to the church and detectives mingled incongruously with mourners. The occasion was bad enough for all who had known and loved Frances. To have her death robbed of the dignity it deserved just made it worse.

Reggie did not speak to the Shea family after Frances was laid to rest. He didn't want to know them; they blamed him for their daughter's death and he blamed them; they said he had always been bad for her and he said they caused her mental problems by trying to pull her away from him. It was pure hatred on both sides.

For Dolly and me, our springtime trip to Spain had not changed anything: we continued to drift apart and by

144

LEFT: The toddling twins: Ronnie (*left*) and Reggie, showing an early liking for the camera.

BELOW: The fighting twins: Reggie (*right*) and Ronnie with our proud mum at Vallance Road.

MAIN PICTURE: Killer instinct: seconds after this picture was taken, Reggie (*right*) knocked out his opponent.

ABOVE: Family affair: me and my brothers with the old man at a Kentucky charity night. Far left is Johnny Squib, one of the many people the twins helped in the sixties.

TOP: Another charity night, with the legendary boxer Ted (Kid) Lewis on the right of young Olympic boxing gold medallist Terry Spinks.

FAR LEFT: Car crazy: Reggie with another acquisition.

LEFT: Helping hands: Reggie (*left*) and Ronnie with former world heavyweight boxing champion Joe Louis in Newcastle.

LEFT: Reggie (*nearest camera*) and Ronnie at Vallance Road.

BELOW: The picture that sparked a scandal: Ronnie with Lord Boothby at the great man's Eaton Square home.

RIGHT: Reggie marries Frances – and even Ronnie is smiling.

BELOW: On the town: Mum and the old man with George Raft at the Colony Club and (*left*) Jim Harris and his wife, Ethel.

LEFT: Ronnie and a friend with American singer Tony Bennett.

BELOW: Dolly before the divorce.

FOOT: Seeing stars: Ronnie, in glasses, and Reggie at London's Stork Club with Judy Garland (*background*). The peek-a-boo face on the right belongs to American singer-comic Stubby Kaye.

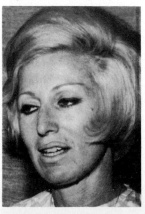

BELOW: Welcome back: me with Mum and Gary on the day I was released from Maidstone Prison.

RIGHT: Mum's funeral: my face tells its own sad story.

FOOT: Cover girl: Diana Dors and her husband, Alan Lake, on the day they popped into our home in Vallance Road to give Mum and the old man a copy of Di's latest book, *For Adults Only*.

RIGHT: Lost and found: me and Diana in 1975 after I'd tracked her down in Leicester.

BELOW LEFT: Star attraction: Reggie arrives, handcuffed, for Mum's funeral.

BELOW RIGHT: Sympathy: Jim Harris, a good friend of Mum and the old man, offers me his condolences after the service.

August I was going through my own domestic crisis. I adored my kids, of course, and was enjoying watching them grow, but the marriage itself was virtually over. The rot had set in the night I learned about George Ince, and the relationship had never recovered. That summer I was ripe for another affair and, when the chance came I threw myself into it with all the boundless joy of a carefree teenager.

Her name was Diana Ward and she had been hired as a waitress for a casino-nightclub I was opening in Leicester with a partner, Trevor Raynor. The club was due to open officially in the autumn and one afternoon I went to Leicester with Tommy Cowley to see how it was progressing. Within a few minutes Tommy spotted Diana. He was knocked out by her beauty and eagerly pointed her out to me. My mind was more on business, and I told him to keep his eyes off the staff. Secretly, though, I admired Tommy's taste: Diana was stunning.

Over the next few weeks, I got chatting to her and learned that although she was married it was not a relationship made in heaven. I was not in a position to ask her out, though. In London I was up to my eyes with my other businesses and I was not able to pop up to Leicester as often as I would have liked.

However, I did have to see how the club was coming along, so I set aside Wednesday as my 'Leicester day'. Diana was on my mind a lot, and as I drove north a warm feeling of pleasure would flow through me at the prospect of seeing her.

What I did not know was that on the eleventh floor of Tintagel House, a towering office block on London's Embankment, behind a door marked 'Krayology', the spider's web was being spun carefully, hour after hour, day after day. A pile of damning documents was growing steadily – detailed reports and sworn statements on the

145

movements and activities of the Brothers Kray by so-called friends and associates, eager to trade a lifetime of loyalty for the promise of freedom.

Suddenly that summer, betrayal was in the air.

Reggie could not cope with the loss of the beautiful woman he had idolized. For weeks after the funeral, he tried to drink himself into oblivion every night to ease the pain. Thanks to the Valium the doctor had prescribed him he found this relatively easy. Mum hated going to pubs every night, but she came with Reggie and me because we were so worried about him. He didn't seem to care about anything any more, he just drank and drank. And when he had drunk too much he would drink some more until the effects of too much gin and Valium would explode in his head making him incapable, and we would take him home and put him to bed.

Reggie had always taken immense pride in his appearance, but in his misery even this went out of the window. Once, someone saw him at five in the morning walking along Whitechapel High Street with no jacket and his shirtsleeves rolled up. Two policemen called out, 'What are you doing?' But Reggie just glared at them and walked on without saying a word. Evidently his look was enough for them to get the message. In the state he was in God knows what he would have done to them if they'd got busy.

Frances had been his life and now she had gone life would never be the same again. If she had not died so tragically young, if she had been around to give him love and a purpose for living, Reggie's entire existence would have taken a different direction. As it was, the whole appalling episode crucified him, and took away everything except an overwhelming desire to destroy himself.

The only reason he had for living, it seemed, was to

die, to join his beloved Frances. He pumped more gin, more Valium, into his body to take him away from the terrible reality of her death, and inevitably his personality began to change. I watched the transformation hopelessly with a kind of dread. Reggie was disintegrating before my eyes and there was nothing I nor anyone could do. He was on a wild, crazy rollercoaster that was hurling him round and round, faster and faster, and he didn't care where it took him or where he ended up. More gin. More Valium. As the heat of that summer of '67 cooled and autumn brought an early warning of winter's chill to the East End streets, the transformation was almost complete and Reggie's death-wish was about to shatter the barrier that separated him from Ronnie, and change all our lives for ever.

Chapter Ten

The early hours of Sunday 29 October 1967. The ringing of the phone shattered the silence of my bedroom. I reached out for the receiver and grunted, 'Hello'. It was Harry Hopwood.

'Something's happened,' he said. 'It's very urgent. You've got to come over.'

'What?' I asked sleepily. 'It's three in the morning.'

'Ronnie said you've got to come over. It's very urgent.' Harry sounded very worried.

'I'll get over as soon as I can,' I said. I put the phone down, wondering what could be so urgent that Ronnie would get Harry Hopwood to ring me in the middle of the night.

As I drove to Hopwood's house my mind ran riot with vivid imaginings. But nothing could have prepared me for the horrific revelation waiting for me at 14 Ravenscroft Road, Bethnal Green.

A distant cousin of ours, Ronnie Hart, opened the door. His face was pale, his expression worried.

'What's going on?' I demanded to know.

Hart motioned with his head to a back room. 'They're in there. You better ask them.'

I strode into the back room: Ronnie and Reggie were sitting in two armchairs.

I looked at Ronnie, then at Reggie. My heart raced with apprehension. 'What's going on that's so important at this time of the morning?'

'We've done McVitie,' Ronnie said in a matter-of-fact tone.

I knew Jack McVitie. He was a small-time villain, who was always shouting his mouth off about what he'd done or was going to do. He was bothered by his baldness and always wore a hat to cover it. He was called Jack the Hat.

He was also a crank; everyone knew it. For weeks he'd been slagging off the twins saying what he was going to do to them. One day they collared him and warned him he was heading for a lot of trouble. Shortly afterwards he went into the Regency, high on drink or drugs, armed with a shotgun, and started shouting that he wasn't scared of anyone – the twins included. He was warned that he was going too far. But he said he didn't care.

I stared at Ronnie. 'What do you mean, you've done McVitie? How bad?'

'We've killed him,' was all Ronnie replied.

I couldn't believe what I'd heard, couldn't take it in. My heart raced faster; my head pounded. I could understand teaching McVitie a lesson. But, murder?

'You've done WHAT?'

'It's true,' Reggie said.

Between them, they told me the story: they'd all been to a party, the Lambrianou brothers, Ronnie Bender, Ronnie Hart and the twins. Someone told the twins McVitie had been shouting his mouth off in the Regency and Ronnie arranged for him to be brought to the party in Stoke Newington. Things had got out of hand.

'That's lovely,' I said sarcastically. 'Well, that's it.' You've gone over the top this time.' I shook my head. 'End of story.'

Typically, Ronnie said, 'Well, it's done now. That's the end of it. He had it coming anyway.'

'He'd been mouthing himself off about what he was going to do,' Reggie chimed in.

Hopwood came in with some tea, and I drank some quickly to calm myself. I glared at the twins.

149

'Nice,' I said sarcastically. 'You have somebody over. Now you ring me up at three in the morning.'

'The Old Bill are going to be buzzing,' Ronnie said.

'So? What's that got to do with me? I wasn't involved. I wasn't there.'

They said nothing.

'What's happened to him?' I asked.

They shrugged. 'I don't know,' Ronnie said. 'Somewhere in South London, I think. The Lambrianous have taken him.'

I shook my head slowly from side to side. I didn't know what else to say to them; but I did know I wasn't involved and didn't want to be. I decided to stay out of it and let them sort it out themselves, so I left the house and went home. Dolly woke up as I went in. I made up some cock and bull story about the twins having a row and told her to go back to sleep. There wasn't much sleep for me. Since the Cornell killing, police pressure had been stepped up. With a second East End murder they would go potty. I'd been woken up from a dream and dragged into a nightmare in which there would be no escape from the ghost of Jack 'The Hat' McVitie.

As I lay there, it struck me that I didn't know how McVitie had met his death. I hadn't asked. And the twins hadn't told me. They never liked talking about their rows.

Later that morning Ronnie and Reggie changed their clothes and set off for Hadleigh, in Suffolk, where we had spent our evacuation. They took Ronnie Hart with them and left Ronnie Bender and the Lambrianous to clean up the flat in Evering Road, where McVitie had met his death.

The twins and Hart spent a week away, keeping on the move among the villages and hamlets of the pretty east coast country. They kept in touch with me by telephone and were relieved to hear that Jack The Hat's disappearance did not seem to have caused any undue police activity. When they returned they were buoyant and overjoyed, carefree almost. The only thing they could talk about was this fabulous Victorian house they had found in Bildeston, a few miles from Hadleigh. It was set in eight acres, with stables, a paddock and a stream running along one boundary. It was called The Brooks and it was on the market for £12,000. The twins snapped it up.

Mum and the old man, who had moved from Vallance Road to a tower block in Bunhill Road, not far from the Bank of England in the City, did not need much persuading to move to Bildeston and for the next few months The Brooks was the centre of the twins' lives.

They spent thousands doing it up and Ronnie took great delight in giving children from the village the run of the paddock, including a donkey which they could ride. Christmas was celebrated in style, with lashings of food and drink, and Mum and the old man were as happy as they had ever been, surrounded by family and friends in a house that surpassed their wildest dreams. The ugly face of villainy seemed a million miles away: a brief glimpse of a strange face in the village or a car cruising past the house were the only reminders that the police were still interested in us.

That period of the twins' lives was hardly idyllic, but the atmosphere was quiet and peaceful and they loved it. For two young men with a couple of corpses on their consciences they were remarkably relaxed. Far from worrying about being arrested, they started talking about retiring from the London scene and becoming country gentlemen.

It was the calm before the storm. For when the twins returned to London early in 1968, the East End was buzzing with rumours that the law had been busy and it wouldn't be long before the Kray Firm was nicked. Typically Ronnie and Reggie laughed in the face of the impending danger. They honestly believed that they were invincible and that no one would dare 'grass them up'. I advised them to go away for a few months, maybe longer, to take the heat out of the situation but they just said, 'Why should we run away? This is our home. No one can touch us.'

Every night they drank in the Carpenter's Arms with their Firm, oblivious, it seemed, to all that was happening around them. Night after night, drinking, drinking, drinking. It seemed to prove something to them: if you went drinking with them, you were a lovely bloke. I did not go drinking every night, with them or anybody. I knew what was looming and I didn't want to get involved. During the day, I kept myself busy with my coat factory and theatrical agency. At night, more often than not, I'd be at home with Dolly and the kids.

But one night I had to see the twins about something and went to the Carpenter's Arms.

All the Firm were there, as usual, sitting around like bit-part actors in a bad gangster movie. Ronnie started having a pop at me; mocking me for never drinking with them, for being hen-pecked, 'under the cosh'.

Then Reggie started putting in his twopenn'orth on the same theme and I lost my temper – 'went into one', as we say in the East End.

'See this lot here,' I said, my eyes sweeping the Firm sneeringly. 'They hang round you. They love whatever's going on. They love the violence. They love being bloody gangsters.'

'You're a nice bloke,' Ronnie said, taken aback. 'All these nice guys . . .'

'Nice guys!' I yelled, feeling all my anger at what was

going to happen to us welling up inside me. 'You know what's going to happen?'

I glared at Ronnie. 'You're going to get nicked.' I glared at Reggie. 'And you're going to get nicked. And I'm going to get nicked, too.'

I glared at the Firm. And they sat there, their mouths open, shocked at dear old Charlie, good old, quiet, straight Charlie, losing his rag.

'And I'll tell you something else,' I said, my voice rising. 'You see all these clever Jack the lads here? They're going to give evidence against you. And I'm going to have to stand there and take it all. For you.'

The twins stared at me disbelievingly. I don't think I'd ever shouted so loudly and been so angry in front of people before.

Finally Ronnie found some words, 'You're being disloyal, Charlie,' he said.

'No I'm not,' I said. 'I don't owe any of them any loyalty at all. They're your mates, not mine. But I can promise you this. You won't get any loyalty from them when the Old Bill gets lively. They'll grass you up as fast as you like.'

I didn't care that the Firm was there. Big Pat Connolly was all right except when he'd had a few and Bender was a bit of a laugh. But the rest I wouldn't give two bob for. I didn't give a monkey's what anyone thought. My views on them and what they would do to the twins was long overdue anyway.

Yuka Stuttgart was a ravishing blonde Swiss beauty who had earned the title Playboy Bunny of the Year in 1966 under her Playboy name, Surry Marsh. She looked me up in London at the suggestion of Joe Kaufman, and when the Leicester club opened she was the perfect partner for

153

me. She turned out to be something else, too – the unwitting catalyst that brought Diana and me together.

The club was bustling with activity that September night. Everyone was done up to the nines and no expense had been spared to give the club a champagne launch. I walked into the club proudly, the sumptuous Surry Marsh on my arm. Heads turned; knowing smiles were exchanged.

Later, Diana came up to our table to serve something. She motioned her head towards Surry, engaged in conversation with someone on the other side of the table. 'I must say you have beautiful friends,' Diana said quietly.

I grinned. 'Yes. She's very attractive.'

Diana's eyes twinkled. 'Well, you'll enjoy yourself there, even if the club's not up to much.'

I laughed. I admired her sauce. She always saw the positive side of situations.

And although it was a flippant remark, just a bit of harmless nightclub banter, there was something in Diana's warmth and friendliness that I found appealing and, in a way, exciting.

Surry and I spent the night together in Leicester and returned to London the next day. The following week I went back to the club, Di accepted my invitation to go for a drink and the affair began. After the dreariness and monotony of marriage to Dolly I found Diana's exuberance and love of life exhilarating and refreshing. She was so much fun she didn't have an enemy in the world, although she was having a very bad time with her husband who had beaten her up a few times; but she kept her unhappiness to herself.

Chemin-de-fer games were all the rage then and Trevor and I opened a new club in Coventry. I had to spend my Wednesdays there, but that didn't stop Diana and I seeing each other. She would ring the Leathrick Hotel to find

154

out if I'd checked in, then get a taxi from Leicester after work at the club.

Diana was such an attractive creature that she was never short of admirers. One of them was Con Cluskey, a member of the Bachelors singing group, which was appearing in Coventry at the time. Con was mad about Di; he would tell me so every time we had a drink. And he was always wanting Diana to dance with him. Happily for me, Di preferred my rough-edged Cockney and didn't fall for the Irish blarney. Those mid-week spells together were joyously happy for Diana and me – welcome breaks from our respective homes where we were less and less content. But as our feelings became deeper, the need to see more of each other grew. When, early in 1968, Diana said her marriage had got so bad she was going to leave home, I knew the time had come for me to make a similar decision.

It wasn't easy with the increasing activity around the twins. Diana was no fool, but she was blissfully innocent of any kind of villainy and I was worried she might hear bad things about the Krays and associate them with me. As tactfully as I could, I explained that the twins had been involved in the odd bit of trouble and had given the name a notoriety. I warned her that it was possible something might happen. Diana, bless her, told me not to worry: she knew me well enough to know I wasn't a villain and that was enough for her. She didn't care what people thought.

Relieved, I decided to tell Mum about the woman I wanted to share my life. But just before I was going round to see her, something happened which I had to put before everything else.

Reggie was having a drink in the Carpenter's Arms one night when two plain-clothes policemen walked in. Reggie told the barman to give them both drinks. They accepted, then asked to speak to Reggie privately. Reggie said, 'What about the toilet?' and they all went in there.

The two men said they were well aware what went on with fit-ups; sometimes they agreed with them, sometimes they did not. They had just come from a meeting where it had been decided to set somebody up. And this time they did not like it at all.

Because the person who was going to be fitted up was me. And everyone knew I was straight.

The plan, they told Reggie, was to plant drugs in my car, then stop me on some pretence. Reggie asked why they wanted to put me into the frame; the cops said the powers that be were upset at some of the things I'd done to get the twins out of trouble. They told Reggie to tell me to make sure my car was secure whenever I left it.

Before they left, Reggie offered them money for the tip-off but they refused, saying that if they took it he would think that was the only reason they had come, when in fact they had come because of the principle. It may be hard for Reggie to believe, they said, but it was true.

After the pub shut, Reggie rang me. He didn't want to talk about it on the phone but asked me to go round to his place very early the next morning.

When I heard what it was all about I went spare. I rang a friend on the *Sunday Pictorial*, Norman Lucas, and told him the whole story. I told other people, too, and I told them to tell their friends. And then, just in case that didn't make the Old Bill think again, I fitted my car with the most sensitive alarm system I could afford; it was so sensitive, the wind set it off one night!

I'm happy to say that, in the end, the fit-up never happened.

Thank God for coppers with principles.

* * *

Mum, as usual, did not criticize me when I finally told her about Diana. She listened intently as I explained that it was over with Dolly, that I'd met someone else who was everything Dolly wasn't, and then she said if that was what I really wanted, she would like to meet Diana. Whether she was tempted to tell me what she knew about Dolly and George Ince I don't know; she didn't say anything. I arranged to bring Diana to the flat the following Wednesday then I walked out along Bunhill Row in the late April sunshine feeling cheerful, and a little light-headed. Telling Mum had made a huge difference; had made it all right in a way. She was going to love Diana.

But Diana couldn't come to London the following week because one of her children fell ill. I was disappointed; I'd been looking forward to introducing the two women I loved deeply. But I wasn't too bothered. There was no rush. I would go to Leicester, as usual, next Wednesday, 8 May, and bring Diana back with me. Seven days wouldn't matter.

Sadly, it was to be nearly seven *years* before I saw Diana again.

They came for me that Wednesday at 6 A.M.

The doorbell rang and there was heavy knocking on the front door. Dolly sat up in bed. 'What's that, Charlie?'

I put on a dressing gown and shuffled sleepily downstairs. I opened the door to the full extent of the safety chain. I didn't get a chance to ask who it was or what they wanted because three plain-clothes detectives shoved against the door, breaking the chain.

'Hold up,' I said, suddenly wide awake. 'What's wrong?'

They all closed in on me so that I couldn't move.

'Let's go in here, shall we?' one of them said. They

157

ushered me into the lounge. One of them eased me into a chair; another took the phone off the hook.

My eyes went from one to the other searching for a clue to what it was all about. All I could think in my confusion was that they were not Metropolitan Police, and that they were probably armed.

By now Dolly had come down with Nancy, wondering what all the fuss was about. Then Gary appeared, looking bewildered. They all stood there, looking at me, hoping I'd tell them what was going on.

I looked at the senior officer and demanded to know what I was supposed to have done to warrant my front door being broken open at six in the morning.

He said I was being arrested on a charge of conspiracy to defraud. I stared at him in shock. I'd never defrauded anyone in my life, was all I said. They cautioned me that anything I said would be taken down and might be used in evidence against me. I decided to say nothing else. There was nothing *to* say: the allegation was utter nonsense.

They told me to get dressed as they were taking me to the nick. The three of them stood watching as I washed. I wanted to shave, but they told me not to bother. Then, after I'd dressed, Dolly made some tea and we all stood around drinking it and making polite conversation like strangers at a vicar's tea party. Finally one of the officers said we were leaving and produced a pair of handcuffs. He asked me to hold out my hands. Flabbergasted, I said, 'Are you joking?'

He ignored me and tried to put the handcuffs on me. But they were too small and he couldn't fasten them. I told him not to be daft; I didn't intend running away. But the officer wouldn't give up and kept pinching my flesh, trying to get the cuffs locked. The top man looked put out, but finally told his colleague not to bother.

I told Dolly and the kids not to worry: I would be back as soon as I'd sorted it out at the police station. Then I was escorted to a police car, a copper on either side holding the sleeves of my jacket.

About an hour earlier, dozens of police had got out of the lift on the ninth floor of Braithwaite House, Bunhill Row. They padded stealthily to Number 12. One of them smashed the door with a sledgehammer then they rushed in, pistols at the ready. Some of the men darted into Ronnie's bedroom; the rest went into Reggie's.

Ronnie woke up with about ten guns pointed at his chest. He reacted with customary coolness. 'I'd be careful with those,' he told them. 'One of them might go off.'

They told him to get out of bed slowly and he said sarcastically, 'What do you think I do – sleep with a bloody machine gun?'

Reggie was in bed with a young woman. Both were naked, and the police ordered them to get out and stand there while the room was searched. Reggie asked if they could put some clothes on. He was told no. He was angry, not only at being arrested, but also because the girl was being degraded. He couldn't understand why they didn't just take him out of the room and leave her alone.

Suddenly the caretaker of the flats came up. He was shocked at the broken door and the mess inside. He made some protest and asked what was going on. A couple of the officers told him, 'Fuck off.'

About half an hour later Ronnie and Reggie were driven to West End Central police station.

As they left the flat in handcuffs, Ronnie looked at the once-beautiful Chinese carpet Mum adored. It was littered with dozens of cigarette butts stamped out by the dawn visitors.

* * *

Getting into the Rover I was not unduly bothered, because my conscience was clear: I was not guilty of fraud and that was that. When we got to Bow Street nick I'd call my solicitor and put things straight.

However, as the car pulled away from the house in Poplar I had a slight feeling of unease: police wanting to arrest someone on a charge of fraud did not force open doors early in the morning and treat the suspect as though he was going to shoot his way out of trouble.

And I knew I was right when the car roared past Bow Street nick and kept heading west. 'Where are we going?' I asked.

'You'll know soon enough,' one of the officers said brusquely.

As we sped through London's sleeping streets in silence, one thought kept coming back to me as my mind reeled with the possibilities of what lay ahead: whatever it was had better be sorted out quickly, because today was Wednesday and I was going to Leicester to see Diana.

I was thinking about her as the Rover swung into West End Central police station in Savile Row.

Inside it was bedlam. Dozens of police were racing around in organized confusion; giving or receiving orders, asking or answering questions, taking notes, speaking on the telephone. I had little time to take it in because I was hustled into a waiting room at the rear of the station, but I did get a fleeting glimpse of some familiar faces that confirmed what I'd begun to suspect: I had been dragged out of bed by something far more serious than an allegation of fraud.

Within minutes, a sergeant read out a charge and cautioned me. The charge had something to do with American bonds and was a load of nonsense. I asked for permission to ring a solicitor, but was refused. All my possessions had been taken from me at home, but I was searched again. Then I was put in a cell. It was now about 8 A.M.

Over the next few hours, there was a lot of rattling of keys, slamming of doors, and raising of angry voices as other cells filled up and people were questioned. Through the tiny bars of the cell's solid door, I saw a lot of faces I recognized: members of the twins' so-called Firm and other East End characters, including Limehouse Willey and Harry Hopwood. The procession seemed endless, and highly significant.

Two faces I didn't see were those of Ronnie and Reggie. When I finally did see them, it was nearly two days later – at 3 A.M.

I was taken from my cell into the charge room and there they were, looking as rough as me: dirty, scruffy, unshaven, and red-eyed through lack of sleep. Ronnie was in a shirt because the police had not allowed him to put on a coat. He asked if I was all right. I would be, I said, if someone would tell me what was going on.

Then all the rest were brought in and senior officers started taking particulars. Sitting at one desk, with inspector's pips, was someone I'd known for years, ever since he was a constable on the beat. He was a terrific rugby player and once, when we both found ourselves in the South of France, I played with him against the French Navy in a stadium at St Raphael. He was plain PC Vic Streeter then, but now he was Detective Inspector Streeter and he was sitting behind a desk taking down my details. We didn't mention the past.

I then had to stand before a young bloke at a typewriter, who asked daft questions such as: 'Do you have blond hair?' 'Have you got blue eyes?' I had not been through anything like that before and I didn't like it; besides, tension and lack of sleep had made me short-tempered. Finally I could stand the bloke's inane ques-

161

tions no longer and snapped, 'Do you need bloody glasses or what?' He shut up.

You could almost feel the tension in that small, crowded room. It needed something to break it and, of course, it was Ronnie who provided it.

Everyone's particulars had been noted and the law were wondering what to do with us, when Ronnie suddenly called out, 'Nipper!'

Detective Superintendent Read turned round. 'Yes, Ronnie?' he answered, respectfully.

'Any chance of a bit of bail?' said Ronnie, po-faced.

The whole room cracked up.

Read coughed quietly. 'Er, I don't think so, Ronnie,' he said, fighting to stop himself laughing.

'Just thought I'd ask,' Ronnie added with a grin.

Early on Friday morning things started to happen: it was orderly and purposeful, with no sign of Wednesday's confusion. I was taken from my cell, closely guarded by two coppers, and ushered into a Black Maria at the back of the nick. I had never seen inside one of those forbidding vehicles and I got a shock. A narrow passageway ran along the centre of what was a converted large van; on either side of the aisle were small cubicles – rather like tiny dog kennels – which allowed the prisoner to stand or sit but little else. Once inside the cubicle the prisoner was cut off from the outside world except for a restricted view from a small window.

When we were all inside, the Black Maria moved out of the yard and the sirens started. They howled deafeningly during the whole journey down Regent Street, around Piccadilly Circus to the Strand and up Bow Street to the magistrates' court, opposite Covent Garden Opera House. Through my tiny window I caught sight of startled pedestrians rushing to get out of the way of the high-speed van and its escort of motorbikes and cars.

It was an elaborate, costly pantomime.

At Bow Street, the twins and I and several others were charged with a number of offences from petty larceny to conspiracy, all of which were merely holding charges that were later dropped.

During the lunch break, we were all shepherded into a large room and left on our own. Something wasn't quite right; I sensed it and so did the twins. Then I realized that a door on the other side of the room led into a corridor which, in turn, led to the street.

'This is a get up,' I said. 'They've put us in here deliberately. They want us to make a run for it.'

I could picture the newspaper headlines: Dangerous Gang In Dash For Freedom. Everyone agreed with me and we just sat around in that room waiting for someone to come in.

When Read arrived Ronnie couldn't resist it. 'We're still here, Nipper,' he said. 'Sorry about all your little Firm waiting outside with their guns. You must think we're silly.'

For the twins, hearing they were being remanded in custody came as no surprise. To me, who had never been inside a jail, it was a great shock. But it was nothing to the humiliation I felt during my first few hours in Brixton Prison in South-West London. I was ordered to strip totally naked in front of two prison officers, then subjected to a most intimate search. I couldn't believe they seriously thought I'd had the foresight to insert money, tobacco or cigarette papers in my rectum, which, I learned, some forward-thinking prisoners do prior to being sentenced. I was told to take a bath. The water was tepid and just nine inches deep, but I attacked my body vigorously and thankfully. I hadn't seen soap or water for three days.

I was then allowed to put on my clothes and was shown into a room, where Ronnie and Reggie were sitting. They seemed in good spirits and Ronnie took great delight in telling us what he'd said to the armed copper who had disturbed his sleep three days before. I was not able to share their light-hearted approach to our predicament; I had businesses on the outside that would not run themselves. I had children who needed me. And what about Diana? But at least the twins and I were happy on one score: Mum and the old man were miles away from the aggravation, safely tucked up in that comfortable house amid the tranquillity of the Suffolk countryside.

We were not allowed to spend long together. We suspected the room was bugged so we kept our conversation to trivialities. Whoever was listening quickly got bored and we were taken to separate cells.

As the massive door clanged behind me, I looked at what was to be my home for the forseeable future: an expanse of painted brick wall around a rectangular area about 11ft by 6ft. To my right was a bed, a stout, tubular steel and wire contraption hinged to the wall. In the far corner an enamelled bowl and jug stood on a triangular table; underneath this was a Victorian-style bedpan. To my left there was a sturdy wooden table with a matching chair.

That was it.

I sat on the bed and thought, and my thoughts were about my kids, and Dolly and Diana, and Mum and the old man, and when I'd exhausted all my thoughts about them I thought about myself and then I started to think about freedom.

It was the first time it had been taken away from me and it was a bad, bad feeling.

* * *

I had always believed in justice. If you did wrong, then were caught and found guilty, you were punished. If you hadn't done anything wrong, you had nothing to worry about. I knew about police frame-ups, of course, but in those first few distressing days in custody I did not think for a second that anyone was out to get me, to stitch me up. Sitting in that cell, day after day, all I could think was that it was a mistake; a massive mistake that had put me temporarily behind bars but a mistake nonetheless. Someone, somewhere would realize that soon, and I would be released, with a suitable apology, to continue earning an honest living on the outside.

I saw the twins every day; we were allowed to take exercise in a small yard for half an hour each morning and we discussed the situation. They were still fairly relaxed and confident: they felt, as I did, that the charges made against them were nonsense and would be thrown out through lack of evidence. Although they had serious problems over the killings of Cornell and McVitie, both were convinced the police would not be able to prove they were responsible. I was not so sure but, from a personal point of view, I was not bothered. Even if someone did come forward to testify that Ronnie had shot Cornell, how could that affect me? I wasn't there. Even if the truth about McVitie came out, how could I be implicated? I'd got a phone call in the middle of the night after the event and knew it had happened; but I'd gone back to bed and left the twins and the others to get on with it. I told the twins this as we took our daily stroll, but they were uncompromising: they said I'd have to take my chance with them and seven of the Firm who were also on remand.

The days rolled into weeks as the machinery of the law moved ponderously along. The monotony of prison life was relieved by interviews with solicitors, noisy, high-speed journeys to Bow Street, and visits by Mum, the old man, Dolly and the children. I was tempted to write to Diana but always decided not to. We had a future together, I was sure of it; but that, like everything else in my life, had gone up in the air. How could I make long-term plans when I had no idea what was going to happen tomorrow? In that cell I thought about Diana a lot. I knew she would have read what had happened and secretly hoped she would get in touch one way or another. But I wouldn't, couldn't, blame her if she chose not to. Leicester was only 150 miles away, but the world in which she moved was a million light years from the one I was now in. How could Diana possibly begin to understand what was going on if I didn't myself? How could I possibly blame her if she had written me off as an exciting, but closed, chapter of her life.

Through the small, heavily barred window high above me, I stared at the blueness of the summer sky and found myself thinking yet again of the appalling injustice: innocent until proven guilty, cried the statute of our beloved, jealously guarded democracy. So why was I here? Why was I being treated like a criminal? Why was I incarcerated behind a massive steel and wood barricade as though already tried and convicted by the courts?

Slowly, my anger turned to bitterness and then, as I saw and heard what was happening around us, I started to worry.

With the twins and members of their Firm locked away on charges that could be thrown out later, Nipper Read got to work on the big stuff. He needed key witnesses – members of the trusted Firm – to betray the twins, to go over to the other side to help put them and others away on the more serious charges. He needed more statements, more damning documents and, with the twins removed, so was the desire to stay silent. With the fear of retribution gone, the men with a lot to say were free to say it, to do deals to save themselves. As London sweltered, first one then another Judas stepped forward to buy his freedom with a pocketful of lies. Now the spider's web was finally spun and out of the labyrinth of tiny, crowded dockland woodwork came the insects, creeping and crawling to the spider, and their names were Ronald Hart and Albert Donaghue and William Exley and Jack Dickson and Leslie Payne and A. B. Cooper and Billy Elvey.

Still the twins were optimistic. Still they had that air of invincibility, the confidence that when it came to it they wouldn't, couldn't be charged with murder. Even when we were put in a specially built two-floor cage, they didn't appreciate the significance of Donaghue, Hart and Dickson being excluded. Even when they heard that visiting friends were intercepted at the prison gates and warned not to have contact with us they didn't see the danger signals.

They were prepared for imprisonment on the lesser charges, though. At one of the early Bow Street hearings, Ronnie was so uninterested in the proceedings that he actually fell asleep during someone's testimony. When I heard the gentle rumble of his snoring I nudged him and told him to wake up. But Ronnie merely grunted, 'Leave me alone. I've got two clever brothers – you listen to it,' and went back to sleep. Suddenly the magistrate noticed and asked if Ronnie was all right. I said I thought so, and nudged Ronnie again. He opened his eyes and thanked the magistrate, saying he felt fine. But about ten minutes later he dozed off again. Later he said he knew they were going down so why should he listen to it all?

Then the twins were charged with murdering Frank Mitchell. The big man's body had never been found after he vanished in December 1966, but Albert Donaghue had told the police the twins had arranged for him to be killed. The charge came as a shock, naturally, but the twins were still surprisingly nonchalant about their worsening predicament. They pleaded not guilty.

My barrister, Desmond Vowden, had given me real hope of getting bail at the next Bow Street hearing. Not one of the conspiracy or fraud charges against me had much substance, he said, and he was confident the magistrate would take a lenient view. My spirits soared; justice was smiling on me, as I always knew it would in the end. The prospect of freedom – albeit a conditional one – dominated my thoughts for the next few days.

At Bow Street, the twins and I were always kept in separate cells, but when we arrived for the next hearing they put us in one together. There, too, was another Mitchell: Charlie Mitchell. We'd known him for years. He was sitting at one end of the cell, away from the twins, and when I walked in he put a finger to his mouth and said, 'Don't speak too loudly. It's bugged.' Then he came up to me, saying to the twins, 'I'm going to say something to Charlie. He'll tell you later.' He whispered in my ear, 'You may hear something you think is terrible. But don't do anything about it because there may be a reason for it.' I didn't understand what he was talking about, but he said, 'Don't puzzle it out. Just remember, I told you.'

A few minutes later, the cell door opened. An inspector said, 'Charlie, we'd like to see you a minute.' I went outside into the corridor. The inspector was joined by another officer, who said, 'Charlie, we're charging you with the murder of Frank Mitchell.'

My mouth fell open. 'You're *what*?'

As we were speaking, Mr Vowden came along the corridor towards us. I told him what had happened. He was kind and sympathetic, saying he knew I'd had nothing to do with any murder, but there was nothing he could do until it came up in court. He did say he wished he could have taken a picture of me at that time because I would have been found not guilty by the look on my face.

I was gutted. For apart from the horror of facing a murder charge, my much cherished hope of bail was gone.

I went back into the cell and told the twins what had happened. They were stunned. Charlie Mitchell said it was diabolical; he was choked for me, he said. Fortunately, this trumped-up, stupid charge was thrown out at Bow Street for lack of evidence.

The cage made life bearable for us as the months rolled on: the beds were more comfortable and there was a TV room which we were allowed into, two or three at a time. But we were not allowed any contact with other prisoners. Nor were we allowed to go to church on Sundays. Security around us was elaborate and efficient, but we managed to find out a lot about what was going on. One new item that filtered through was that Nipper Read was visiting Brixton in various disguises for his growing Kray dossier.

The months rolled on and on and then, hard though it was for us to believe, it was Christmas. Mum and the old man, who had sold The Brooks and returned to London permanently, sent in as much food and drink as allowed, although money was beginning to be a bit short. It was my twentieth wedding anniversary but Brixton Prison is far from ideal as a venue for such a celebration. As the festivities passed and we moved on to yet another New Year, I thought of Diana. Had she, I wondered, followed through that decision to leave home? Whatever had happened, I hoped she was happy.

And then it was 7 January and the Old Bailey was set for the trial of the century. The cockney canaries had sung their hearts out to Nipper and his men. And when

169

the twins and I, with seven members of their so-called Firm, emerged from the cells into the famous No 1 Court that morning it was not to face the relatively innocuous charges of conspiracy to defraud but varying charges of murder and complicity in murder.

Far from being worried, I was relieved. Eight months in prison without trial by jury had drained me, knocked my self-confidence, left my nerves in tatters and almost wrecked my spirit. Now it was all over and twelve ordinary citizens and a fair-minded judge were going to see through all the lies and deceit and set me free.

Justice, I'd always been told must be seen to be done. That cold Tuesday morning I couldn't wait for the world to see it.

Chapter Eleven

People who have never been in trouble with the police will find it difficult, if not impossible, to understand why I didn't go into court and tell the truth about that terrible October night in 1967. That way, I could have thwarted every attempt by police and prosecution witnesses to convict me for something I did not do. But, quite simply, that was not the way we did things in the East End. Nobody – me included – thought for a moment that the twins would plead anything but not guilty to everything, which meant that I would have to deny all knowledge of Jack McVitie's murder and take my chances along with everyone else.

Lying, I appreciated, would make things difficult for me, because I *had* received a phone call in the middle of that Saturday night and *had* gone to Harry Hopwood's house, and both Hopwood and Ronnie Hart were going to say so. I wasn't unduly worried, however. Hart, the star prosecution witness, had traded his conscience for freedom, and had proved at the Bow Street committal hearing that he didn't give a toss for the truth. But my counsel had reserved my defence, and not one of Hart's damning false allegations had been challenged yet. Now, before an Old Bailey jury, the gloves would be off: Vowden would be the aggressor and every one of Hart's lies, every careless slip of the tongue – not only by him, but by all the prosecution witnesses – would be seized on and torn apart.

I honestly didn't think Hart's evidence would affect me too much. He had a grudge against the twins, may have hated them even, but I'd never done anything to make him want to frame me. He'd lied in the lower court but surely under fierce cross-examination he would crack and admit I wasn't involved in disposing of McVitie's body.

Standing in the famous No 1 Court at the Old Bailey that first morning with the nine other accused I felt supremely confident. For at the end of the day the charge against me *was* unfounded. That night in 1967 I had not even seen McVitie's body, let alone got rid of it. And anyway, as Mr Vowden had explained, if the impossible happened, if the preposterous lies *were* believed, the onus was still on the prosecution to prove I was guilty, not on me to prove I was innocent.

I looked confidently at the jury. They all appeared to be intelligent human beings, capable of distinguishing between fact and fiction, simple truth and barefaced lie. I looked at the judge – Melford Stevenson, the epitome of justice. Experienced, knowledgeable, wise. He, too, looked as if he would be eager to protect an innocent man from the falsehoods of his corruptible accusers.

The cases against the twins, their so-called Firm and me went on for thirty-nine days. The popular papers labelled it the Trial of the Century and the financial cost of the whole affair – over £150,000 – earned it a place in the *Guinness Book of Records* as the most expensive criminal hearing ever. If you want a strictly accurate, blow-by-blow account of all that went on, the statements of claim, the pleadings and submissions, wrapped up in colourful and complicated legal mumbo-jumbo, plus all the heated exchanges between accusers and accused that made the headlines, your local library will probably be able to provide you with details. Certainly I'm not going to attempt to do so here. The whole business, from the moment of my early-morning arrest on 8 May 1968 to my sentencing on 5 March 1969, was the most nerve-racking, nightmarish experience of my life, and at the end of it all I was in no position to remember much about the proceedings except what had directly or indirectly affected me. Everyone there, from the judge and jurors to the men in the dock, the barristers in their wigs and gowns and the spectators in the gallery, saw the trial differently. For me it was a mixture of highs and lows, from times when I was amused, hopeful or quietly elated, to others when I was worried, acutely disappointed or hurled into dark despair. Since this is my story, these are the moments I shall concentrate on.

The basis of Ronnie Hart's evidence against me was that I had driven with him in his mini to Freddie Foreman's pub, the Prince of Wales in Lark Street, Southwark, in the early hours of Sunday 28 October. The purpose of the visit, said Hart, was to tell Foreman to get rid of McVitie's body. This was, of course, a blatant lie, which I thought was made clear when Harry Hopwood, another prosecution witness, told the truth, which conflicted with Hart's claim. Hopwood told the jury, quite rightly, that I had indeed gone to his house but had set off home alone about half an hour later. Moreover, he added that Hart himself had not left the house. Men have been acquitted on less corroboration and my hopes were high. But I did not realize then that this was more of a political trial than a criminal one. In case the jury were having thoughts of believing Hopwood, Mr Justice Stevenson pooh-poohed his evidence. 'In things like this, people *do* get mixed up,' he told them. 'It must have been a bit of a shock for him; he must have forgotten. But at least he is telling the truth, or so he thinks. He's just mixed up. We have the proof from Ronald Hart.'

It was at that moment, I think, that I glanced up at

Mum in the gallery. Throughout my life she had drummed into me how important it was to tell the truth. How I wished right then that I could have done just that, backing up Hopwood's accurate statement and redressing the balance in my favour after the judge's appallingly biased comment. My fears that my fate was in the judge's hands rather than the jury's grew when he unexpectedly called an adjournment thirty minutes early – at a crucial moment in Hart's evidence.

Hart had been telling the court about a visit he allegedly made with me to Foreman's pub a week after McVitie's murder. He said he remembered Foreman leaning over to me and saying, 'When I found that body it was all glistening, like he had vaseline on him.' The pub was noisy and Hart said he couldn't hear anything else. Just that sentence! It was all too pat and I was sure the jury would not believe it. Then, during Vowden's cross-examination, Hart made a slip that sent my pulse racing with excitement. Having just stated that I was with him that day he then said in a loud voice that I wasn't. As Hart was about to get himself deeper into trouble, however, Mr Justice Stevenson interrupted the cross-examination and said the court would adjourn for lunch. It was 12.30. The court normally rose at 1 P.M.

During the break I was very worried, sensing trouble. The judge had been so biased against all the defendants that I felt sure he had called for an adjournment early to protect Hart. Vowden told me I was being over-sensitive. The slip was significant, he said, and the judge, realizing this, had called for an early lunch because the case against me would be thrown out that afternoon.

I was not convinced, and no sooner had Hart got back on the stand than the judge reminded him, 'You said earlier that you weren't with Mr Kray that day.'

174

And, of course, dear old Ronnie had had a change of heart!

He had been thinking about it over lunch and was now sure that I *had*, indeed, been with him. Vowden couldn't believe it, but I could. I may not be as eloquent or as academically brilliant as a university-educated barrister but I am sharp-witted, and astute enough to know when the dice are loaded. No one will ever convince me that Stevenson didn't save the prosecution that day, or that its star witness was not given a gentle prod in the right direction over lunch.

Even with Hart giving an Oscar-winning performance to try to convict me, there was so much doubt clouding my case that I should have got off. One of the twins' Firm, Scotch Jack Dickson, for example, was hopelessly trapped by Vowden, only to be saved by the judge who excused his mistake.

Dickson was adamant that he had been with me in a Mile End café owned by Terry Pellicci the morning after McVitie's murder. He claimed I had told him the twins had killed McVitie, and that I knew all about it. Something bothered me about his testimony. Apart from the fact that it was all a load of cobblers designed, like Hart's, to plunge me deeper into the prosecution net, there was something else, something not right. I thought long and hard about it that night in my Brixton cell and finally it hit me.

It was impossible for me to have been in the café with Dickson. It was impossible for anyone to have been in the café at all that day . . . because it wasn't open on Sundays!

Again, my heart beat a little faster. Surely this was important. Surely a prosecution witness lying on oath was good for my case. Surely all that Dickson had said, whatever it was meant to imply, would have to be struck from the record, or the jury told to disregard it.

In his cross-examination, Vowden let Dickson go on and on about his café conversation with me. Was it Sunday? Yes. Are you quite sure about that? Absolutely. Is there just a chance, a mere possibility, that you're mistaken; that it was another day, the Monday morning, perhaps? Not a chance, sir, it was a Sunday. I remember it clearly. Thank you. Mr Dickson. That is all.

Enter Terry Pellicci for the defence. Now, Mr Pellicci, did Mr Dickson and Mr Kray come to your cafe? Yes, sir, I saw them together several times. Was one of those times Sunday 28 October? No, sir. Are you quite certain of that, Mr Pellicci? Yes, sir. How can you be so certain? The café isn't open on Sundays, sir, I haven't opened on a Sunday for seventeen years. Thank you, Mr Pellicci. That is all.

Dickson's jaw dropped. There was a flurry of activity among the prosecution barristers, much hurried whispering and looks of surprise and consternation. Vowden sat down, the faintest look of satisfaction on his face. I fought to stop myself grinning. It was a bombshell for the prosecution all right.

And then Mr Justice Stevenson stepped in to save their blushes again. 'It is clear Mr Dickson has made a mistake with the day of the meeting,' he said. 'As it couldn't have been the Sunday, it must have been the Monday.'

And that was that. For although Vowden made the point over and over again, it was what the judge said that in the end made all the difference.

Naturally I was gutted. But although the lies were making the case against me look very black and the judge, for some reason, seemed to have it in for me, I still clung to my strong belief in British justice. I had *not* disposed of a murdered man's body, so come what may I was not going to be found guilty of doing so.

I consoled myself that it was still early days; there

176

would be other ways in which the prosecution's liars could be exposed. One of these came in the shape of two honest men who ran a garage off Vallance Road. Hart's version of events during the early hours of that Sunday morning could not be right, they told Vowden, because the mini Hart said we drove in was parked in their garage all Saturday night and Sunday morning. They were not mistaken, they stressed, because the mini had blocked some taxis and efforts had been made to trace the owner. To me the men's joint evidence seemed manna from heaven, but apparently the police got wind of it and told them not to interfere. Despite the garage men's protests, they were not even allowed to appear in court.

Even so, there were other holes in Hart's testimony that should have made the jury suspicious of his motives. On his own admission he had been a witness to murder, yet I was supposed to have suddenly appeared on the scene and taken over. He said I made him stand by the mini outside the Prince of Wales at 3 A.M. while I rang the bell and woke Foreman up. On one hand he said he was too far away to hear all that was said but on the other he had no doubt that he heard me telling Foreman to get rid of the body. It did not add up.

Hart claimed the Lambrianou brothers had taken McVitie's body from the house in Stoke Newington 'over the water' to South London, but he and Hopwood said the brothers were not in Hopwood's house when I arrived. So how was I supposed to tell Foreman where the body was? Unless I'd driven around South London, found the Lambrianous and asked them, I would not have known. If I didn't know where the body was, how could I have disposed of it?

It was a dream-like experience, sitting there listening to people relating in sincere tones, as if butter wouldn't melt in their mouths, what I was supposed to have done. There seemed to be so many conflicting statements that I got totally confused and lost track of the plot, as it were. Most of the time I found myself thinking: if only the twins hadn't told Harry Hopwood to ring me. If there hadn't been that phone call, none of this would have happened and I wouldn't have been in the frame. But the fact that I *had* gone to the house gave the police and their witnesses the foundation on which to build their lies.

In court there was so much happening, so much to take in and concentrate on that I had little time to feel angry. But at night, alone in my cell in Brixton, my feelings would boil up and my insides would ache with fury, not only at the twins for roping me in so unnecessarily and thoughtlessly but also at their short-sightedness and naïvety so far as their damned blasted Firm was concerned. Ronnie and Reggie had always attracted people and been surrounded by large groups who enjoyed their charisma. And they loved it, probably needing it to boost their own ideas of themselves as powerful leaders of men. But with one or two exceptions, the idiots who went around with them hanging on their every word were not worth two bob. The Firm were physically tough but not very bright characters with overblown ideas of their own importance. Having little ability themselves to make anything worthwhile of their lives they settled for a grubby twilight existence basking in the dubious reflected glory of the twins' reputation as fearless hard men, and grabbing the easy money that came from being their henchmen. Despite what Ronnie and Reggie believed then, or now, the Firm revelled in the violence and wallowed in their roles as self-styled gangsters.

In my lonely cell I often conjured up pictures of that fateful evening in Evering Road. I knew enough of the Firm's mentality to realize what had probably happened to prompt Ronnie to have McVitie brought to the flat from the Regency, and I would play the imagined scene over and over in my mind, a worthless exercise in masochism that served no purpose except to make me even angrier and more frustrated.

''Ere, Ron,' I could hear one of them saying. 'McVitie's in the Regency mouthing off again. Says he's going to blow you and Reg away.'

If that had got no reaction some bright spark – maybe even Ronnie Hart himself – would have stoked him up. 'You're not going to stand for that, Ron. You're not going to let him get away with that, are you?'

Such was the mood at that gathering that Ronnie bit on the bait, telling the Lambrianou brothers to fetch McVitie – which they did, not from fear of Ronnie, as was suggested at the trial, but from a sadistic pleasure at witnessing a hated man's humiliation at the hands of a more powerful individual.

No one will convince me that the Firm that night didn't egg on the twins to sort out McVitie once and for all. If it was all Ronnie's idea, if they were worried for McVitie and wanted to spare him his ordeal, why didn't they just go to the Regency and tell him to make himself scarce? No one would have been the wiser if Chris or Tony Lambrianou had said, 'Do us a favour and go, so we can say we didn't see you.' As it was, they loved it all so much that they raced off to the Regency and gleefully brought McVitie back to meet a violent death.

In the early hours, when my fury had cooled, the irony of my own situation would hit me. I had received a phone call *after* the event, which had implicated me, but if someone had rung me *beforehand* it would never have happened, because I wouldn't have let it. Just as I had told Scotch Jack in the Starlight Club that he wasn't going to shoot Connie Whitehead, so I would have told the twins and the idiots around them that it was madness to wipe out McVitie.

This is why no one even tried to suggest at the trial that I was at the party. If I had been, there would have been no murder. As it was, McVitie was lured to the flat and confronted with men in no mood for mercy. Reggie, out of his mind on drink and Valium, taunted him that he wasn't much of a man because he had thrown his wife out of a car, and that although he had had plenty to say about him and Ronnie he wasn't so big now. Reggie pulled out a gun. He fired, but it didn't go off. McVitie tried to dive out of a window but was pulled back in by the Firm. Then there was a struggle and Ronnie was holding McVitie, supposedly urging Reggie to kill him, and suddenly Reggie had a knife in his hand and was plunging it into McVitie's throat, the drink and drugs transforming him into a mindless killer with no regard for his victim or for himself.

Even today, more than twenty years after this terrible event, I cannot take in that Reggie did that. Yes, he could be violent, but, unlike Ronnie, he had always held back. Much was made at the trial of Ronnie's alleged comment, 'I've done mine. Now you do yours.' I do not know whether he did say it because neither twin will discuss it with me. They did not volunteer information at the time and when I've brought it up since then, they can't understand why I'm interested in something that happened so long ago. They say, 'What difference will it make if we tell you?' To me, it doesn't *seem* like the kind of thing Ronnie would have said; he'd always been more inclined to do things himself.

One thing is certain: if Frances had not died, Reggie would not have committed that crime, spurred on by a death-wish. If Frances had been alive and they were living a happy married life, with children perhaps, he would have been a different person. When guns had come on the scene he would have thought it through and seen the sense in getting out. As it was, Frances met a tragic end and Reggie lost all interest in life, becoming just like all the others. When those idiots who called themselves friends egged Ronnie on that Saturday night, the lethal cocktail of drinks and drugs helped Reggie enjoy it all as much as everyone else, and he was to pay the price.

Despite all the prosecution lies, all the inadmissible evidence, and my own barrister's reluctance to put me on the witness stand, I still believe I would have been cleared – or at least received a far lighter sentence – had it not been for Melford Stevenson. Before the case police and lawyers alike were saying that he was the worst possible choice for the men on trial, and I was to find this hard to dispute as the hearing went on and on. It was not just the words he used, it was his tone and mannerisms, his tut-tutting and sarcastic comments that were quite obviously designed to leave the jury in no doubt what he felt about a particular witness's evidence.

The transcript of the hearing does not tell the full story. If it had been taped and filmed, one would be able to see how Stevenson swayed the evidence in the prosecution's favour and then meted out the unbelievably harsh sentences that appeased his pals in high places but shocked nearly everyone else.

The small things drove me and the twins mad: the way Stevenson treated our Aunt May, for instance. May had never been in a court in her life, and was married to a man who had worked in the same company for fifty years and was so straight that he'd never even been given a parking ticket. She was a religious woman who went to church regularly, but Stevenson treated her abominably with a total lack of respect just because she was speaking on behalf of the twins. In contrast, Ronnie Hart's girl-friend was treated like a lady by Stevenson. It really wound us up, but there was nothing we could do except sit there and take it.

We took it for thirty-nine days; days in which the smooth, efficient, well-rehearsed case against the twins, their Firm and me rolled on and on to its inevitable conclusion. Many days were filled with legal mumbo-jumbo which I found hard to follow; others were filled with stories of the twins' reign of terror, which I found equally hard to swallow. But there were moments of humour, too, like Ronnie's comment when he was charged with being involved in the McVitie murder. Warned by Nipper Read that anything he said would be taken down and might be used in evidence against him, Ronnie replied, 'I presume that your presumptions are precisely incorrect and that your sarcastic insinuations are too obnoxious to be appreciated.' As he watched a fellow detective write it on the charge sheet, Ronnie added, 'Bit hard to spell, that one, isn't it?' I'm not sure what the elaborately worded sentence meant, but Ronnie liked the sound of it as a child and had learned it parrot fashion. He said it to the police because he didn't give a damn. He was obviously philosophical; he always thought he'd get thirty years. His cheeky answer to the charge had to be read out at the Old Bailey, of course, and provided welcome light relief to the heaviness of the proceedings. I think the laughter in court even woke Ronnie up.

If there was going to be any humour, even black humour, it was bound to come from Ronnie. And he made me smile one day when he more or less ordered the judge to let him give evidence after making it clear to defence and prosecution counsels that he would not. Ian Barrie, charged as an accessory in the Blind Beggar killing, had just stepped down from the witness box and

Ronnie suddenly said loudly, 'I'm going to give evidence now.' Some bigwig – probably the judge – told him it was most irregular: Ronnie had chosen not to testify and had instructed his counsel, Paul Wrightson, accordingly. That cut no ice whatsoever with Ronnie. 'I can change my mind if I like,' he said. 'I want to give evidence. And I'm going to. It's my right.'

I couldn't help smiling at the turmoil he caused. Courts, naturally, have set rules of procedure and officials don't like the protocol being upset. But Ronnie couldn't have cared less; once he decided to do something he usually did it. He got his way that day, and the court buzzed with expectancy as he took the stand.

Prosecution counsel, Kenneth Jones, a little Welshman with a resounding Richard Burton-type voice that seemed too big for his body, couldn't believe his luck. He tore into Ronnie with relish, determined to goad him into losing his temper and, perhaps, betray signs of the violence that was an integral part of the prosecution case. Much to the eloquent Mr Jones's chagrin, Ronnie was far from intimidated by his cultured tones and cunning approach. He was in the mood to antagonize everyone and he matched Jones's skill with a cheeky arrogance.

'Among your Firm, you are known as the Colonel?' asked Mr Jones.

'I was a deserter from the Army, so how could I be a Colonel?' Ronnie replied.

'You gave money to charity,' Mr Jones said later.

'Is that a terrible thing?' Ronnie asked.

'There are stories that it might have been £10,000. Where did you get that money from?'

'I don't think that matters,' Ronnie countered. 'I had it. That's all that matters.' When that didn't seem to satisfy his interrogator, Ronnie shouted, 'If you want to know, my father gambles for me. He's up there in the gallery, so ask him. I know nothing about gambling, so there's no point in asking me. I may have clubs, but I know nothing about gambling.'

The judge broke in to tell Ronnie not to shout. But Ronnie just said 'Why? I'm here to speak. And I'm answering.'

Jones went on and on and finally Ronnie had had enough. 'Listen, you fat slob,' he said, making me cringe. 'You've been going on enough. You're Welsh, aren't you? Down the mines would have been a more fitting profession for you than being a prosecutor, I promise you that.'

Naturally, this attitude did not endear him to the judge or jury, but Ronnie was convinced, as ever, that he was going to get thirty years, innocent or guilty, and he didn't care: it had just come into his head that he wanted to say something, so he said it.

Something Ronnie did not say, however, despite my encouragement to do so, was what his so-called pals, particularly Hart and Albert Donaghue, had got up to during the twins' so-called reign of terror. These two supposedly tough individuals loved the villainy. Late one night they got drunk, forced their way into the Regency Club and demanded £50 a week from the owner Johnny Barrie. The next day, having sobered up, they were worried and went to Ronnie to own up. He went spare, wanting to know why they had done that when the Firm had a share in the club anyway. Hart and Donaghue admitted they had made a mistake but begged Ronnie to say he'd sent them round because Barrie might get the police involved. Typically, Ronnie helped them. He told Barrie he'd had the hump the previous night and had sent Hart and Donaghue round. He said he was sorry and asked Barrie to forget it.

To my disappointment, Ronnie didn't tell that story in

court. Nor did he tell how Hart and Donaghue went to Freddie Foreman's pub and tried to 'nip' him for £25. When I asked him why he hadn't seized the chance to redress the balance that was swinging ever more heavily against us all he said that nothing would ever make him sink as low as those 'rats'. He had his principles and he would stick to them.

But I know he was sick to the stomach over a blatant lie Donaghue told the police when he was trying to get himself off the hook in the McVitie case. During the meeting with Donaghue and our solicitors, shortly after the arrests, Ronnie asked for the address of Donaghue's mother, saying he wanted to send someone round with some money for her. It was a genuine offer of help but when Donaghue turned Queen's Evidence he twisted the story to put Ronnie in a bad light, claiming that Ronnie wanted the address because he was going to arrange for the old lady to be murdered. In those days, Ronnie seldom worried about anything, but that allegation hurt him. Set up an old woman to be wiped out! Ronnie used to get the hump if anyone even swore in front of women. But when his chance came to hit back against Donaghue he still chose not to.

I never found out whether that lie was Donaghue's idea or the police's. Certainly Nipper Read and his team weren't fussy about the tactics they used to blacken our names and reputations. The disgraceful lie about Reggie and Connie Whitehead's son, for example, takes some beating.

Reggie idolized Connie Whitehead's little boy – also named Connie – and used to take him to a boys' club to see Father Hetherington. When the balloon went up, Whitehead tried to get himself out of trouble by writing a letter to the police saying that Reggie had threatened his wife and son. Our solicitor heard of the allegations and told the twins, but made them promise not to touch Whitehead. It was very hard for them because Reggie had stayed with the Whiteheads and had done nothing but try to help them. Ronnie seemed even more wound up about the lie than Reggie, and when he saw Whitehead in jail he said, 'I see. You wrote to Old Bill and said Reggie threatened your wife and kid.' Connie had no idea the twins knew and he went white, fearing the worst. Ronnie would have broken Connie in half if he hadn't promised to tell the truth.

Connie did admit in court that the police had made him say it, but as far as the twins and myself were concerned that did not make things right. What sort of man agrees to utter such a lie to make things easier for himself?

Most of the courtroom battles were, of course, won by the prosecution, but Reggie did score a couple of victories which, although they did not affect the outcome of the cases, did give him some satisfaction.

One was when Kenneth Jones brought up Frances. Reggie immediately got to his feet, his face white with fury. He was gripping the rail round the dock so tightly I thought he was going to break it. 'What has Frances to do with this case?' he demanded to know.

Jones made an attempt to justify bringing up her name, but Reggie interrupted him. 'This has nothing to do with her,' he said. Then he added, quietly but menacingly, 'If you continue involving her name, I'll be over this dock to you. I know all the police here are armed, but no gun will stop me.'

Reggie thought Jones was going to bring up Frances' suicide to make him look bad. So did the rest of us in the dock, and we all stood up to support Reggie's objection. It was like a scene from a film.

For several tense seconds Jones and Reggie glared at

each other. Then the barrister gulped and said to the judge, who was also shaken by Reggie's fury, 'In view of the circumstances, my lord, I think we'll move on to another subject.'

It proved the point, I think, that Jones was out of order in mentioning Frances. If he had been right, surely he would have insisted on carrying on, despite Reggie's threat.

The longer the trial went on, and the more the jury were swayed by Stevenson's interjections, the less confident I became that I would be found not guilty: all the signs pointed to the lies triumphing over the truth. My fears proved well-founded on Tuesday 4 March when the jury returned after seven hours' deliberation to find myself and everyone else in the dock guilty of their respective crimes. Sentencing was put off until the next day, probably to prolong the agony, and the twins, their Firm and I were taken back to Brixton to think about what sentences we would get.

Ronnie was still philosophical about it: thirty years was what he expected. Reggie was now thinking the same. And me? Well, all I prayed was that Stevenson, despite his biased performance throughout the whole thirty-nine days and particularly in his summing up, would see my position for what it was and treat me leniently. Many of the Brixton prison staff who believed in my innocence kept telling me I'd get no more than two years and, much as I hated the idea of doing any time at all for something I didn't do, I hoped they were right. With remission for good behaviour, that would be down to about eighteen months and since I'd been in custody for a year that would mean I'd be out in six months or so.

I was far from happy at the prospect of spending more time behind bars, but I wasn't in the depths of despair. I finally dropped off to sleep, having convinced myself that even if Stevenson did his worst I could reasonably expect nothing more than three years. I'd take it on the chin, make sure I kept my nose clean in prison, then pick up my life where I'd left off.

When we arrived at the Old Bailey the next morning, one of the officers in the cells offered me a bottle with some liquid in it. It was a tranquillizer to calm me down and he wanted me to take it before I went into the dock.

'No thanks,' I said. 'I'm quite capable of accepting anything Stevenson dishes out.'

Other officers pressed me to take some, but I still couldn't see the point. Then Ronnie urged me to take it to keep everyone happy, so I did. I can't say for certain what that odd-smelling mixture did to me. I did feel a bit strange, but then the whole experience had been strange, like a disturbing dream where all sorts of people pop up in the unlikeliest places, saying and doing the craziest things; where one minute everything is clear and certainly happening and the next, it's fuzzy like your imagination, and then you finally awake, not knowing where you are, and you can't tell the things that happened from the things that didn't.

I was sitting in my cell in a sort of trance when one of the officers came by. 'Charlie,' he called quietly, 'they've got thirty years.'

I stared at him, the dream focusing sharply into reality. *Thirty years*! It was what they had expected, what they had prepared themselves for. But it was still dreadful to hear. My twin brothers were to be caged until they were old-age pensioners, banished from the outside world until just one year from the end of the twentieth century.

It was hard to take in, and the officer's face and words began to fade behind a cloud of unreality, then I was floating and the next thing I knew I was standing in the

188

dock looking at Mr Justice Melford Stevenson, feeling the heavy silence of the crowded court but not sure whether I was really there.

Then the judge was speaking, not so much *to* me but *at* me, relating incidents about my past that I'd long forgotten. I listened, trying to take in what he was saying, but it was as though he was talking about someone else, someone I'd known very well but hadn't seen for years; perhaps someone from another life.

He spoke for only a minute or so but it seemed like forever, and then he got to the point of his monologue, the denouement of my personal tragedy that had been played out on the greatest criminal stage in the land.

'Charles James Kray,' he said slowly, 'you have been found guilty of being an accessory to murder. It may well be that you were not a member of what, in this case, has been called the Firm, but I am satisfied that you were an active and willing helper in the dreadful enterprise of concealing traces of the murder committed by your brother . . .' Stevenson paused. He looked down at Kenneth Jones. 'For accessory after the fact the maximum sentence, I believe, is . . .'

My breath caught in my throat. I could see the word forming in his mouth, grotesquely enlarged like some surrealistic painting. Was this all happening, or was it a dream? Was I here? Or was someone pretending to be me?

And then he said it and I swear my heart stopped. . . . 'life.'

Jones sprang to his feet. 'No, m'lud' he corrected. 'The law has been changed. The maximum sentence for accessory after the fact is ten years. And I don't wish . . .'

Then my heart pounded. Don't wish what, Mr Jones? Say it. Go on, tell him you don't wish to press for the maximum sentence. Tell him you don't believe all the lies

189

nor do you wish for a man to get ten years for something he didn't do. Go on, Mr Jones, tell him . . .

But the judge was motioning to him to sit down. 'That's enough, Mr Jones,' he snapped. And he turned to me. 'I sentence you to ten years' imprisonment.'

I stared at him, suddenly understanding, even in my dreamlike state, the meaning of the phrase 'absolute power'.

'Take that man down.' The words seemed to come from a long way off and I was floating again and the next thing I heard was Ronnie banging on the door of the first cell, asking what had happened.

'I got ten years,' I said.

Ronnie went mad. He started kicking the door, then he began shouting. 'Ten years! The rats gave you ten years!'

There wasn't much else I could say. I was taken to my cell, where I sat, saying over and over in my mind, 'Ten years. Ten years. Ten fucking years!'

Then Freddie Foreman and Connie Whitehead were put in the cell with me. Freddie had got ten years for supposedly disposing of McVitie's body. Connie had got nine; two for having a gun and seven for complicity in the McVitie murder.

I could hear Ronnie still creating in his cell. An officer passed by and motioned towards the first cell. 'He's making more fuss over your ten than his thirty,' he said.

Shortly afterwards the officer came back. 'Charlie,' he said. 'Ian Barrie's got twenty years. He's in a state. I can't pull him out of it. Can you have a word and try to calm him down?'

I did my best. I told him I was sorry but he had to calm down. There was an appeal coming up; his sentence was bound to be reduced. I didn't really believe it, but it was all I could think of to quieten him down. Hope was all I could offer.

190

When I went back to my cell Connie was sobbing. 'Nine years,' he kept saying.

'Connie,' I said as gently as I could, trying to hide my irritation, 'Freddie and me have got ten years for doing nothing. How do you think we feel?' I sat down on the cell bed and put my head in my hands. Reality was forcing through the numbness as the effects of the tranquillizer began to wear off and I found myself trying to get to grips with what ten years meant. I was coming up to forty-three years old. Even with full remission I was going to be more or less fifty when I came out. Fifty!

I looked at Freddie. What had happened to bring us here? What hand of fate had decided to make us the fall guys? Why us? With the daunting prospect of spending vital middle-aged years incarcerated behind bars hitting home to me now, I was at my lowest ebb, frail and weak from nearly a year in custody, drained dry from hearing my reputation blackened in thirty-nine dizzy days of courtroom drama. And then the cell door opened and my solicitor Ralph Haeems walked in. Detectives Read and Cator were upstairs and they wanted to see me, he said.

My heart leapt. Maybe, I thought, they were shocked at the severity of my sentence; maybe they were going to make a submission for it to be reduced. Crazy thoughts, I know, but I was so low I was ready to clutch at any straw. I looked at Ralph hopefully, but his face was grim. 'What do they want to see me for?'

Ralph looked down, shamefaced, embarrassed. 'They're going to charge you again with the murder of Frank Mitchell.'

I froze.

Ten years for something I hadn't done was terrible enough. But to face a life sentence for a murder I had nothing to do with . . .

* * *

The previous summer the murder charge against me had been dropped through lack of evidence without the case going to trial. But since then a law known as a Voluntary Bill of Indictment had been passed, which meant that I could be charged again. The new legislation made it possible for the prosecution to put the accused straight before a judge and jury without bothering with committal proceedings in a lower court.

I looked at Read and Cator with contempt, but they couldn't bring themselves to look at me. They knew full well I had had nothing to do with Mitchell's murder. They charged me and asked if I had anything to say but I said nothing. What was there to say?

That night in Brixton, I learned from prison staff that it was common knowledge in the nick that the police were determined to stitch me up on the Mitchell case. They had not liked the charge against me being dropped at Bow Street the previous July. I ached with despair. Was there no end to the police vendetta? Wasn't ten years enough? Did they really want me to go away for a lifetime too?

I was standing on a chair in the security wing looking out of a window when Tommy Cowley called up from the remand block below. 'Charlie, I know how bad you feel. But there's no way you can be found guilty on this Mitchell thing.'

I grunted sarcastically. 'You all said they wouldn't be able to get me in the McVitie trial, but I ended up with ten years so please don't say anything now.'

Tommy simply repeated that I couldn't possibly be found guilty. I thanked him for trying to make me feel better, and I hoped he was right, but I felt it was a useless, stupid thing to say. If the police wanted to get someone they had plenty of ways of doing it.

I had learned my lesson from the Bow Street hearing

and I was going into the witness box, come what may, to say my piece. I had nothing to lose. At the committal proceedings I'd listened to Vowden's advice and it had rebounded on me: by not going into the witness box I'd left myself open to all sorts of allegations which, because of my silence, must have been believed. The most outrageous of these, which would have been funny in less dire circumstances, concerned Leslie Payne's accountant friend, Freddie Gore, whom the twins and I had had some dealings with during the Great African Safari.

The only harsh encounter I'd had with Gore had been when he walked into an office I shared with Payne in Great Portland Street and interrupted a conversation we were having. I didn't approve of his manners, but let it pass. About ten minutes later, however, he came back and did the same thing.

'Mr Gore,' I said angrily, 'don't do that to me again. It's an insult. Remember, you work here and can be sacked. If you must say something privately, do it outside.'

After our arrests, when they were holding us on all sorts of weird and wonderful charges, Gore walked into the witness box at Bow Street and was asked by the prosecution, 'Have you ever been threatened by anyone?'

'Yes – one person.' Gore replied.

'Do you see that person anywhere in this court?'

Gore looked at the twins and me and the others in dock and pointed. I looked around to see who he was pointing at, but Ronnie nudged me and whispered, 'He means you.'

Shocked, I stood up. 'I threatened you?' I said. 'I've never threatened you in my life.'

During the lunchtime adjournment I told Vowden about the incident in the office – the only time I'd said anything remotely harsh to Gore – and said I wanted to go into the witness box to set the record straight.

Vowden would not hear of it. 'Don't worry,' he said. 'Wait till we get to the Old Bailey. We'll get him there.'

'But at least ask him how I was supposed to have threatened him,' I pleaded.

Vowden would not budge. He did not want to commit himself, he said, in case we gave something away that might be useful to the prosecution.

I argued with him. Since there were no reporting restrictions Gore's allegation was going to be all over the papers, with no response at all from me. To people who didn't know me, it would look as though I was admitting the threat, and I was sure that would be bad for my case. But Vowden told me I must be guided by him in matters of law, so I swallowed it. The next day, the papers made a meal of it: 'GANG BOSS THREATENS WITNESS!' screamed the headlines.

Nice! I was choked, and I couldn't resist asking Vowden if he'd seen the papers. 'Unfortunately, I have,' he replied, embarrassed.

When I appeared at the Old Bailey on the McVitie charge Vowden was again against my going into the box, repeating that if I didn't say anything, nothing could be used against me. My gut reaction said he was wrong, but I went along with him because he was the legal expert.

As it was, the decision *not* to give evidence was disastrous for me. In his summing up, Melford Stevenson made an issue of it, saying, 'If Charles Kray was innocent, would he not have gone into the witness box?' He made it look as if I had made the decision not to give evidence!

Afterwards I told Vowden I'd been made to look an idiot. He tried to console me by saying that it did not matter and that Stevenson should not have said what he did. Sadly, that didn't do much for me.

Barristers are very highly trained but they are not very worldly. I don't think Vowden was 'got at', either at Bow Street or at the Old Bailey, but I do think he gave me bad advice (albeit in good faith) in a case that was to ruin my life. So when the Mitchell trial opened at the Old Bailey in April 1969, I made the point strongly to Vowden: I was not going to be set up twice; I was going into the box, come what may. And I did.

I'm sure that giving evidence helped me, particularly since the judge Mr Justice Lawton was fair-minded, totally aware of what was going on and, unlike Stevenson, eager to see that justice was done. For example, when the prosecution counsel – Kenneth Jones again – tried to belittle me over my earnings as a theatrical agent Lawton stepped in to let everyone know what was right.

Jones, who obviously knew nothing about the theatrical agency business, implied that I was trying to cover something up concerning a bank statement, which the judge then asked to see. Within seconds he said the statement was in order and he understood it perfectly. Jones was angry at being put in his place and tried to take it out on me. He quoted five people who had given a different version of events from the one I had sworn, and said, 'Come, come, Mr Kray. What reason do you give for their telling lies? All five of them?'

'That's quite simple,' I said.

'Oh, is it?' Jones replied. 'Why is that?'

'Because they are sitting there and I am standing here,' I said.

He did not have an answer to that. I sensed the judge nodding in agreement. He seemed to be aware of who was telling the truth – unlike Stevenson whose preoccupation, it seemed, was to find people guilty. Lawton appreciated very early in the trial that the case against me was extremely slim. One particular piece of evidence, concerning where I had been on two days in December 1966, was vital, and thankfully I was able to prove that I was not where the police said I was because I was at home in bed with quinsy. Fortunately, a Dr Morris, a child psychiatrist with a practice in Wimpole Street, came to my home to visit my son Gary, who he was treating for suspected rheumatic fever, and he wrote to the court confirming I had been in bed. Lawton told the jury that a letter from such a professional gentleman should be accepted, and from then on I was home and dry.

It was the judge who actually led the prosecution into dropping its case against me. After hearing all the evidence he ordered the jury to leave the court while he had a discussion with Kenneth Jones.

'Regarding Mr Charles Kray,' said the judge. 'Four people have testified that he was at a meeting to kill Frank Mitchell. A lot of things have been said at this trial, but let us say they were right: he was there and they all discussed it. He could have said, 'No, thank you, I want nothing to do with it.' Because we don't hear very much about Charles Kray afterwards, do we? Whatever they say, it is not very safe at all, is it?'

Mr Jones agreed it wasn't.

'Do you want to carry on with the case against him?' asked the judge.

'No, m'lud.'

'Then I am stopping the case against Mr Kray,' said the judge.

And in the dock I found myself weeping with relief. I was too caught up in the emotion of the moment to be embarrassed or ashamed of my tears. Anyone who has been in a major court, fighting to prove their innocence will appreciate my feelings. The relief was indescribable, and at last I felt that the nightmare of the Axeman was over.

I was wrong.

The police, not satisfied with my ten-year sentence in the McVitie case, had another card up their sleeves: if I didn't actually help to murder poor Frank Mitchell, they argued, then I had helped plot his escape from Dartmoor and had harboured him in London. More rubbish, of course. But more agony, too. I was beginning to feel that their persecution was endless.

Thankfully, this case was eventually thrown out too, but not before I'd been reduced to tears again in the witness box.

Fuelled by more and more lies from Albert Donaghue, Billy Exley and Harry Hopwood, the persistent prosecutor hammered away at me, insisting that I must have known about the arrangements for springing Mitchell. I took it for what seemed an age, and then the terrible injustice of having to defend myself against lying idiots finally got to me, overwhelming me, and I cracked. Trembling with emotion, I said: 'I didn't have anything to do with it. They did. You have to remember, my name is Kray and if anyone makes a statement and puts the name Kray on it, they are believed by the police.' I gripped the frame of the witness box tightly as I felt my voice going. I fought in vain to control it. 'I'm doing ten years for nothing because of all these lies,' I choked.

And as I wept again with the frustration and injustice of it all, Mr Justice Lawton adjourned the court.

The high tension of the Old Bailey saps one's energy; adrenalin starts to flow as soon as the building comes into sight. I had had more than 300 tortuous hours which had done my brain in, leaving me mentally drained and ragged, my nerves in tatters.

When they finally took me back to Brixton and opened my cell, I walked in with my shoulders hunched in dejection, what little pride I'd clung to in court all gone. I fell on the bed and curled myself into a tight ball, enjoying the silence and the solitude.

I think then I knew how a fox feels when he finally shakes off the hounds.

Chapter Twelve

The full weight of what had happened hit me when I walked into the security wing at Brixton that evening. I went into the room with four cells, and the Governor, assistant governor and chief prison officer were standing there, solemn-faced, like a bizarre welcoming committee. They were not sure what to say, but they knew enough about convicted men not to be flippant or sarcastic. On a table in front of them were cardboard boxes for our clothes. For eight months on remand and for more than a month of the trial we had worn our own clothes, but now we had to exchange them for prison issue. We put our clothes in the boxes and knew it would be a long time before we saw them again. They took away the boxes and banged us up. I wanted darkness to cover me, so that I could be alone with my thoughts, but we were all A-Category – maximum security – men and a red light was left on all the time. I didn't feel suicidal. But I *was* depressed. The prison clothes felt awful, the atmosphere in the cell was terrible, and all the time that red light was on and the prison officers looked through the flap in the cell door, invading my thoughts. I thought again of Mum and the old man and the rest of our family and wondered how they were taking the sentences. I sat there, my eyes closed to that insensitive red light, trying to work out how it had all happened. Ten years! It sounded like a lifetime. And for what? Just for keeping my mouth shut. I fell asleep through sheer exhaustion. I felt as if I'd been digging a road all day.

That first terrible night as a convicted criminal was worse than anything I'd experienced in my life.

In the morning the red light had gone out and the wing was bright with March sunshine. Ronnie came out of his cell and clapped his hands. He looked at the prison officers. 'Good morning, gentlemen. What a lovely morning.'

The officers looked at him strangely.

'There's no point being downhearted,' Ronnie said. 'We've got to carry on.'

One officer turned to me and said, 'He's something else.' I said he'd always been like that and would never change.

The cheerful banter continued while we had our breakfast and then it was time for exercise. As we were on our way out Ronnie was laughing with one of the officers, a tall, heavily built bloke in his early forties.

'What I'm going to do today,' Ronnie said, 'is write off for a world cruise because that's one thing I want to do when I get out.'

The officer was half-laughing with Ronnie and before he knew what he was saying the words had slipped out. 'Oh, well,' he said. 'You've got thirty years to save up for it.'

He knew he had said the wrong thing. But it was too late. Ronnie went white and moved forward threateningly.

'Ronnie,' said the officer quickly. 'I'm so sorry. I apologize. You were larking about and I forgot and said it without thinking.'

I believed him. So did Ronnie. He calmed down immediately and told the officer to forget it. But, he said, it wasn't a nice thing to say. After exercise, the officer came to my cell and asked if Ronnie was still upset. The incident was still playing on his mind, he said, and it was such a stupid thing to say. I said Ronnie had forgotten it, but I don't think the officer believed me, because he went up to Ronnie at lunchtime and apologized yet again.

Later that day Ronnie sent off for some brochures.

That officer's slip of the tongue was sparked off by the tension that surrounded the twins. And that tension was not helped by some idiots in a cell about fifty feet away on the opposite side of the square; a section full of drunks doing a month, or creeps finishing six months or whatever for petty crimes.

One day, as we were exercising in the square, two chaps – young by the sound of their voices – called down mockingly, 'I've got another ten days to do – and you've got thirty years. How do you feel about that?' Then they laughed.

The taunts went on and on for a couple of days. Finally Ronnie could stand it no longer; the tormentors were probably cowards who would have topped themselves if they had been given thirty years and he wanted them silenced. He asked the security wing's chief prison officer to tell whoever was responsible to shut up.

The Prison Officer was delighted to step in. He thought it was unfair when Ronnie and Reggie were taking their punishment so well; also, he would have to deal with the problem if Ronnie lost his rag. Later that day, he told them, 'By the way, I found out who it was. I don't think you'll be hearing any more from them.'

While we had all been in the square on exercise the officer had stood in a cell, waiting and watching. When the two idiots stood up and started their cowardly shouting, he noted their cell and went round. 'Hello, you brave little pair,' he said. 'Those blokes down there are doing thirty years, but I'll tell you something – at least they're

201

men. You snivelling idiots are causing us problems by upsetting them, so I'll tell you what I'm going to do. If I hear one more peep out of you I'll bring Ronnie and Reggie through here on our way somewhere and leave them with you for five minutes. I'm warning you – one more peep.'

The two guys, in their mid-twenties, were the type who would mug old ladies, or pick on victims who couldn't fight back, the type who tease animals through bars, the type with no bottle. Not surprisingly, we didn't hear another word from them.

One day the twins and I were staring at the security cage and saw three guys taunting a tall, spindly, ginger-haired bloke who looked like an office worker. The three bullies just wanted to have a go at someone and we were not going to stand for it. We shouted out to them that they were nothing but cowards, that they were brave only because there were three of them. The men took one look at us and decided to leave it out. As they walked away, the weak-looking 'office worker' looked up and nodded his thanks. We discovered later his name was Paddy Sullivan and he was a major in the IRA. He was waiting to come up for trial.

Six months later I got a message from Freddie Foreman. His son, Gregory, had been called in by the headmaster at his public school and asked to give his father the message: 'Paddy Sullivan sends his regards and best wishes to Charlie.' Apparently the headmaster knew Paddy well and had been to visit him in Wormwood Scrubs.

Paddy was obviously one of those people with a long memory.

* * *

When I got sentenced it seemed like the end of the world. But I never thought of trying to escape. When the Mitchell case was thrown out, it helped me come to terms with the ten years. It was still terrible being punished so severely for something I didn't do, but at least it was not a life sentence. I figured I would be out in seven years if I kept my nose clean: short of being beaten up and forced to retaliate I reckoned I could keep myself under control.

But if I had been sentenced to life on the murder charge I do think I would have changed – and tried to escape at every opportunity. I would probably have been killed, but what would it have mattered? The twins know that they did certain things and they do not cry about their sentences, but I would not have been able to accept it like that, because I was innocent. I dread to think what sort of twisted, hateful character I would have turned into had that Mitchell rubbish been believed.

As it was, I did my best to accept that what was done was done, and nothing was going to change it. It would have been easy to give in to my hate and bitterness, to lose control and smash things up in frustration, but I knew that could destroy me. So, as the days and weeks and, eventually, the months wore on, I gritted my teeth and battled to keep myself under control.

It was not easy though. And when I was finally moved from Brixton to Chelmsford in Essex thirteen months later, I still had not come to terms with the fact that I was caged like an animal for something I did not do.

My world at Chelmsford consisted of just ten other A-Category prisoners in a small, maximum-security block with cameras watching every move. We were treated like children. Normal prisoners walked freely to their work but we were led everywhere and led back; we would have to wait for prison officers to fill in the pass book and to log the time. When we left for lunch we had to wait for someone to escort us fifty yards or so. It was frustrating beyond belief.

There were thirty cells for just ten prisoners, and my fellow inmates got so bored that they would move from one cell to another for something to do. Because we were in such a confined space we were allowed certain freedoms to save us going out of our minds. If you wanted to work, you did; if you didn't, no one made you. I felt I needed to keep myself busy; one week I would go into the workshop and saw iron for traffic triangles; the next I would wash the rubber floors. I even got into cooking: the kitchens would send the food to us and we would try to make it appetizing.

But it was the outside exercise I lived for. We played volley-ball – every day for two years – and football. The exercise period was one hour, and cameras in the four corners of the playing field watched us all the time while a helicopter hovered overhead. Such expensive security was senseless – one needed to be Superman to clear the wire and barbed wire on the high walls behind the playing field. The prison officers were hand-picked and as good as gold, and I'd ask them about the vast amount of money being squandered unnecessarily. They would merely shrug and say, 'Don't ask us, Charlie, we only work here.'

On Mondays we were taken into the main prison – an elaborate process in which we had to pass between electric doors and bullet-proof glass windows. But it was worth it. The library was there and we were allowed to spend fifteen minutes picking books. It was like a holiday.

In the evenings, once or twice a week, a woman would come in to teach us handicrafts. She was a lovely lady, in her fifties, and we looked forward to her visits. You have to give her credit: she was very brave, although I think she knew she was perfectly safe. We all thought so much of her we would have died rather than let anything happen to her.

I told her once that what she was doing was worthwhile, and that I admired her. I promised myself I'd take her some flowers when I got out but, sadly, it was one of the things I never got round to.

Wally Pobyn was a clever bloke. He was the man who arranged John McVicar's escape from Durham Prison by knocking a hole in a shower and covering it with papier mâché until it was time to go. Wally was due to escape, too, but something happened and only McVicar got away. During the riots at Durham in 1964 some prisoners locked themselves in an office and read reports written on them for the parole board. The men could not believe the terrible, untrue things the prison staff had written: it seemed incredible that a prison officer had the power to poison a prisoner's record with the stroke of a pen if he didn't like him.

Suddenly it became all-important to me to know what my report said and Wally knew an officer who promised to find out. Nothing could have prepared me for the shock of hearing what that report, which my immediate future depended on, said. The exact words were: 'Charles Kray. This is not his natural attitude. It is all a pretence. This cannot be his normal behaviour, because he is too nice. He has caused no problems since he has been in this prison, but we know this is a big act.'

I was shell-shocked. Just because I said 'Hello, please and thank you' and didn't go around hitting people, they thought something was wrong. I tried to treat the report with the contempt it deserved, but it was impossible: the injustice of it all burned into me deeply and there was nothing I could do about it.

As I entered my second year at Chelmsford, my bitterness at being robbed of important years of my life began to fade and I softened a little. I formed close bonds with some people I might not have wanted to know outside. Somehow, when people are thrown together in jail, one doesn't think of their crimes – you just get on with the business of living.

Someone I did get close to was John Duddy, a small, grey-haired man sentenced to life, with Harry Roberts, for the Shepherds Bush murder of three policemen in the early sixties. It choked me one day when he told me he'd decided to tell his wife they were finished. I felt he should not do it, because they had been married many years and were still in love. But he said he knew he was never going to get out of prison and he didn't want her to waste her life. She was too good for him, he said.

His wife didn't want to know about a divorce and she told him she would still come to see him whether he liked it or not. John was pleased, of course, but insisted she should visit less frequently, to give herself a rest. He was a very unselfish man and over the next year we got very close.

One Sunday evening about 7 P.M. I was called in to see the Prison Officer and told I was being moved to another prison early the next morning. At about 8 P.M. John Duddy came up to see me. He was pleased for my sake that I was going, but sorry to see me go because 'things have been good since you've been here'. Close to tears, he said he wasn't going to wait until 9 P.M. to 'bang up', he was going in early. But he asked me to knock on his door in the morning to say goodbye. It was all rather emotional; you do get close to people in a short time in prison.

At 6 A.M. the following morning I was handcuffed and taken to a security van by six Prison Officers. My report,

I was reliably informed, read: 'We have come to the conclusion that this is not an act with Charles Kray. It is his normal behaviour.'

It had taken someone two years to work that out and now I was being transferred to Albany on the Isle of Wight, a couple of hundred yards from Parkhurst, where the twins were held.

While I was in Albany I heard that John Duddy had died of cancer.

We travelled through London on the journey to the Isle of Wight and my stomach knotted when we hit the East End. It was a weird feeling, looking through the darkened windows at all the old, familiar places: it hurt, but at the same time it was lovely. So Poplar and Bow and Mile End and Whitechapel were still there! The joke in prison is: 'Don't worry – over the wall, the world's still there.' And now I could see it for myself. The driver pulled up at some lights and I told my six guards that I'd lived only a minute away. I'd got quite close to them in two years and one of them said, 'If we had our way, Charlie, we'd nip you down there for a quick cuppa.' But, of course, the security was so tight that it was out of the question. The van was in radio contact with police stations at different points en route, as if someone expected a helicopter to drop out of the sky and pluck me to freedom. We moved away from the lights and suddenly we were in White-chapel Road; there, staring me in the face, was my old factory with the sign, Berman and Kray, still there. What I would have given to walk along that street just then, even as a roadsweeper! But soon the van was picking up speed towards the city, pulling me away from the warmth of my nostalgia.

I got my chance to breathe fresh air when we stopped at a police station for my guards to use the toilet. I stayed in the yard, basking in the exquisite feeling of the hot summer sun and cool breeze on my face and in my hair. I stared up at the sky, marvelling at its blueness. I'd seen the sky in prison, of course, but somehow it was different looking at it on the outside. It was only a tiny police station yard and I was in handcuffs but for those few minutes I felt I was in heaven. I could have stayed there all day, but soon we were on the move again, passing through Central London and South London suburbs towards the A3. All the way through Surrey and Hampshire I talked little and just stared out of the window, drinking in the beauty of the countryside, thinking, as I had a thousand times in prison, that you don't know how much you'll miss something until it's taken away from you.

Then we were on the ferry and I was transfixed by a kaleidoscope of colour that took my breath away. In prison I'd been surrounded by dowdy greys and blues month in, month out, but now in front of me were greens and reds and yellows, all bright despite the darkened windows of the van. It was warm and sunny and there was a holiday atmosphere. I took in the men's suits and shirts and watched them drinking beer out of cans; I watched women talking casually and children running around playing. Everyone looked happy. I'd seen smiles on the faces of people in prison but, like the sky, it was different. I wanted to get out of the van, close to the children's laughter, but it was forbidden, so I stayed there looking out through the dark green glass at the unfamiliar scenes, feeling as though I was from another planet.

When we got to Albany one of the six guards unloaded my box of gear and we waited in a little room for the prison staff to take me to my cell. When the time came one of them said, 'Well, that's it, Charlie. You're here. They'll be giving you something to eat in a minute.' And then they all shook my hand, promising to give my regards to all the people who had become my friends in Chelmsford. The Albany staff looked shocked: a Kray brother in the nick, shaking hands and exchanging good-natured pleasantries! They could not be blamed for being surprised. The publicity about the family would have made anyone expect the worst. In my case, they were to discover that the image bore little resemblance to reality.

Within a few minutes my cell was full of people wanting to say hello. I was pleased and was polite, but after a short time I wanted them to go: I had been in a world of just nine other inmates for two years and the talk and noise sort of did my brain in. I wanted to be on my own, to shut my eyes and think about the countryside and the ferry and pretend I was going on holiday. Slowly, agonizingly slowly, they drifted back to their own cells. But one bloke, a Scotsman, hung on, and when the others had gone and we were alone he started telling me how he had stabbed and killed someone. We were similar, he said, we were both doing ten years.

We were about as similar as Jekyll and Hyde!

He loved talking about his violence, thinking I would enjoy it, but it sickened me; violence always has. He was one of those idiots who have wanted to be in prison all their life. He loved it. But I was doing ten years for nothing, and all I could think about was getting out. Finally I could stand him no more and told him to go.

Alone that night, I thought back over my day. It had been an enjoyable trip: it had done me good, put me in a better frame of mind. I lay on my bed and brought the colours of those holidaymakers into focus, filling my head with the laughing faces of those happy children.

Oh, yes, over the wall the world does exist, I thought, my eyes full. I'd seen it.

* * *

For a while, Ronnie had been alone in Parkhurst, on the Isle of Wight. But Reggie was moved from Long Lartin Jail, in Leicester, to calm him down.

Ronnie has been taking four different tablets every day since his breakdown in the fifties. He understands that they keep his paranoia and uncontrollable temper at bay and insists he has the prescribed dosage four times a day. One day in Parkhurst a new officer in charge of the high-security wing chose not to understand Ronnie's problem.

When Ronnie went into the office and asked for one of his tablets, the new man was difficult. He was on his own, in the middle of a shift change, he said, and Ronnie's request would have to wait.

Ronnie, who knew his body's danger signals well, told him the matter couldn't wait: he was due a tablet now and he had to have it.

The officer checked his records. Yes, he agreed, Ronnie was right: four tablets a day and one was due now.

If he had simply taken out the appropriate pill and handed it to Ronnie, all would have been well.

As it was, the officer seemed anxious to prove a point. 'I'm afraid I can't give you the tablet,' he said.

'Why's that?' asked Ronnie.

'Because I don't know which one you're supposed to have right now.'

'It must say which one in my records,' said Ronnie.

The officer shook his head. 'It doesn't.'

'Don't give me that.'

'You'll have to wait until my relief comes back.'

'I'm telling you, I need to take that tablet. I know I have to have it.'

'You'll have to wait till the other officer comes back,' said the new man. And he added cockily, 'And I wouldn't bank on him giving you a tablet anyway.'

Whether it was the bloke's arrogant attitude or the

urgent need for that tranquillizing tablet I don't know, but Ronnie snapped, as anyone who understood him would have expected. He felled the unsuspecting officer with a right hook, then picked him up and vented his anger and frustration in a severe beating.

Ronnie's polite request for a tablet landed him in the chokey block for fifty-six days – with a diet of bread and water on and off for fifteen days.

When he came back to the maximum-security wing, he was very disturbed. Bobby Welch, one of the Great Train Robbers, was standing at the top of the stairs and said something. Ronnie told him to get out of the way, then picked up a chair and proceeded to smash everything he could see: lights, tables, other chairs, and the glass on the inside of the barred windows. When his frenzied moment of madness was over he turned to watching prison officers and said, 'You'd better take me to the chokey block again.'

I heard the story from Welch when he was transferred from the security wing at Albany. He said it was awful; he couldn't believe what they had done to Ronnie.

Obviously someone did. For Reggie was quickly brought down from Long Larten and asked to tell Ronnie he would be allowed out of the block the next day if he promised to behave himself. It did the trick. Ronnie got it all off his chest and said he'd had enough of the screws treating him badly. He knew he needed tablets to keep him calm.

Perhaps next time they would believe him, he said.

I had come to terms with being robbed of my freedom. But I was becoming more and more bitter about being on the A-Book and all the stringent security that went with it. To be regarded as a constant threat, someone to be watched twenty-four hours a day, is bad enough when you've done something to deserve it. When you have done nothing and are non-violent and easy-going it is terrible, and impossible to accept. What made it worse for me was that all the prison officers could not understand why I was on it in the first place. My case kept coming up, of course, but I was always turned down. Someone somewhere very high up had clearly made a decision about me. My name was Kray and that was that.

The attitude of Home Office officials did not help my mental state either. After seven months at Albany I had served a total of three and a half years, qualifying for parole. I was taken upstairs to a cell where a young man in his middle-to-late twenties was sitting at a desk, ready to interview me. There was a young woman there, too.

I sat down and he said, 'Kray?'

'Yes,' I replied.

'Ten years,' he said. 'Well, you aren't going to get parole, you know.'

'Oh, I'm not,' I said, failing to keep the hard-edged sarcastic tone out of my voice. 'And who are you to judge that?'

He said nothing, just looked at me.

'Why are you wasting my time bringing me up here for an interview if the decision's already been made?' I said. 'You give all the sex cases, all the perverts who are a real danger, parole. But normal people don't get it.' Before he could say anything, I went on. 'Anyway, if the decision has been made in my case, I don't see any point in talking to you.' And I got up and walked out.

I was seething. All right, it was my first interview for parole and I didn't expect to get it. But why build me up then put the knife in before I'd been asked one question?

Later the Chief Prison Officer said he would try to get me another interview, but I told him not to bother; it

212

would be exactly the same, and I didn't need the mental strain of false hope.

A few weeks later I was given the job of helping an officer with the inmates' workshop time sheets. When we were on our own he said, 'I wish you weren't on the A-Book. I could give you this job; it would be a bit of extra money for you. You could work up to being in charge of the workshop.' He paused and grinned. 'We could have a coffee together and a bit of the wife's cake.'

In the outside world that would be nothing. But after three and a half years in prison on the A-Book it seemed everything. I could think of nothing I'd like better than to sit down with a nice bloke and share some of his wife's cake over a coffee, without a camera watching my every movement.

'That would be lovely,' was all I said.

He said he would have a word with someone because there was no logic in keeping me on the A-Book. I didn't hold my breath, which is just as well because I didn't hear anything for about twelve months. Then one day the maximum-security wing's Prison Officer called out, 'Charlie, I want to talk to you!'

I walked over, wondering what stroke they'd pulled now. But he was grinning; maybe he'd picked a winner and won a few quid.

'Charlie,' he beamed. 'You're off the A-List. I've got the papers. You're a normal prisoner.'

He shook my hand. 'I'm so pleased,' he said.

I was delighted, of course I was. And relieved. But I couldn't resist a sarcastic jibe. 'Thank you,' I said. 'But I wonder if you can tell me how the Home Office can decide overnight that I'm no longer a threat to society when I'm no different from when I came in?'

The P.O., I must admit, was sympathetic and understanding. 'Don't ask me, Charlie. *They* make the decisions.'

Perhaps the workshop officer had put in a good word,

for within a couple of weeks I got the job in there working out the timesheets. I did them every Friday and I felt amazing; it sounds so little, so unimportant and menial, but it was a huge triumph in my life. No longer did I have to go to work with someone escorting me, opening and locking doors all the time.

I was still an inmate, deprived of my liberty. And I was only halfway through my sentence. But for the first time I felt normal, a member of the human race, if still an imprisoned one.

Now I began to enjoy my visits. It was a long haul from London, involving train, boat and taxi, and I was grateful to my parents, Dolly and the kids for making the effort. Those two hours every fortnight were a highlight of my existence and I treasured them. Sadly, though, my cell always seemed lonelier than ever after I'd said my good-byes and was sitting there thinking over what had been said. After one particular visit by Dolly and Nancy I was feeling more depressed than ever when I heard some news that sent me into a wild panic.

An Isle of Wight ferry had overturned outside Ports-mouth harbour. A TV news report said that a woman and a little girl were among those missing. My world seemed to stop. The time of the tragedy fitted in with when Dolly and Nancy would have been on board. I was inconsolable, convinced they had drowned, and it was all my fault for being the reason for their visit. I begged the prison authorities to make enquiries to find out if that woman and little girl were Dolly and Nancy. Things had not been perfect with Dolly and me, and, yes, I had been thinking of leaving her to live with another woman. But in times of extreme crisis you push these things to the back of your mind: she *was* still my wife, and we *had* had some marvellous times together, and she was the mother of my lovely children; I couldn't bear the thought of her and my darling Nancy ending their lives so horribly. I waited and hoped and prayed, then finally, hours later, someone came and told me that Dolly and Nancy were safe.

They had not been on that fateful ferry. They had missed it – just.

I thanked the prison officer for telling me and added, 'Thank God.' I couldn't trust myself to say more: the feeling of relief was so exquisitely warm and spine-tingling that it coursed through my entire body and tightened in my throat, leaving me choked with emotion.

Not all the people who came to see us were family and friends. We had visits from an American judge – and even half a dozen monks. The judge was travelling all over Europe inspecting the jails and when he visited Albany he asked to speak to me. Of course I was delighted to talk to someone like that and was introduced to him in a little room the authorities made available. He was in his late fifties and informally dressed in a lounge suit. He arranged two cups of tea and we started talking.

At first I felt a little strange talking to a judge, but after a while I relaxed and started to enjoy telling him what life was like for me in prison. He asked about my case and I explained that I was serving a sentence for something I didn't do. I don't know whether he believed me, because prisons are full of people who claim they are innocent, but he seemed genuinely interested and sympathetic. He echoed my own thoughts when he said that the laws in Britain are antiquated. They can say one thing and mean another, and can be bent and twisted by clever lawyers to suit their case. In America, the judge was quick to point out, the laws are not so wishy-washy; they are black and white and it is clear what is meant. I didn't want to make a big thing of my case but, since he asked me about it, I went into some detail. He listened then said that if I'd been in America I could have pleaded the Fifth Amendment, i.e. I could have refused to give evidence against the twins because I did not want to implicate myself.

I amused the judge when I told him that the conversation we were having could not happen with a British judge. They were not living in the real world, I said, and I made him laugh when I recounted the story of a judge who made the headlines by asking in the middle of a major High Court case, 'Who are these Beatles?'

After we'd talked for an hour or so, the American thanked me for agreeing to see him. But I said it had been my pleasure: apart from being highly intelligent, the judge's views were refreshingly democratic, and his opinions had had a striking effect on me. I went back to my cell feeling pleasantly high on having had a conversation of real substance with a humane gentleman who felt genuine compassion for people who had fallen foul of the law.

The judge left the prison that day, but the monks who came to visit stayed a week to see what it was like to be a prisoner. They ate the same food as we did and slept in two cells on opposite sides of the wing. I had a chat with one of them, a charming young man in his middle twenties, and told him I admired him for what he was doing. 'At least you know how we feel,' I said.

'Yes,' he replied, 'but only up to a point.'

I looked puzzled.

'If I wake up at two in the morning and decide I don't like being caged any more, all I have to do is ring a bell and ask to be let out. You can't do that.'

I smiled. How right he was.

I wondered later whether anyone thought of searching the monks when they came in. I decided that someone probably did: no one is trusted in jail. They would probably frisk the Archbishop of Canterbury.

Chapter Thirteen

During Christmas 1972 they told me I was being moved on again. Someone somewhere, some faceless civil servant who had never met me, had decided that one year in the hard, high-security island prison had changed me, that I'd learned from the tough oppression and constant vigilance, and that the threat I'd posed had passed, and I was ready for some rehabilitation to prepare me for my return to the outside world.

The establishment they chose for this worthy exercise was Maidstone Jail in Kent. I welcomed the move; it was a more relaxed prison, and would cut out travelling problems for my visitors. Chatting in unnatural surroundings, conscious all the time of prying eyes and cocked ears, is bad enough, but it is even worse when your loved ones and friends are whacked out by a five-hour trek over land and sea. Maidstone, in contrast to Albany, was a comfortable hour's drive from London.

Quickly, my world became brighter. I was given a job in the kitchen in charge of the hotplate, took French lessons, organized volleyball competitions, kept in shape in the gym and generally made the most of prison life. But, like everyone else, I lived for my visits and when Dolly and Nancy arrived, and Nancy ran to me and I took her on my knee and held her close, it hit home to me how much I'd missed.

Spring came to Maidstone and I started counting the months to my release. I had kept my nose clean from the moment my sentence began and I worked out that, with full remission, I would be a free man in January 1975.

The thought was warm and comforting. But it led me on to think about Dolly and the children, and what our life would be like. I was far from happy. I had to face facts: Dolly and I had gone from bad to worse and it was unlikely to be any better on my release. I was going to need a lot of help to adjust and Dolly, neurotic and unstable, was not the supportive kind. I had to be careful not to stick my head in the sand and pretend our problems didn't exist. Having been unjustly robbed of precious years I wanted to come out and make the most of life with someone who cared about me. I had two years to think it through and to work out what I really wanted to do with the rest of my life. I was determined there would be no more mistakes.

It was not long before Diana came into my mind again. She had rarely been out of my thoughts, but her lack of contact had made me think that, sadly, the relationship was dead. What was she doing? Where was she working? Had she left her husband? Was she happy? The questions filled my head night after night, and I decided it might be a good idea, with my release date looming nearer, to ask a departing inmate to try to track her down. Yes, I know it was a wild, crazy idea. But after five years in prison wild, crazy plans seem perfectly logical and sensible. I began keeping my ear to the ground for Leicester-bound inmates.

On 2 May 1973 George Ince appeared at Chelmsford Crown Court accused of murdering Muriel Patience at the Barn Restaurant in Braintree, Essex, the previous November. Seven days later the jury returned saying they could not agree and a retrial was ordered. It began on 14 May, still at Chelmsford but with a different judge – Mr Justice Everleigh. As the second trial got under way, the newspapers started running stories of a 'mystery witness'.

I knew immediately who it was but when Dolly visited me I didn't say a word; nor did she. Then the papers started referring to a Doris Gray – the name to which Dolly had changed by deed poll three years before – and I knew for certain I was right. The mystery woman, it seemed, was going into the witness box to say that George Ince could not have been at the Barn Restaurant in the early hours of 5 November because all that night he had been in bed with her. Reading that, I went cold. My stomach knotted in fury, and I paced up and down my cell, my mind running hot with vivid, masochistic imaginings of the man walking into my home, talking and playing with my children before climbing into bed with the woman who was still my wife.

Suddenly my brighter, more hopeful world was shrouded in a gigantic black cloud of despair. I fought to control my self-torture, but agonizing thoughts kept invading my mind. How often had Ince been to the house? Had little Nancy been encouraged to call him Daddy? Did he walk about the house half-naked like I'd done? Did she . . . did she see or hear her mother moaning in ecstasy as Ince made love to her in my bed?

It was a terrible, terrible experience and I was impotent in my frustration, unable to vent rage on anything except my cell wall. And then I was told Dolly was coming to see me.

The prison promptly ordered six extra officers to be present at the meeting. After more than five years, they still didn't know me; they had no idea how I thought or how I reacted to situations.

'Nice,' was all I said to her as she sat down.

She started gabbling on nervously about it. I cut her short. 'All I want you to tell me,' I said curtly, 'is whether Ince has got something on you to make you give evidence. Or did it happen? Were you with him?'

219

'Do you want someone to get thirty years, like the twins?' she said.

I ignored the fact she had avoided the question.

'I don't want anyone to go down for anything,' I said. 'I just want to know, Dolly.'

She opened her mouth again, but I shut her up. '*I just want to know, Dolly.*'

She was quiet for a few seconds. Then she looked down. 'He *was* with me,' she said softly.

I didn't say anything. Silence was a massive wall between us. Then, deciding attack was the best form of defence, she started to get hysterical.

'What do you expect?' she screeched loudly. 'You've been away all these years!'

'That's not the reason,' I said, still calm. 'It happened before, I know.'

'Not like you think,' she snapped. Then she started blaming me. 'It's your fault. You went away. What do you expect me to do, sit indoors all my life?'

'I didn't expect you to take him home. I didn't expect you to screw him in front of Nancy.'

'Anyway, he *was* with me. And I *am* going to give evidence. How can I let a guy go away for thirty years?'

I took in what she said. I didn't like what I'd heard, but I felt she had no choice. 'Quite right,' I said finally, amazed at my tight self-control. 'If that's the truth, go and give evidence.'

I meant what I said. I knew Ince *could* get thirty years and I didn't want to see that happen to an innocent man. Not even Ince. 'I don't like it,' I added. 'But you have to do it.'

With it all out in the open Dolly started running off at the mouth. 'I couldn't help it . . . all the problems I've had . . . It's been one thing after another . . . I had to do something . . . you don't know what it's like . . .'

220

'Don't make excuses,' I broke in. 'You've done it. You've probably been doing it for years. The thing I can't stand is that you've let him in our house with Nancy there. With me here and him there it's blowing the kid's brain.'

She didn't say anything. There wasn't much she could say. We talked about it a bit more, then I said I wanted to be alone to think what I was going to do about her now.

It didn't take me long. Dolly hadn't reached her Poplar love-nest before I decided that I didn't want to know; our marriage had run into stormy waters long before and it was now lying smashed to pieces on the rocks. Divorce was going to be painful for Gary and Nancy, but that was the price that would have to be paid.

Dolly did give evidence and George Ince walked out of Chelmsford Crown Court a free man. I hated the idea of seeing Dolly again but I had to because of the children: we needed to talk about what was going to happen to them after the divorce. On her next visit I told her we were finished, but she refused to accept it.

'Why?' she asked. 'Everything is going to be all right now. It's over between George and me. We'll go away when you come home. It'll be nice.'

'What?' I said incredulously. 'We're not going away anywhere. I don't want to know. It's over. End of story.'

But still she couldn't believe I meant it. 'I got twenty thousand from a newspaper for my story of my affair with George. I can put some of it away till you get home. We can go away somewhere.'

'Listen,' I said. 'I don't need holidays or anything else with you. I don't want to know about that money. Give Gary some and keep the rest. As far as you and I are concerned, we talk about the kids and that's it.'

221

Over the next few months, she kept trying to make me change my mind. Once she brought a friend with her, who said I really should forgive Dolly and make an effort to patch things up.

'I don't really want to discuss it any more,' I said.

'The thing with George is over,' she told me. 'Dolly isn't seeing him any more.'

By then Ince had been arrested on a charge involving a gold bullion robbery and was in Brixton awaiting trial. News travels fast on the prison grapevine and during the next few days I heard that Dolly had visited him. So much for it being finished, I thought.

Dolly's friend came again. 'I know what you're going to say,' she began.

'Well, *did* she see him?' I cut in brusquely, not wanting to waste time on it.

'Yes,' the woman replied. 'But it was the last time.'

'Do me a favour,' I said. 'Tell her to come and see me. I want this over. Now.'

The following week Dolly arrived with Nancy and Gary. She looked dreadful: thin, with bags under her eyes, untidy make-up and her hair a mess.

'What's the matter?' I asked. I meant it. I'd never seen her look like that.

'Why should I look well?' she replied defensively. 'All the problems I've had.'

I almost choked. '*You've* had problems!'

She talked rubbish for about two minutes. I looked at Nancy, then Gary. I felt for them, but I couldn't stand it any longer.

'Do me a favour,' I said quietly. 'Get out of here. Now. And start divorce proceedings. I can't do it from in here.'

We sat there glaring at each other. Nancy and Gary were quiet. They didn't know what to say; I suppose they were frightened.

Finally Dolly said, 'I will do that.' And she took Nancy's hand and half-dragged her out of the hall, leaving Gary sitting there with his eyes full of tears.

I put my hand on his. 'I'm sorry about that, Gary.'

'I'm not,' he said. 'I'm glad you said it.'

We sat there for a few seconds, not knowing what to say. My heart went out to him.

Finally I said, 'You'd better go. She'll leave without you.'

'I don't care,' he said. 'I don't care any more.'

We sat there and finished the visit. When Gary left he found his mother waiting in the car for him. The journey back to London must have been awful.

That was the last time Dolly visited me.

My darling, adorable Nancy, just eight years old and so lovely and innocent. How I idolized her! The thought of her being hurt cut through me as I sat in my cell that evening, but I knew there was nothing I could do, especially from prison. It really was all over with Dolly, and the sooner the break was made, the better. Nancy would come to terms with it, I consoled myself: kids always do.

But later that night the pain was deep as my mind ran back over all the precious years I'd missed of Nancy's growing up. She had been three when I was arrested. One minute I'd been free to come and go as I pleased, to take my child wherever I wanted and care for her like any normal working father, the next I was caged like an animal, stripped of all parental rights except an unnatural, stilted chat in a sombre prison visiting room a couple of times a month. Five years I'd missed, years that should have been carefree and fun-filled, lovingly memorable. And I was to miss more. Even if all went well and I was released in January 1975, Nancy would be coming up to ten. Another two years and she would be in puberty, then a teenager. Before I knew it, she would be asking me to give her away in church.

Sitting in my cell, alone yet again with my thoughts, I concentrated on memories of Nancy until I could summon up a mental picture of our holiday together in Sitges. How pretty Nancy had looked that April, her blond hair bleached even lighter by the Spanish sun and her little body bronzed deep brown. She was a water baby, always in the hotel pool – only two years old but totally fearless, running and jumping into the safety of my arms then, as her confidence grew, jumping into the deep end on her own. When I reprimanded her with fatherly concern she would climb out then leap straight back in, going under and coming up again, clinging to me and giggling with childish joy as she rubbed the water from her eyes.

Yet, as always when I thought of Nancy, the doubts surfaced in my mind despite my attempts to push them away. That night after I'd seen Nancy dragged from the hall without a chance of a loving goodbye kiss the doubts stared me in the face, again, and this time I had to accept they were real. Deep down I knew Nancy was not my child.

It wasn't easy to accept, of course, and for a long time I'd refused to believe it. Not mine! That laughing, giggling, squealing, shrieking little ball of wide-eyed innocence, that cartwheeling bundle of energy, that adorable impish little girl? Not mine!!

As a loving father it was something I had never ever questioned or considered. Cradling Nancy as a new-born baby, watching with pride as she tottered on her first unsteady steps, holding her hand as she toddled along East End streets, talking to her softly as she lay in bed exhausted after a play-filled day . . . the very idea that the little girl I worshipped might be someone else's flesh and blood was absurd. No, impossible. And then I had heard it from the mother of the child herself and for six years the horrible haunting question had hung over me like a thunder-cloud.

Dolly told me during a row when Nancy was two. I was getting ready to go to Leicester on business and Dolly didn't like it. 'You think more of that bloody club than you do of me,' she said.

I groaned inwardly. This was an old chestnut and I wasn't in the mood for it. I wanted to get on the road. 'You know I've got to keep an eye on things,' I said, fighting to keep the exasperation out of my voice.

But Dolly *was* in the mood for a row. She'd been tense all day, building up to it. 'It's probably not the only thing you keep your eye on,' she sneered.

'What do you mean by that?' I snapped.

'You certainly don't seem interested in me. You don't want to know.'

I ignored that and carried on dressing.

'You don't want to bloody know!' Dolly raised her voice, trying to provoke.

'Leave it out, Dolly.' I said calmly. 'Not now. I'm late.'

'Business. Bloody business. It's business all the time. When's the last time you took me out?'

I felt it best to ignore her and not rise to the bait.

'Come on,' Dolly persisted, more loudly. 'When's the last time?'

'Keep your bloody voice down. What's the matter with you?'

And then she went into one, shrieking hysterically, accusing me of ignoring her, not wanting her any more, moaning that I let the twins run my life. Her voice got louder and louder and then she shouted, 'It'd serve you right if I found someone else while you're enjoying yourself up there.'

225

I snapped. 'Shut your mouth, for Christ's sake!' I said fiercely. 'You'll wake Nancy.'

'Why should you worry about that?' Dolly bellowed.

I didn't understand what she meant, so I said nothing.

'I don't see why you should worry about someone else's kid.'

Silence. Then I said, 'What are you talking about?'

'What I say. Nancy's not yours, you know.'

I froze, then just stared at her, searching her hard green eyes, unblinking now in blazing hatred.

'She's not, you know.' Her mouth curled and twisted with arrogance, enjoying my pain.

What she had said roared in my ears, deafening me with its implications. I felt suddenly weak. A thousand responses hammered in my head but my brain was too numb to make sense of them, then one single thought forced its way to the front of my mind, pounding and pounding away: 'Don't let it be true. Don't let it be true. Please, please don't let it be true.'

But Dolly, cocky in her desire to hurt, just stared at me in silence, enjoying my anguish.

Later, days later, she took it back, said it was a lie dreamt up in the heat of the moment. But it was too late. She had sowed that seed of doubt and it was to grow and grow until it was always there in the back of my mind.

And now in my cell, swimming around in a sea of warm memories of little Nancy, Dolly's damning declaration began to dominate my thoughts. I remembered all the odd coincidences, the strange happenings that somehow didn't add up, and I remembered, too, the innocent slips of Nancy's tongue telling me 'George' had been round.

All those wasted, precious years when my little girl had needed the influence of a caring father. Well, I had to stop tormenting myself. For my own sanity I had to accept once and for all that Nancy had indeed had that father's influence all the time I'd been away.

His name was George Ince.

Mum and the old man were not surprised, of course, by my decision to divorce Dolly. When the papers revealed the affair with Ince Mum admitted she'd known about it for some time but hadn't said anything because she felt it was not her business. 'I didn't like it,' she said, 'but I felt you had enough problems. I knew you'd have to decide for yourself one day.'

Dolly, ever ready to see the worst in people, always blamed Mum for telling me about Ince, but that simply wasn't true. Mum was not the sort of lady who liked making waves and causing problems. When the mystery witness story broke I told Mum I hoped Diana would read it and get in touch with her, in which case she was to be sure to bring her to see me. I was tempted to ask Mum to try to find Diana herself, but decided against it because she had enough on her plate earning a living, taking care of the old man and visiting the twins and me in different parts of the country. I'd been keeping my ears open for departing inmates going to Leicester but had not heard of any so far.

I'd spent hours describing Diana to a little Jewish man called George who was in for fraud. He often said I talked about her so much that he felt he knew her personally, and he told me nothing would give him greater pleasure than to go to Leicester to try and find her. But of course that's easy to say when you're locked up more than 150 miles away. George was coming up for release and due to be given a little job in a hostel to prepare him for life outside.

One day he came looking for me, beaming all over his face. 'Charlie,' he said, excitedly, 'I've got the hostel.

They're offering me London.' He paused, then grinned. 'Or Leicester.' He stood there, waiting.

I didn't know what to say; it's difficult to ask someone to organize their life in a certain way just to help you find a lost love. But it was as if George was reading my thoughts.

'Charlie, I've got no family to worry about. It makes no odds to me where I go. I'd love to go to Leicester to try to find Diana.'

I was lost for words. Prison life is not known for its generosity of spirit, for humane gestures that demand nothing in return. Finally I said, 'That's really nice of you, George. I'd love you to try to find her.'

George beamed. I think it made his day.

Sadly, George had no luck. The club in Leicester had closed and he could not find anyone who had worked there. He did the rounds, asking in pubs and so on, but drew a blank. I was disappointed, naturally, but told myself it was probably for the best. If Diana had got her marriage sorted out she certainly wouldn't need an ex-jailbird knocking on her door and asking her to renew a romantic relationship with someone she had probably forgotten long ago.

And yet, as the months towards my release wore on I could not get Diana out of my mind. She had been so beautiful, so kind, so loyal; so much the woman of my dreams. I knew I was still in love with her and had never stopped loving her.

And I knew, despite everything, that I would not be able to stop myself trying to find her to tell her so.

Chapter Fourteen

I could see the road from my cell. Day after day I would gaze out, lost in thought about the horrors of yesterday and the hopeful tomorrows waiting for me on my release. I would watch the cars on that road and think of the people in them, trundling along in comfort, peace and freedom. One day, I thought, I'll be on that road. One day, I'll be free; free to prove to my captors, my prosecutors, my friends even, what a terrible wrong I had suffered in the name of justice. One day . . .

At Maidstone there is a reception area where inmates arrive and depart. One morning I had to go there for something connected with my job in the kitchen and I found myself staring at four cubicles, each with a prisoner's name on the outside. I peeked into one of them: there was a long mirror, and a jacket and trousers hanging on a hook. There was also a clean white shirt, some socks and on the floor were some shoes. The cubicles were for inmates leaving for good or for a pre-release weekend. I looked at the clothes, then at the names on the doors. One day it will be my clothes hanging there, I thought. One day it would be my name on the door. One day . . .

Two or three months later, in July 1974, a prison officer told me to go to reception again. It had nothing to do with the kitchen, so I guessed it was about my pre-release weekend. A wave of excitement surged through me; I felt like a schoolboy being given an unexpected day's holiday. Sorting out the clothes I needed for my weekend was a tingling experience: nylon socks, not coarse woollen ones, white cotton pants, not drab prison issue, a blue blazer, and neatly pressed light-brown trousers. I didn't need to try them on, but I did, even the socks. Then I looked in the mirror at myself. It was an indescribable feeling, the first time in more than six years that I'd worn normal clothes.

They told me I was being released on Friday 23 August for three days and I went back to my cell, walking on air. Over the next few weeks I could think of nothing else but putting on those clothes and walking out of the door, breathing the sweet, fragrant scent of freedom. And then it was the Thursday before the Friday and I was so excited that I felt I'd never drop off to sleep. But I did and slept wonderfully peacefully. I was woken twenty minutes before other prisoners so that I could get washed and shaved. I could not do it all quickly enough: I was quivering all over with excitement like a child on Christ-mas Day.

There are many people in prison who are not worth two bob, but there are others who are genuinely sincere and really care about people other than themselves. I'd struck up friendships with several people and later that morning as I sat around waiting to be called to reception they came over to me. 'Have a lovely weekend, Charlie . . . Enjoy yourself, mate . . . Don't do anything I wouldn't do, my old son . . . Don't forget to come back, Charlie . . .' They were all pleased for me and I didn't hide my excitement, then someone was calling my name and I was on my way to reception, half-running to taste the freedom I'd dreamt about for over six years.

A prison officer told me there were some people waiting outside, reporters and photographers mainly, but I couldn't care less. My day had come and I would talk to anybody about anything. Not for long, however, because Mum was meeting me to drive me to London and I was going to make the most of my three days, squeezing the

230

maximum enjoyment and pleasure from my short-lived liberty.

The Press were great, as they always had been to me, then I was in the car and Mum, bless her, was putting fifty pounds in my hand and we were driving away from the grim establishment that had been my home for the last eighteen months.

I glanced back and caught a brief glimpse of my cell. Yes, I would be back there on Monday, I knew that. But for the next seventy-two hours I was going to push my hatred for that lonely cage out of my mind. My 'one day' had come and I was going to think of nothing but catching up with the world that had left me behind so cruelly on 8 May 1968.

That evening, Mum and the old man suggested going to the Blue Coat Boy pub in Bishopsgate; just a quiet drink, they said – there were a couple of old friends who were dying to see me again. We walked into the downstairs bar and chatted to a few people. I was a little baffled; I certainly knew the people there but only to say hello to – they were hardly old friends. But I was enjoying myself anyway, so I didn't say anything.

Then Mum said casually that we ought to go upstairs where there was a bigger, more comfortable lounge.

And I nearly fell over.

There were not a few friends who wanted a quiet drink with me, there were over two hundred! Everyone I'd known down the years, it seemed, was standing there waiting for me, wanting to shake my hand and say how good it was to see me again. There was a beautiful buffet laid out, the drink was flowing, and all the time I was being taken from one person to another, exchanging a piece of news here and enjoying a bit of nostalgia there. Suddenly, around closing time, I started feeling dizzy: I'd spent more than six years with just a handful of people –

sometimes only one or two – and the hustle and bustle and heady party atmosphere was getting to me.

As if by magic, the chap who owned the pub came over and asked me to go downstairs with him; he had something important to tell me. The pub had now closed, and in the welcome tranquillity of the downstairs bar he sat me down and grinned. 'I haven't got anything specially important to tell you, Charlie,' he said. 'Your mum saw it was all getting a bit much for you so she asked me to get you away for a few minutes. She could see it was doing your brain in.'

I laughed. It was typical of Mum; she didn't miss much.

After I'd got my breath back we rejoined the fray, and the drinking, eating, laughing and joking went on until 4 A.M. I was so high on excitement and joy I was neither tired nor drunk, and when some of us went back to Braithwaite House I happily sat there, drinking one gin after another, with no thought of going to bed. We talked about prison but it seemed a long way off. It was as if those six years had never happened.

I spent the whole weekend in the East End, strolling around to see how much of the old place was still standing, and chatting to other people I'd known before I went away. They were a highly charged, emotional few days for me and of course they couldn't last. Before I knew it, it was Sunday night and I was making plans to return to the prison at 10 A.M. Mum wanted to come back with me, but I did not want her to have the upset of seeing me walk back through that door again. So, around 8 A.M. the next day, it was my old mate Tommy Cowley who drove me through South London and on to the A20 to Kent.

The Press were there in force, not so much to record my arrival, I think, but to be on the spot if I failed to turn up; that would have been a far better story. Tommy and I sat chatting until a couple of minutes to ten, then I walked to the gate and pressed the bell. The cameras clicked and I forced a smile I didn't feel. 'Fooled you, didn't I?' I cracked. 'Bet you thought I wouldn't be back.'

The newshounds liked that.

It was weird being back inside. It was as if I'd never been away and those three marvellous days as a free man had never happened. But they had, of course, and my friends wanted to know all the details – what I'd done, who I'd seen, whether things had changed, and whether I'd enjoyed myself. They would not taste that freedom for many years, so I drained my seventy-two hours of every little detail and they hung on every word. What I told them could have been put over in five minutes; I made it last a week.

Of course, one of the things they wanted to know was whether I'd slept with a woman. Like any normal man I'd missed sex desperately and had thought of going to bed with someone – probably a professional lady – on my first day out. But when it came to it, so much had been arranged for me, so many people were wanting to see me, that I simply did not have time. And anyway, deep down, the only person I wanted to go to bed with was Diana and I didn't even know where she was.

My mates in prison thought it hilarious that I'd been too busy for sex.

Everything, they say, comes to those who wait. And the one thing I'd been waiting for – my full release – finally arrived on 8 January 1975. My name was on one of those reception cubicles again and I changed out of my prison gear for the last time. All the excitement I'd felt five months before was still there, but this time it had a hard edge to it, tinged with a fierce determination that once I was out of prison I would begin a campaign to prove I should never have been jailed in the first place.

Several days earlier I'd been told that, despite our divorce, Dolly had rung the prison governor asking for details of my release. No doubt she wanted to make a big show of meeting me to squeeze some more money out of a newspaper. Fortunately, the governor had told her she had no rights, and the only people who met me that nippy winter's morning, apart from the Press, were Mum and two dear friends, George and Sue Dwyer. Driving down that road I looked back at the retreating prison wall, then up to where my cell was. For a few brief seconds memories of my prison existence swam around in my mind: the boredom and frustration, the anger and bitterness of maximum security, and the joy of coming off the A-List; the callous prison officers who loved making life difficult, and the sympathetic ones who bent the rules; the stupid inmates who drove me mad by talking rubbish and the mild-mannered ones who became my friends. These memories sped through my mind like a fast-forward video and then suddenly seemed to switch off. As on my pre-release weekend, it was as if those years, all that never-ending forever, had never happened.

As we left the town and headed towards the A20 and London, I sank back in my seat and closed my eyes, trying to take in that from that very moment I could do precisely what I wanted when I wanted with no questions asked, no permission to be sought. I was a free man, and it was a blissful, blissful feeling which sent a shiver of exquisite pleasure through me.

I cannot remember a more enjoyable hour's drive.

One of the first things I did was persuade Mum to give up her office cleaning job. On my pre-release weekend I'd been shocked to learn that she was getting up at four in the morning for this, then waiting on tables at the Blue Coat Boy at lunchtimes. She said she needed the money to be able to afford to go on prison visits, but it made me ill to think about it. All the people who had had money from us over the years! You would have thought somebody would have helped her out with a few quid. I didn't mind her doing the pub work, because she was an outgoing type who enjoyed company but I hated the idea of her getting up in the middle of the night to clean bloody offices. So when I was home for good I told her that that was the end of it. Mum, bless her heart, said she couldn't give it up – the cleaning company boss was a lovely man and she did not want to let him down; but I persisted and eventually she rang him and said she was quitting. He was very understanding and thanked her for all she had done.

Mum had started with nothing, suddenly had everything, and now she was back to nothing again. Yet she never complained, never moaned. I was so pleased for her and the old man that they still had that flat in Bunhill Row. When we bought the house in Bildeston, people suggested we should sell the flat, but I said: supposing something happens and we're not around, what would they do? Well, something *did* happen, and the house had to be sold. But Mum just went back to living in the flat and took on two jobs to make ends meet. Living the high life in the West End or on the breadline in the East End, she was still the same lady.

Money was a nightmare. I'd gone into prison with a lifetime's experience of threepenny bits, tanners, half-crowns and ten-bob notes, and I came out to the complexities of decimalization. The old half-crown had bitten the

235

dust and the much-loved half-a-quid note was now a fifty pence piece.

For a while it was like a foreign currency and, on my second night home, it hit me just how much I had to re-learn. I was staying with George and Sue at their home in Orpington and while I was in the local pub I decided to ring Gary. Without thinking too much about it I went to the phone, but I couldn't work out how to use it. Coping with the new money was bad enough, but the phone system had changed too. I went back to George and Sue, feeling pathetic. 'I can't do it,' I said, like a child. They fell about.

Once I had picked it up, I seemed to be on the phone all the time, trying to pick up the threads of my life as fast as I could. I was always flying about, always in a hurry. I couldn't bear the thought of standing still; I'd idled away nearly seven years of my life, and I was determined to make up for lost time.

For two weeks I didn't think of driving, even though my licence was up to date. But then, after a night at Mum's, I asked George if I could drive us back to Orpington. Like swimming, or riding a bike, driving is something you never forget, and I drove the twenty miles as safely as if I had never been away from the wheel. After that, I was eager to drive everywhere. But I was still in a hurry: if I needed to stop for a paper or cigarettes, I'd see a shop then think, 'I'll wait for the next one.' Then I'd do the same at the next shop. It was as if I felt I'd be missing something, losing my place in the queue of life, if I allowed myself to pause. The changes took a bit of getting used to: I lost count of the number of times I took a sharp turn into what I thought was a traffic-beating back-double, only to find myself facing a block of flats or a one-way street that had not been there before. Then when I did calm down and took Shanks's pony I'd find the traffic had increased so much that crossing the road was a major, life-risking event.

There were people who were wary of me because of my name, but on the whole I found nearly everyone very friendly. I never took anything for granted, however, and was always on my guard. One night in the Chinbrook pub in Grove Park, South London, I was aware of a man at the next table staring. Then he said something to his wife, who looked over; it was obvious they were discussing me.

I felt a bit awkward – rather like an animal in a zoo – but ignored them and carried on chatting to George and Sue. The man continued to stare and I began to feel uneasy: the Kray trial had affected a lot of people and even though seven years had passed one couldn't be sure of people's reaction to meeting one of the convicted men.

Finally, George, Sue and I got up to leave. The man got up too, and walked towards me. He was about sixty, but huge – about six foot six. I tensed inwardly. This is it, I thought. He's going to take a pop at me, or slag me off. He certainly didn't look the type who wanted my autograph.

The gentleman looked me in the eye, but instead of giving me a load of abuse or even a right-hander he merely extended his hand and said, 'I hope you don't mind me asking, but how are you?'

I replied, 'I'm very well, thank you.'

'Oh, that's good,' he said. 'I'm so pleased. I'd like to wish you all the very best for the future.' And then he shook my hand warmly.

He was a middle-class, confident sort of man who, I believe, said what he meant and meant what he said. I left the pub with Sue and George, feeling buoyant. The encounter boosted my confidence no end.

* * *

I decided I had to talk to Dolly. Even though I knew Nancy was not my child I still wanted to see her; the upset of that last prison visit when Dolly had half-dragged her out still bothered me and I was missing her more than ever. I went to the flat in Poplar, which I had handed over to Dolly along with everything else, and discussed visiting arrangements. Dolly agreed it was best if I popped up whenever I liked and for the next few weeks I did that. For a while it was quite friendly; Dolly often cooked a meal and I looked forward to the visits, which I found rewarding and enjoyable.

Suddenly everything changed, however. For some reason Dolly decided she didn't want me to see Nancy any more and I got a summons ordering me to go to court to fight over custody. I was shocked then angry, thinking this is all I need – court! I could not understand what it was all about. I didn't want Nancy to leave her mother and live with me; I just wanted to see her once a week or so. Surely that could be arranged without the hassle and expense of going to court?

I started wondering what possible legal argument could be put forward to stop me seeing Nancy whenever I wanted. Surely Dolly wasn't going to come clean and tell the truth about Ince? When Dolly's solicitor eventually told me, I burst out laughing. 'One of the points we shall be making,' he said pompously, 'is association.'

'Oh, yes,' I said. 'And what do you mean by that exactly?'

'That it is not in the child's interests to be associated with you, a convicted criminal.'

I laughed in the solicitor's face. Well, what a joke! Dolly knew full well that I had served a sentence for something I didn't do, and here she was, living with a man who had done time for something he admitted, yet it was me who was not a good influence on Nancy.

238

The court case went ahead. I won the right to see Nancy once a week and did so for a while. But it became clear that Nancy was not bothered about seeing me and gradually I stopped going round to the flat altogether.

Once I'd got back into the swing of normal life again, I turned my mind to tracking down Diana. The first weekend I could, I drove to Leicester. But seven years is a long time and I couldn't find anyone I knew who could give me some leads to try to trace Diana. George, my old Maidstone mate, had discovered that she and her husband had once owned a pub, so we did the pub circuit again, but with no luck. Leicester is a fairly big city and Diana could have been anywhere. On the other hand, she may well have left the area entirely. I returned to London none the wiser.

George and I agreed to try again the following weekend, but during the week I got involved in some work that made it difficult for me to get away. George rang me and I explained that our private detective business would have to wait a week. An hour after I put the phone down, George rang back. 'I bet you'll come up now,' he laughed.

'Why?' I asked.

'I've found her,' George said.

Suddenly I found myself short of breath.

George had discovered Diana's pub was called The Carousel and had rung there. He had learned she was still married, and was ready to put the phone down if her husband answered, but luckily it was Diana who picked it up. When George told her he had a message from a 'mutual friend' Diana, who later said she knew that the 'mutual friend' was me, was pleased, but also wary; she had been questioned by the police after my arrest and didn't know if what she'd read about the murders was true. Anyway, she told George, she didn't like talking to strangers on the phone. George immediately went to the pub, discreetly introduced himself to Diana and told her that I'd been thinking about her for nearly seven years. Diana was not totally convinced but agreed to go to a Leicester hotel a couple of days later to meet me again. The agreed time was 8 P.M.

As a boxer, I never suffered from butterflies. I knew I was good and could handle myself, and always walked from the dressing room to the ring with no tummy rumblings at all. But waiting for Diana in the hotel room that evening I went slowly but steadily to pieces. By 8 P.M. I was almost a nervous wreck. Seven years was a long time, I kept telling myself. Things change; people change. Before the arrest, I'd been a happy-go-lucky man about town – a wealthy businessman with a neat line in chat to match my expensive clothes, not bad-looking for my forty-four years, and supremely confident in myself because of my business success. In short, a winner. But I knew that prison had changed me. Seven years for something you did was hard enough to take; seven years for something you didn't do was a knockout blow that was bound to take a heavier toll. I looked at myself yet again in the mirror. Yes, I had lost weight, and I was seven years older. But would Diana detect something lacking in me? Would she feel that the happy-go-lucky spirit that had attracted her all those years ago had died? That my eyes had lost their sparkle? That the effervescence and cavalier approach to life had been replaced by a quieter, almost inhibited, shyness? That seven years locked away from society had robbed me of my personality, leaving me a shadow of my former self? Would she see not the winner she had once admired, but a loser to be avoided?

In the end, I bottled it. After all the build-up, I couldn't face the confrontation and the accompanying possibility of rejection. Not in the hotel foyer, anyway. If the reunion was not to be how I had imagined and dreamt throughout all those imprisoned years, I wanted it to take place in the privacy of the room, where we could at least be polite and brief and make small talk, then go our separate ways without too much hurt and certainly without any fuss.

So, at 8 P.M., I asked George to go down and bring Diana to the room. As I started on yet another packet of cigarettes new worries started banging away in my brain. What if she was scared to go to a hotel room with a man she had met just once? What if she wasn't just scared, but mightily offended? What if she just walked out? What if . . . ? I was piling one obstacle on top of the other when the door opened and there she was standing before me, blonde and beautiful, just as I remembered her. As we stood there looking at each other, smiling shyly, I knew it was going to be all right, and I walked over to her and gave her a kiss.

'Well, I think I'll be going,' said George, bless him. And he went out, closing the door quietly behind him.

Diana and I talked and talked. She was eager to tell me how much she had wanted to get in touch; how many letters and cards she had written, only to tear them up because she didn't want to cause me problems. In the end, she said, she reluctantly decided that she would leave it to me. She was so pleased that I'd tracked her down and had felt confident that I would do so. For my part, I was eager to tell her that I felt the same about her as I had done before I went away, but I stressed that if everything was all right in her life I didn't want to spoil things and cause her problems. She immediately reassured me that I'd come back at the right time. She had left home once while I was away, but had returned; now she was so unhappy with her husband that she was on the point of leaving again. When she had read that I'd been out for a pre-release weekend she'd considered ringing, but had feared that I'd be too busy.

The talking went on and on, and then, quite naturally it seemed, we went to bed. I would like to be able to describe the sheer joy of holding, caressing and making love with a woman you adore after nearly seven years without any female contact whatsoever, but it is beyond me; I would think it is beyond most people.

There is only one word to describe my feelings that night – they were wondrous.

I started to pop up to Leicester regularly, and eventually Diana decided to leave home. It was a difficult decision for her because her daughter, Claudine, was only twelve, but she felt it was best for everyone involved, so she moved in with a girlfriend in Beulah Hill, at Crystal Palace in South London.

Diana was so good with people, particularly the elderly, that I couldn't wait to introduce her to Mum and the old man. I felt sure they would adore her as much as I did, and I wasn't disappointed. The old man did not make friends easily, but he took to her at once; Diana really cares about people and the old man quickly realized this. They got on really well. Mum thought she was great and said it was a pity I hadn't met her years before. Mum never spoke badly of Dolly, but she went off her after the shabby way she behaved over the Ince affair. More than once Mum said my life could have been so much happier if I had met Diana first.

A friend of mine, Wilf Pine, former manager of the hugely successful rock band Black Sabbath, kindly loaned me a house, and Diana and I moved in together. Immediately after the breakup Claudine and her brother Ian stayed with their father in Leicester, but it wasn't long before Diana and her husband agreed that it was best for the children if they moved to London. Some loyal pals made sure I had a few quid to help put mè back on my feet and I was able to buy a flat in Worcester Park in Surrey. The kids came down and soon we were all living happily under one roof.

Sleeping had never been a problem for me. I'd always had the knack of being able to cut myself off from the hassles and aggravation of everyday living, and I managed this in prison, despite all the problems. But when I started living with Diana I would wake up in the middle of the night, shouting at the top of my voice. A dream would set me off and I'd wake up in a sweat but I could never remember what the dream was. It did happen once in prison – at Maidstone – and I woke myself up shouting. When it happened at home I would get up and have a coffee then go back to bed but then I'd have to get up again, and it would be backwards and forwards like that all night. Diana was worried, and a little frightened to begin with, but as soon as she senses the build-up now she shakes me and I slip back into a peaceful sleep.

I found I could go on television to talk about the past and my time inside, but in one-to-one situations – particularly with women – I'd find myself stumbling over my words with embarrassment. So you can imagine how awkward I felt when people actually wanted my autograph.

I'd got a job working on a big cutlery and silverware stand at the Ideal Home Exhibition at Olympia and attracted a lot of publicity. Around 80,000 people passed through the Exhibition each day and after a while I started feeling as though many of them were looking at me and pointing me out to their friends. One day a couple of girls asked me for my autograph.

Not knowing what to do, I said, 'You must have got me mixed up with someone else. I'm nobody famous.'

One of the girls laughed. 'We've seen your picture. And read about you. You're the Kray twins' brother, aren't you?'

Of course I signed my name for them, but I did feel funny doing it. And then it happened again, and again. A *London Evening Standard* reporter must have noticed, because he came up for a chat. He mentioned I was working, as though it must be a new experience for me. I told him I'd always worked, despite the notoriety.

'But ten hours a day?' He was shocked.

'I like it,' I said.

The next day I picked up a copy of the *Standard*. The reporter had written an article saying Charles Kray was working at Olympia and signing more autographs than he was selling cutlery. I thought it hilarious.

Communication with Dolly became cold and casual. We only spoke to each other about our son Gary but I knocked even that on the head when she did something I'll never forgive her for. Dolly would be the first to admit that she is a hard, unemotional individual, but what she did to my family, particularly Gary, was quite spectacular in its selfishness and brutality.

When George Ince had been released from prison, Dolly had decided it was not convenient for Gary to live with her. She did not discuss it with him but waited until he went out one day, then packed all his belongings in a suitcase and left it on the doorstep for Gary to find when he came home that night. He went to live with Mum and the old man in Bunhill Row. But I always made sure he kept in touch with Dolly.

I had always got on well with Dolly's mother and was very upset one day to hear she was ill. She was staying at

244

the home of Dolly's elder sister, so Gary and I went round there with some flowers. She was a lovely woman of about seventy and thought the world of her grandson. We had a nice chat and before we left she whispered, 'Just because I'm getting old, they think I'm senile. But don't worry, I know exactly what's going on.'

I smiled and took her hand. 'Well, you know what we think of you,' I said. 'I'll be running around, but I'll be back to see you in a couple of weeks.'

Early one morning, about ten days later, I was going on a visit to Parkhurst and left a note for Gary reminding him not to forget to ring his mother.

When I came back from Parkhurst around 7 P.M., an awful atmosphere hit me as soon as I walked in the door at Bunhill Row. Mum and the old man were in tears. I wondered what the hell had happened, then Mum said, 'Charlie, I've never said anything about Dolly, but I think this is terrible. After you left this morning, Gary phoned her.'

I nodded. 'I told him to.'

'He asked how she was, and said can I come and see you today? She didn't want him to. Then . . .' Mum was finding it hard to speak through her tears. I put my arm round her. '. . . then Gary asked how Nana was.' Mum couldn't speak for a few seconds, then she said, 'Dolly just told him, "Dead and buried," and put the phone down.'

I went numb. Then cold fury swept through me. How could Dolly not tell us her mum had died? How could she not give us the chance to pay our respects at the funeral? It was almost unbelievable.

'That's it,' I snapped. 'That's the end.'

Seething, I got on the phone and rang one of Dolly's brothers, Raymond. 'Dolly's taken a right liberty,' I said, and told him what had happened.

'Charlie,' he said sympathetically. 'We never thought our sister was that bad. We thought she'd let you know.'

'Somebody should have rung, Ray,' I told him.

'We thought you were away.'

That didn't cut any ice. 'I respected your mum, Ray. If I'd been in China, I would have come home. It's bad enough me not being there, but Gary . . .' I was so angry I couldn't speak, then finally I said, 'Anyway, that's the end for me. It's the most terrible thing to do to anyone.'

After that I told Gary I didn't want to have anything to do with the family.

Dolly felt guilty about Gary. For the next few months, she would ring him a couple of times a week, but it was purely because she felt she had to, not because she wanted to. She is incapable of feeling much for anyone other than herself. I would have expected Dolly to take Gary home to her flat, but she never did. I would have thought she could have taken him to see Nancy; after all they grew up as brother and sister. But she never did. Perhaps I should not have been too surprised. Dolly was jealous of Mum's popularity and stopped Nancy from visiting because she knew the child loved her. Every one of Dolly's relations said it was a bitchy, hurtful thing to do but Dolly didn't care. She was the only person who didn't like my mother. And the reason? She knew she couldn't compare with her in any respect as long as she lived.

At one time both Gary and I missed Nancy terribly, so when a young bloke I knew said he often saw her, I asked him to set up a meeting with her for us. I told him to let us know if he wouldn't be seeing her so we wouldn't be waiting unnecessarily. Well, we waited. Nancy didn't turn up, and neither did the bloke who was due to see her. That was the end for me and I decided not to bother any more. It was painful because I'd thought the world of her. Even though she was another man's child.

Chapter Fifteen

I started visiting the twins while they were together in Parkhurst. I didn't moan to them about my ten years because they were sentenced to three times that. We did discuss the events that had put us away but neither Ronnie nor Reggie wanted to know about the problems I had faced because of the Kray notoriety. I was out and they were still inside, they said; they would love to have my worries.

I did mention that I'd warned them not to trust those idiots, the so-called Firm, particularly Hart and Donahue, but the twins, as usual, took the view that it wasn't worth talking about: it was a thing of the past, finished; nothing could be done to change what had happened so best forget it.

For two criminally minded people, the twins are strange in that they do not like talking about crime, or violence. As young men they never discussed it and in prison all the talk of villainy and boasting drove them round the bend. Because of their name and reputation other inmates used to seek them out to try to impress them, and it bothered the twins so much that they would ask to be put in cells on their own. For years they were marked men, as they had been on the outside. And sometimes the pressure got to such a pitch that they exploded.

During the first few months of my freedom Mum phoned me, saying that there had been an upset in Parkhurst: Ronnie, it seemed, had gone into one and belted a couple of prison officers. They had injected him to sedate him, and chucked him in the chokey block. Mum and I were on our way to Parkhurst at once.

They told us we would have to see Ronnie in his cell, because he wasn't well enough to go to the visitors' room. That surprised us, but it was nothing to the surprise we got when we saw the state of Ronnie – and the cell, which was filthy and stank to high heaven. Even I, who had spent years inside, was shocked, and it knocked Mum bandy. I couldn't believe the authorities had allowed us to see the state of it; I suppose they felt it better to let us see Ronnie in those conditions than stop the visit altogether, in case we thought something was wrong.

There was just an iron bed in the cell and Ronnie was sitting on it. He looked awful: his eyes were lifeless, with bags under them, his skin sallow, and his normally neatly combed hair was dirty and straggly.

The twins and I were never demonstrative towards Mum, despite our deep love and respect, but that day, as Mum leaned towards him, Ronnie grabbed her by the arms and kissed her warmly on the cheek. He was ashamed of the cell and upset that we had been brought there. Mum said that it was terrible to see him looking so dreadful in a place like that, but Ronnie just said, 'Mum, I had a fight. I hit a couple of screws. What do you think they're going to do? Give me a medal?' He always took what they dished out without moaning or complaining.

We sat at the foot of the bed talking to Ronnie for nearly two hours and at the end of the visit Mum said that, despite everything, she felt better for having seen him. Ronnie replied quietly that he was pleased we'd come; he had needed to see us. It was an emotional and highly personal visit, and a prison officer sat behind us all the time listening to every word.

* * *

Mum's stamina was amazing. She hardly missed a visit, every week, winter or summer, from the moment we were arrested and on remand in Brixton, to the time when we were sent to far-flung prisons in Durham, Leicester and Chelmsford, then Albany, Parkhurst and Maidstone. It was a feat that only a deeply caring, loving mother could have achieved. Remember, she was getting up at 4 A.M. for her office cleaning job then working in the pub at Bishopsgate.

But there was one visit I forbade her to make – to Long Larten in February 1982. Reggie had been transferred there from Parkhurst and Mum was all set to go after receiving a distressing phone call from a prison official. I told her the visit would be awful and would make her ill.

For Reggie had tried to kill himself.

Early one morning in February Mum had rung me in tears at my home in Crystal Palace. 'Reggie's tried to commit suicide,' she sobbed.

'What!' I couldn't believe it. Ronnie had told me he had a feeling all was not well with Reggie, but I put it down to the change of jail; he would get used to Long Larten after a few weeks.

'He tried to slash his wrists,' Mum said. She was in a dreadful state.

'I'll be right over,' I said. 'I'll ring the prison from your place.'

I covered the fifteen miles in less than half an hour and rang the prison. It was true, they told me: Reggie had tried to slash his wrists. It was a nasty incident, but he was recovering and everything was under control.

I was not convinced. I asked if I could visit him that day and they agreed. Mum wanted to come with me, but I felt it better if I saw Reggie's condition first. Obviously things were bad and I didn't want her upset more. Also, I sensed trouble and I wanted someone other than family with me, someone honest and trustworthy with no criminal record who would be a reliable witness. I chose an East End mate, Laurie O'Leary, and we arrived at Long Larten that afternoon.

Reggie was in the hospital wing. He had been feeling depressed and wanted to be on his own, we were told. Ah, I thought, so they knew he wasn't well. What else did they know about my brother that had led him to try to take his own life? As we followed a prison officer to Reggie's cell I wondered what state he was going to be in. Nothing could have prepared me for what we were about to see.

Like our father, Reggie had always been fussy about cleanliness. As a young man he kept himself spotless: you rarely saw Reggie unshaven or with untidy hair, and he was always dressed in clean, neatly-pressed shirts and suits. So the sight that greeted me when I looked through the flap on Reggie's cell door jolted me. He was sitting on his bed, his clothes creased as though he'd slept in them, his uncombed hair standing on end, and with two or three days' growth of beard. He looked like a raving lunatic who had been locked up for twenty years.

Laurie and I went in and, after the usual pleasantries, I motioned towards one of his arms, which was heavily bandaged. 'Why did you do it, Reg?' I asked. There was no point in beating about the bush.

Reggie shook his head. 'I don't know.'

'There must be a reason,' I persisted.

'I don't know what's wrong with me,' he said. 'People keep saying strange things to me. They keep taking a pop at me.'

I looked at Laurie. It did not sound like the Reggie we knew and I didn't know what to do for the best. I looked at his arm again. 'How on earth did you do all that?'

'With my glasses,' he replied.

Apparently he broke his glasses in half and used a piece of a lens to saw into his wrist. Listening to him describe it made me go cold. He had been alone in his cell and no one had seen him until an officer had spotted him covered in blood. I stared at Reggie as he talked. I could not get over the state he was in. I'd never seen him like that in my life and all I could think was that no one in their right mind breaks their glasses and saws into their wrist. I had to ask him, again. 'But why, Reg?'

It's strange with people who have gone over the edge: when we had arrived, he was reasonably okay, although not like the Reggie of old, of course. Then suddenly when I asked him that question he seemed to break up in front of our eyes, and finally cracked. Close to tears he told us that he'd been depressed because he was causing everyone so many problems, and had decided that if he was out of the way it would make life easier for everyone, particularly Mum and me, what with the visiting and everything. 'It seems it will never end,' he said quietly.

I told him not to be so stupid, not to think like that. No, the visiting was not much fun for Mum, who wasn't getting any younger. But she wasn't complaining; she could cope. Hadn't she always? 'She loves you and wants to see you,' I insisted. 'And Ronnie. You'd break her heart if you did yourself in.'

Reggie listened, but I could see he was not convinced. There was a dullness in his eyes, a look of defeat. I asked him if he had been taken out of the cell. He nodded. 'They've just brought me back up.'

'From where?'

'The chokey block,' he said.

I stared at him disbelievingly. He'd sawn his wrist, lost a lot of blood and they had put him in the chokey! I knew that people were stripped naked and left on their own in there with just a blanket. Sometimes there wasn't even a bed, just a mattress or a sheet of canvas.

I knew Reggie was not himself, so I asked him if he was sure. Then I left the cell and demanded to speak to the Chief Prison Officer, who confirmed that Reggie had spent the maximum twenty-four hours in the chokey block. I went spare. The block was meant for normal prisoners who went off the rails and needed time on their own to quieten down. Why, I wanted to know, had Reggie been taken there and kept there all day and all night in his condition?

'He was put in the chokey for his own protection,' the P.O. said, 'so he couldn't do anything else.'

But that didn't wash with me.

'You didn't have to put him in the strong box for that,' I protested. 'Someone could easily have watched him in his own cell.'

But the P.O. did not want to know, saying the prison was not to blame for Reggie's condition. He felt Reggie was in a perfectly balanced frame of mind and had probably cut his wrist deliberately to cause trouble. He even suggested Reggie was trying to "nut himself off" so that he would be certified insane and sent to Broadmoor where Ronnie had been transferred three years before. I lost my cool and told the P.O. that he was out of order. Reggie did not want to go to Broadmoor; he had always said that once you go there, you're in for ever. After a heated exchange I went back to the cell, seething. The whole thing was a disgrace but what could one do?

When I told Reggie what had happened he didn't take much notice and didn't seem with it at all. Then he said something that convinced me I had to take the matter further.

'That bloke who found me in my cell,' Reggie said. 'He

asked why I'd cut my wrist. He said people usually hanged themselves with a piece of sheet or something.'

Dora Hamylton is a Leicester magistrate who has taken an interest in the twins' cases. After meeting them several times and starting work on a biography of our mother she had become a friend of the family, and I rang asking her to come to Long Larten with me to see Reggie and the prison authorities.

She could not believe what she saw. Reggie had been cleaned up but he was still in a terrible state, nothing like the person she had seen when she had last visited him. The chief male nurse asked to speak to Dora alone, which made me suspicious, but there was nothing I could do about it. I learned later that he told her he thought Reggie was putting on an act. She said he could not be serious: she had visited Reggie many times and knew him well enough to know that he certainly wasn't acting; he had gone over the edge. Whether the nurse was convinced I don't know, but some good came out of the talk, because he promised Reggie would not be put in the chokey block again.

We then went to see the assistant governor. I demanded to know why Reggie had been driven to cut his wrist and why he had been treated the way he had. The assistant governor went round and round the houses before saying that he wasn't sure whether Reggie knew what he was doing. I cut him short by telling him I knew what was on his mind: he felt Reggie was trying to work his ticket to Broadmoor to be with Ronnie. He admitted that I was right.

'Well, you can forget it,' I said. 'Ronnie or no Ronnie, that's the last place Reggie wants to go. He's always said so.'

The assistant governor simply looked at Dora and me with a total lack of concern.

'You don't seem at all bothered that one of your inmates has tried to commit suicide,' I went on. 'Have you seen what Reggie did to himself?'

He said he hadn't.

'He broke his glasses and actually sawed into his veins with the lens,' I told him. 'Do you think anyone could do that as an act?'

The assistant governor did not have an answer to that.

'Would you have been happy if he'd managed to kill himself?' I asked.

'No, I wouldn't,' he replied casually.

Getting angrier by the second at the man's offhand attitude, I told him that the prison staff should have known what was happening to Reggie to make him so depressed and should have been aware of the pitch he was reaching. The assistant governor mumbled some stock reply but I knew from my own experience what had gone on. Prison officers are not aware of such things because they think there's a hidden ploy behind everything. They write reports on people every minute of the day but they don't seem to notice the things that matter.

Then Dora put her bit in. Reggie was not at all well, she said. She had not liked what she had seen, nor what she had heard, and she trusted something would be done about it.

I let a couple of weeks go by before I took Mum to the prison. Reggie was a little better but still not right, and the sight of him really upset her. I'm glad I didn't take her with me on that first visit or she would have collapsed from the shock.

Reggie continued to progress. And then one day I got a phone call from the prison authorities, saying they

254

wanted to see me because he had got out of control and attacked four officers. I went the next day and asked Reggie what it was all about.

'They're driving me mad,' he said. 'I ran into them and they all jumped on me.'

It didn't make sense to me. He had had no problems in Parkhurst but Long Larten was bringing out the worst in him. I'd been dubious at first, but now I believed Reggie when he said that the officers there provoked him. In the end it all worked out well for him because Long Larten said they couldn't handle him and he was sent back to the Isle of Wight. Reggie was delighted and relieved.

After he had been at Parkhurst a couple of days, I went to see the Chief Prison Officer, who told me that Reggie still wasn't one hundred per cent but they would have him back to normal in a few days.

Within a week, Reggie was as right as rain and able to talk coherently about what had been a four-week blitz on his brain. He said the move to Long Larten had unsettled him and he had never been happy there. His letters had either been late or stopped altogether and officers tried generally to provoke him, as if they were seeing how far they could go and how much he could take.

And he remembered being told that people 'usually hang themselves with a piece of sheet or something'.

'That was a very irresponsible thing to say,' Reggie said. 'Or maybe they really did want me to top myself.'

Ronnie had known before any of us that Reggie was heading for a crisis. Reggie did not talk about his problems in his letters but Ronnie picked up that something was wrong. Even if Reggie had not written at all Ronnie would have sensed the trouble ahead, for the amazing telepathy they shared as children was still there.

Mum never ceased to be amused by it, even though she

had grown used to it over the years. Ronnie, for example, would write to her from prison saying she should go on holiday for a couple of weeks, then Reggie, from a different prison hundreds of miles away, would write saying the same thing, even though the twins themselves had not discussed it. She would go to see one of them and talk about a certain subject, then when she visited the other one, he'd bring up the same subject, and Mum would find herself having an identical conversation. She would come home and laugh. 'Would you believe it, it's happened again!'

So it was hardly surprising that Ronnie knew Reggie was suffering in Long Larten. One thing is certain: Ronnie would have understood Reggie's desire to be left on his own to avoid listening to all that talk about violence from idiots. For Ronnie had gone through the same problems himself, first in Durham then in Parkhurst. He liked being on his own so much that I'm sure it wouldn't have bothered him to stay in the chokey block for six months, not twenty-four hours. Broadmoor is perfect for him: most of the inmates there are in for domestic crimes and not caught up in the supposedly glamorous side of villainy. The novelty of having a notorious Kray twin in their midst has worn off and Ronnie can now go off and sit on his own for an hour without being bothered. It took him a long time to get to this comfortable stage, though. After he arrived so many people from other parts of the hospital wanted to chat to him that it got on his nerves and he didn't go out for two years.

One would have thought that after all the medical reports on Ronnie the staff at Broadmoor would understand that he doesn't need people nor does he want to buy friendship. But they are still puzzled by his charitable nature.

The Superintendent called me in once, a concerned

look on his face. 'Ronnie keeps giving things away,' he said. 'What do you think the motive is?'

I smiled to myself. I knew he kept half his ward in tobacco, and at the last count he'd given away thirty watches. 'He likes giving things away,' I said. 'He's done it all his life.'

The Superintendent was not convinced.

'What possible motive could there be?' I asked.

The Superintendent shook his head. 'I don't know. That's why I asked you.'

'If you think he's bribing people so they'll be on his side, so they'll help him in some way, forget it. You should watch and see what sort of people Ronnie picks out. You won't find any tough six-footers, I can assure you.'

It was true. All their lives the twins have had an over-whelming compassion for the underdog – the little man who can't protect himself from the bully, the old lady who is ill or down on her luck. Often I've been sitting in the visiting hall at Broadmoor when Ronnie has spotted an old lady he's never seen in his life. 'Look at that old lady, Charlie,' he'll say. 'Bless her. Get her a box of chocolates, will you?'

I do it for him because I believe in it. I've always been soft-hearted too.

I realize that I knew this side of Ronnie for more than thirty years before our arrest, but one would expect an institution that has supposedly been monitoring his health and behaviour to understand that acts of good-natured charity are part of Ronnie's character and nothing to get worked up about. In Broadmoor, he gives away so many watches that he is nicknamed 'the watchman'. Wilf Pine gave him a watch on one visit which Ronnie immediately sold for £50, giving the money to someone who was having an operation for throat cancer.

Once he gave away a chain which I had just given him. I was quite angry and said, 'I didn't buy you a present to give away.'

'If you gave it to me, it's mine,' Ronnie replied. 'So I've got the right to do what I like with it.'

'But I expect you to keep it,' I told him. 'I bought it for *you*.'

'If it gives me pleasure to give it away there's no harm in that, is there?'

There was no harm in it, I suppose, but it was galling to think that a chain I wanted Ronnie to wear was being worn by someone else who I had not even met. 'Anyway,' I said, 'I'd prefer it if you didn't give my presents away.'

Ronnie assumed that look of determination, the look that said: Don't you argue with me. If I want to do something, no one is going to stop me. 'If *I* want to give them away, I think it's better that I do,' he said. 'I would accept it if you did it. Why can't you?'

And Ronnie *would* accept it. But then he can go one way or the other.

Other inmates must think the world of Ronnie. He will give away half his tobacco allowance, borrow some back when he runs out then buy them some more. Sometimes inmates are allowed to buy meals and Ronnie will pick ten people he feels are in need and treat them. Once Wilf took him in a platter of seafood and Ronnie immediately said, 'We'll have a party tonight.' If he gets money, he'll buy a dozen steaks and share them round. It goes on all the time. He'll never change.

Life as a free man was wonderful. But there was always something nagging at me that would not allow me to enjoy it to the full. It was that unfinished business of injustice.

I had had six years and eight months taken off my life for something of which I was totally innocent. I'd sat in jail seething with frustration at the injustice of it all. I'd driven myself almost round the twist discovering people who had received far lighter sentences after pleading guilty in similar cases. But I'd resisted the temptation to write letters because I felt them to be a waste of time. However, something had to be done about it and I decided to wait until I was out then go to the International Court of Human Rights in Strasbourg. If there was one place that could put right the wrong that had been done to me and mete out the justice I'd been deprived of all those years before, that was it.

Day and night, night and day, throughout the agonizing, mind-numbing tedium of prison existence, I had thought and dreamt . . . and fantasized about the wonderful moment when the truth about me would scream across the pages of the British Press and people would know they should not tar me with the same brush as my twin brothers.

Then, just three months after my release, I abandoned all those dreams after an emotional talk with an eminent psychiatrist.

Ronnie had just been transferred to Broadmoor, and while I was visiting him one afternoon he asked me to do him a favour: he wanted me to go to Dr Klein, a psychiatrist he knew, and enquire about Ronnie's current mental state. Ronnie had known Dr Klein for many years before being arrested, and in fact the psychiatrist had been to Broadmoor to visit him. Ronnie felt he could rely on the doctor to get accurate information from Broadmoor's medical staff and tell him the truth.

I fixed an appointment to see Dr Klein at his Harley Street office. We were talking about Ronnie, but also about me, and after a while it dawned on me that Dr Klein was analysing me. I asked him if this was the case and he admitted it, saying he found it worrying that I seemed so full of hate and anger, even though I had served my sentence.

'Wouldn't you be if you'd been jailed for something you didn't do?' I said.

He had assumed I'd helped dispose of Jack McVitie's body, so I put him right as succinctly as I could. He sat back, behind his desk, deep in thought. Then he leaned forward and looked at me. 'Charlie,' he said earnestly. 'Don't waste your time trying to prove your innocence.'

'What!' I snapped. 'I've thought of little else for nearly seven years. I'm taking the case to Strasbourg.'

Dr Klein shook his head slowly, sadly.

'No matter what you do, you won't be allowed to win.'

I didn't understand.

He explained. 'Even if you did succeed in getting the case to Strasbourg and the court did agree you were wrongly convicted that doesn't mean the British Government would do anything about it.'

'They would have to,' I said.

He shook his head again. 'It would cause some embarrassment, but that's all. They certainly wouldn't issue a pardon.'

'But it's the principle,' I insisted.

'Even if the principle's right, the whole exercise would be futile because you've served your time. You can't get back those seven years.'

I said nothing. I stared back at him, unable to think of anything except that his last point was spot on. Nobody could give me back seven years of my life.

He let the silence continue, allowing the profundity of what he had said to sink in. Finally he said softly, but very warmly, 'After being away so long, don't you think you should just enjoy your life? Don't you think you owe that to yourself?'

'Of course I do,' I said quickly. 'But I'll enjoy my life more if I can clear my name, make people aware I didn't do what they believe I did.'

Dr Klein shook his head. 'If you carry on your fight, it will become a full-time occupation that would ruin your life. It could ultimately destroy you.'

I didn't reply, and he asked me if I respected him and his advice. I told him I did.

'I know you will never completely forget the injustice,' he said finally. 'But try to put it to the back of your mind and put all your energies into living. That is the best advice I can give you because you will never be allowed to win.'

As I walked out of his office and along Harley Street I thought of what he had said. I hated the idea of not going through with what I'd promised myself, but there had been something in Dr Klein's warm sincerity that warned me I should consider his advice very carefully indeed. I was no fool. I knew no one was going to admit I was wrongly convicted, because that would throw a huge question mark over the whole case. The authorities had been given all the evidence they needed to release me when Ronnie Hart tried to kill himself and left a note admitting that he had lied about me in court. But even that had made no difference to my appeal.

Over the next few weeks I pondered Dr Klein's advice: it dominated my thoughts, nagging away at me as I tried to get back into the swing of daily working life, hammering inside my brain as I fell exhausted into bed at night. And then, one day in the summer of 1975, one lovely day when the sun was shining and the East End was bustling with happy, smiling, contented people, I knew what I had to do.

Dr Klein was right in everything he said; I think, deep down, I knew that all along. But it was something he didn't say that made me decide to drop my plans for taking the case to Strasbourg. Life was precious, but short, and I was one year away from my fiftieth birthday. I was fit, strong and as alert as I'd ever been – a youthful fifty – but no matter how I looked or felt, time was not on my side. As Dr Klein had said, taking on the Establishment would be a full-time occupation; to give myself even half a chance of success I would have to drop virtually everything else I was involved in, all the little business deals I was trying to pull together for Diana and me. I would have to dedicate myself singlemindedly to the whole business, think, talk, dream about nothing else twenty-four hours a day, seven days a week. And not just for a year; I'd read of human rights cases taking years. And for what? Dr Klein's words came back to me, filling my mind: *'You will never be allowed to win.'*

Did I want that? Did I want more pressure, more aggravation, more courtroom confrontations, more legal mumbo-jumbo, when the odds were stacked so heavily against me? Did I want to go through yet again all the mental anguish of trying to convince people of the truth of that terrible October night when they had had enough facts to convince them already, and had chosen to come to the wrong conclusion?

Did I really want all that in my life as I approached my half-century? And, just as important, did my darling Diana?

On that sunny day, with the East End and its people so full of life, I decided once and for all to stop dreaming about getting a pardon or even a court victory for wrongful conviction. I would take Dr Klein's advice and I would take it from that very minute.

I would never be able to forget the trauma and indescribable agony of it all. But at least I could try to push it further and further back into my mind until it was just a memory, not a crusade. I would not allow the Establishment another victory by destroying myself. I would rediscover my zest for living and get back into the business of making money to provide for the woman I planned to marry.

After the darkness of prison, where nothing is easy, I would revel in the sunshine of a free life, where everything is possible. I would throw myself into it with all my heart, determined to try to catch up with my lost years by making every moment count.

Chapter Sixteen

I cannot thank Maidstone Jail enough for teaching me artificial resuscitation. I passed the elementary exam so well one morning that I was asked if I wanted to take the advanced test in the afternoon, and passed that with honours. This was great for me but even better for Diana a few years later. For it helped me to save her life. Three times.

Diana suffers from asthma, and towards the end of an evening at Joe and Rose Rankin's pub in Hackney she suddenly found it hard to breathe. I suggested we leave, and soon we were heading down Kingsland Road on the way to Ewell in Surrey. I did not realize how serious Diana's asthma attacks could be until I looked at her in the passenger seat and realized she was passing out. I needed to get her home as fast as possible so I put my foot down, assuming that if I was stopped the police would be sympathetic. Fortunately, there were no police cars to be seen that night and I got her home in double-quick time. Without a booking.

I helped Diana out of the car and sat her in an armchair while I made some coffee. When I came back she was on the floor. Out of my mind with worry, I picked her up and put her on a settee.

I felt for her pulse. There was none.

I felt to see if she was breathing. She wasn't.

I picked up the phone despairingly. It was out of order.

Trembling with panic, I moved Diana gently back to the floor. She was lifeless. And she would stay that way unless somebody did something quickly. Well, there was nobody else. Only me. I knew I had to find out just how well I'd learned artificial resuscitation in jail and I prayed I'd learned it well enough.

My Diana was not going to die on me.

I took a deep breath, filling my lungs with as much air as I could, and blew into her mouth – first one big blow; another deep breath; another blow, then another. Next I hit her on the sternum to start the heart.

She didn't move. Didn't breathe.

Another deep breath. More air, more life-giving air. I hit the sternum again, harder this time.

Come on, Diana, come on!

But nothing.

And then again, and again and yet another rib-crushing thump on the sternum. Come on. Come on. COME ON! Breathe, my darling. BREATHE!

And then, finally, she did. She took in the air I'd given her and started breathing it. From an inert, lifeless body, she started coming back to me again.

I got up and dashed across the road. I knocked on a door urgently and a young girl of about fourteen opened it, alarm on her face at the sight of a strange man on her doorstep at 11 P.M.

'Don't worry, darling,' I said, not wanting to frighten her. 'There's a lady across the road having an asthma attack. She's in a bad way. Can you ring for an ambulance?'

I left her to it and ran back into the house. Diana's breathing kept stopping then starting and I prayed I could keep her going until the ambulance arrived. Just then the girl came in, looking terrified. The ambulance was on its way, she said. At that moment the ambulancemen came running into the house, carried Diana out and put her on oxygen. I jumped in the ambulance and we were racing to the hospital with someone radioing ahead to tell them to prepare for a major emergency. And all the time Diana's breathing was stopping and they had to keep starting it again.

At the hospital they put her on a machine, then on to a bed which turned upside down so that a pipe could be put down her throat. It seemed like hours before the ambulancemen came out and told me I could relax because Diana was breathing normally.

I thanked them for all they had done, then, as they started to leave, one of them turned to me and said, 'By the way, you saved that lady's life. Where did you learn resuscitation?'

I shrugged, embarrassed. Somehow, the place did not seem right to get involved in a conversation about prison. 'It was years ago,' was all I said.

Diana was told she was being kept in overnight but I was allowed to see her once she was settled. She was sitting up, looking perky and right as rain.

'How do you feel?' I asked.

'Like a fool,' Diana replied. 'I feel perfectly well enough to go home.'

'Well, you're not,' I said. 'We're not taking any chances.'

I told her how the whole business had opened my eyes: I hadn't realized asthma attacks could be so lethal. 'You were completely out,' I said.

Diana smiled. 'I know. They told me who saved my life.'

'Well, now you're in my debt,' I joked. And we both laughed.

I left her at 3 A.M. and suddenly remembered my car was at home in Ewell. I got a cab easily in Epsom town centre, but I was so brimful with relief I could happily have walked all the way.

* * *

In 1984 we had another drama while at a wedding. Diana swallowed a couple of mouthfuls of brandy, then felt so ill that we decided to leave for home, which was now in Crystal Palace, South London. Diana's brother, John, and his wife Dede, who were over from Canada and staying with us at the time, were surprised to see us home so early. But it was nothing to the shock they got when Diana slumped in an armchair and stopped breathing.

Dede went into a panic. John told her to quieten down: he had been a medic in the Navy and was now medical director of a hospital. He was calm; he knew what had to be done.

What a relief! I thought. My memories of the first crisis were still quite fresh and quite honestly I didn't want the responsibility of trying to pull Diana through again: the thought of failure petrified me. Thank God this time someone was on hand who knew more about medicine than I'll ever know.

But when I saw what John was preparing to do I knew Diana's life was in my hands again. He was taking a carving knife out of a drawer, saying that Diana needed a tracheotomy.

'What are you doing?' I asked, shocked.

'It's the only way, Charlie,' he replied. 'It's the only way to make her breathe.'

'No it's not,' I said sharply, my panic and concern for Diana giving a rough edge to my tone. I knelt beside her and took a deep breath, then I whacked her sternum hard, probably harder than necessary but I was taking no chances.

Looks of relief swept our faces as Diana started to breathe again. Dede had called an ambulance and I went with it to the nearest hospital. I told a doctor what had happened, but he was very offhand and seemed to think

Diana had been drunk and it was all a waste of time. After a check-up she was allowed home.

The next day, her doctor hit the roof. He rang the hospital, demanding to know why Diana had been treated so shabbily, despite her medical history, in such a dangerous situation. He asked Diana for the name of the doctor who had treated her so that he could take it further, but she persuaded him to drop it.

Things go in threes, they say, and we did not have long to wait for Diana's hat-trick of crises. We were having a meal at a Crystal Palace restaurant when Diana said she was going outside for some air. She promptly collapsed on the pavement.

The first I knew about it was when a girl came running in, saying a lady had fallen down, hitting her head. I dashed outside while someone rang for an ambulance. Diana's breathing had not stopped this time but she was out cold so I turned her over and started giving her the kiss of life anyway. I didn't manage to bring her round, but then the ambulancemen arrived and took over. Diana finally came to fifteen minutes later and was soon feeling well enough to insist that she was okay and did not want to go to hospital. To this day, we don't know what brought that attack on.

I was getting quite a dab hand at the kiss of life. And my prison training in medical crises was to come in useful again, in tragic circumstances.

During the early eighties the twins' telepathy was working strongly. In their letters to each other neither had mentioned confessing to their respective crimes, yet they both did so at roughly the same time. I don't know the reasons; they haven't told me and I haven't asked. I think, perhaps, they both decided they had served so many years that it didn't matter any more.

They owned up in front of a panel reviewing their cases for parole, and one of the questions each twin was asked was: 'Do you feel any remorse?'

Ronnie decided he could not lie just to get parole. He said he was unable to feel remorse because of the situation behind the killing: he knew George Cornell was going to kill him, so he killed him first. And, he said, he would do the same again in similar circumstances. He accepted that the panel would not agree with him; they would probably let the other person shoot. But that was not his nature, he said.

Reggie said he *was* sorry about what had happened. But it did not do him any good. He was told his parole was being turned down and he would not be released until the 1990s.

I was bitterly disappointed at that decision, but delighted that Reggie had confessed to the McVitie murder because it meant, at long last, that I could tell the truth about my involvement that fateful October night. Family loyalty means everything to me – no matter how terrible the circumstances – and all the time the twins denied killing McVitie I had to pretend I hadn't gone to Harry Hopwood's house. However, with the admissions came my chance to get the truth out in the open and clear my name once and for all.

My first thought was to seize the chance quickly with both hands. I remembered my anger and bitterness throughout my years in captivity, my fantasy about seeing my reputation redeemed in blazing newspaper headlines. Well, here was the perfect opportunity to hit those headlines and make all those pompous prosecution legal eagles see that, in my case at least, they had got it wrong.

It would not give me back six years and eight months of my life; it would almost certainly not win me an official pardon. But it would make me feel better and make the rest of my life taste sweeter. I thought and thought about it, trying to convince myself I should go against Dr Klein's advice, but in the end I didn't. His words, '*They won't let you win,*' hammered away inside my brain and convinced me that no matter how much I wanted the world to know that 'Charlie Kray is innocent, OK?' the battle was not going to be worth it – even though Reggie had confessed.

Dr Klein is more experienced than me. He has studied for years and years and knows about life. I am positive he was right in everything he told me and I am so, so glad I decided *not* to go back on his advice.

Even today, I could be locked in some courtroom battle, fighting the lies all over again.

Although Ronnie and Reggie have shown little concern for the years I lost on their behalf I visit them regularly still – Ronnie in Broadmoor and Reggie now in Gartree – and run around trying to make things happen on the outside that might make life more comfortable on the inside. I've been liaising with former rock star Roger Daltrey over a film of the Kray Story, and secured a sizeable advance payment for the twins. Negotiations have been going on for four years and, although it is a frustrating business, one hopes the film will eventually be made. The twins are fascinated by who will play them on the screen. In addition I have put together a deal involving Kray Twins' merchandising – T-shirts, calendars, mugs etc. – which will also earn a few bob over the next few years.

Both the twins are as impatient and impetuous as ever, particularly Reggie. When they were free they got things done quickly – often literally overnight – and they still feel that should be possible. But of course many things have changed since those relatively carefree days of the sixties, and one of them is people's attitude to business in general and the Kray twins in particular. Neither Ronnie nor Reggie can accept it, but the notoriety their exploits earned them is as strong today as ever. Annoying though it may be to them, people who might be useful are more than a little wary of getting involved, no matter how commendable or financially sound a project might be.

Ronnie has not lost his sense of humour and is popular among inmates and staff alike in Broadmoor. Reggie, however, has become more and more intense, probably due to the disappointment at not getting parole. He was always a thorough individual, keen to pay attention to detail, but nowadays he goes into everything more deeply than ever. It can be quite a strain sometimes.

Much has been said and written about the twins' aggression, but little has been said of their compassion or, indeed, their kindness. In the East End in the sixties, hundreds, if not thousands, of old people and children had good reason to be grateful to the twins, who always reached into their pockets if the cause was worthy enough. Hospitals and other charities, too, benefited from boxing tournaments and showbiz gala evenings that were not all arranged with personal Press publicity in mind. Even now, with their own problems to think about, Ronnie and Reggie are charity-minded. Throughout the time they have been in jail they have painted pictures which have then been auctioned for deserving charities. If they read in the paper about a handicapped child the chances are that they will arrange for something to be made – either a teddy bear or some other toy – which they send to the family.

Not all their compassion is restricted to children and frail old folk, however. A few years ago each twin wrote to a man they had read had tried to kill himself. They succeeded in snapping him out of it and each received a letter from the poor man's wife saying how grateful she was to them for saving her husband's life. The cynics would say they had done that for publicity, to show how caring they were, but they didn't tell a soul. I want to make this point because most of the traffic has been one-way: the media always refer to the twins as 'evil gangland killers', but no one seems to want to know that they have a gentle, generous and kind side to their natures.

Whether it was the painful memory of Frances's suicide that prompted Reggie to write to that poor man I don't know. Certainly that tragic episode in the early summer of 1967 still haunts Reggie and probably always will. Even today he will not – cannot – talk about her death. For the burial he imported a beautiful stone from Italy and bought a plot in Gants Hill Cemetery. I go there regularly and sit by the grave, not only for Reggie but for myself, too, and when I see him in prison I tell him I've been there and taken flowers and he thanks me, but can't talk about her. She was everything to him and the hurt is too great even now, twenty-one years later.

The Shea family put a few flowers down in the months following the funeral, but the stone grew grubby and when Mum was buried in an adjoining plot Reggie asked me to arrange for Frances's stone to be cleaned. It cost £150 but it looked better, more cared for, and it made Reggie feel a lot happier. I took some photographs of the new-look grave, and Reggie was pleased, and sat looking at them a long time, but still did not want to talk about her.

Frances was the only girl he wanted to marry. When he comes out of jail I cannot see him remarrying. There might be a woman who could pull him out of despair over Frances but she would have to be someone truly exceptional.

* * *

Just before 9 A.M. on Tuesday 5 April 1983, the phone rang at my home in Crystal Palace. It was Gary, calling from the flat in Bunhill Row, where he was living with the old man. Gary was sobbing. He had woken up and found the old man lying at the bottom of the stairs. I told him to ask a neighbour to ring for an ambulance; I would get over as fast as possible. As I got ready, I knew what had happened, and ten minutes later an ambulanceman phoned to confirm it. The old man was dead.

The ambulanceman was kind and gentle and told me to take my time; there was nothing anybody could do and he didn't want me to have an accident. He and a colleague would wait until I arrived.

On my way through South London to the City I saw a crowd of people standing round a man on the ground. They were just staring at him, not knowing what to do so I stopped the car and ran over. After suggesting that someone ring for an ambulance immediately, I loosened the man's tie and checked his pulse and breathing. They were fine – the man, who was a postman, had just fainted. I put him in the coma position and told the crowd that he was going to be all right but that I couldn't wait for the ambulance because I had an emergency of my own. I got back in the car and carried on to Bunhill Row.

Five days later, we buried the old man next to his beloved Violet. The prison authorities made it clear that the twins would be given permission to attend the funeral, but they didn't ask for it.

The old man did not want another circus. Neither did they.

I don't mind the visiting side of my life: it is something I have to do. I go to see the twins regularly and I go to the cemetery at least once a fortnight, often more. If the weather is bad I don't go, but then I feel guilty.

It's lovely and quiet in that cemetery and I'll go there

273

with Gary to put flowers down, clean the stone and sort it all out. I'll read the stone for the millionth time: 'May you both rest peacefully. Our love and memories are always with you. May God bless you both.' I'll talk with Mum and the old man as though they were there. Afterwards we'll go to the car and look over and I'll say, 'We're off.' Driving away I always feel better for having gone.

That grave is the first place Ronnie and Reggie will visit when they are released.

Epilogue

The longest, costliest trial in British history branded the twins and me with a notoriety that lasts to this day. For Ronnie in Broadmoor and Reggie in Gartree that notoriety has ceased to affect them. In the early years of their sentences, they found it difficult: certain inmates, jealous of their 'star' status, tried to make a name for themselves by taking on the twins. Prison officers too took a delight in winding them up, seeing how much they could take, and putting unnecessary obstacles in their way. Over the years, however, everything seemed to calm down. The twins did not like the prospect of being locked up for thirty years but they were determined to take their sentences like men without whingeing. They settled into the mundane routine of prison life, causing no problems and, in return, were treated with respect by prisoners and staff alike. The notoriety of their name is still there, of course, but it does not adversely affect their lives. If anything, it helps them and gives them an edge, because even now certain individuals adore basking in the reflection of what they misguidedly see as Kray glory. For me, however, the notoriety destroyed my life.

When I came out of jail the first and most important thing on my mind was to try to pick up where I'd left off, to get involved in some legitimate venture that would put me back on my feet financially and restore my pride, which had taken a beating since my arrest. However, I quickly discovered that the minor irritations the name Kray had caused me before my sentence were now major problems. The headlines and long-running stories that had followed each day's Old Bailey evidence were, it seemed, indelibly printed on everyone's mind. In restaurants and bars people stared at me with curiosity, distrust, perhaps even fear. Acquaintances who before were only too pleased to offer help were 'unavailable'. Business contacts, who had once seen me as a reliable, feet-on-the-ground skilful operator, now did not return phone calls. The name Kray, I quickly found out, spelt NO in giant capitals, not only in London but throughout the whole country.

The twins have no idea of the terrible effect our name has on people, even today. I have tried to explain, but they have been cut off from normal everyday working life for so long now that it is impossible for them to understand. I doubt that they will *ever* fully comprehend the strain their activities have put on me. What made my blood boil when I first came out was not so much that I'd been locked up for something I hadn't done – although that was bad enough – but that people refused to give me a chance. Their minds had been made up for them; they assumed that what they had read and heard must be true, and that was that. People who had never seen me, let alone met me and listened to what I had to say, took it for granted that, because I was a Kray and the twins' brother, I was a gangster – a ruthless, nasty piece of work who should be avoided at all costs.

I didn't expect it to be easy when I left Maidstone, but nothing could have prepared me for the wave of distrust, bordering on hatred, that my surname inspired. It meant I had to try harder with everything. And I did. I fought to conquer the inferiority complex and shame my conviction had given me. I battled to revert to my former self, to recapture some of the good-humoured personality and energy that had endeared me to many people and helped make my businesses successful. I even tried to convince the cynics that I was an innocent party in all that had happened, a victim myself, caught up in tragic events that were beyond my control. But it was like bashing my head against a brick wall. People, in the main, did not want to know.

Once I decided to take Doctor Klein's advice and forget about fighting a legal crusade to clear my name I became a happier, more contented person. It still bothered me that people could dislike me without knowing me but I forced myself to accept that this was merely an additional price I would have to pay.

Several people suggested that the simplest way to solve the name problem was to change it. But that's something I never considered and never will. I have always been proud of my mother and father and the name they gave me, and I'll never forget the pride that surged through me when I saw that name on my boxing trophies, before and after my Navy life. It's terrible that the name will now live forever because of the twins' violence, but I, like them, will have to live with that. The mere thought of going through a legal process to rid myself of that connection makes me feel quite sick. It would be a betrayal of our dear, much loved mum, and I couldn't live with that.

Now, for my own sanity, I put people into two categories: those who don't know the truth and are wary of me are inconsequential to my life and don't matter; and those who do know the full story know I'm all right anyway. Sadly, though, prison life took its toll, and I've got to the point where the only people I truly care about, deep down, are Di and Gary. I still like people and I want them to like me, but I won't beg to be liked. If someone isn't prepared to take me as they find me today – whether they believe I was innocent of complicity in the McVitie murder or not – then that's tough, I'm afraid.

* * *

The last thing I want to do is make excuses for Ronnie and Reggie. What they did to George Cornell and Jack McVitie cannot be defended and, rightly, they are paying a high price for those crimes. But I do want people to know – whether they were around at the time or whether they were too young and have only read about the twins – that they were the victims of parliamentary pressure. What was sensationally labelled The Trial of the Century was a political exercise. Someone somewhere had decided that the Kray brothers – me included, presumably – had become too powerful, too influential, knew too many powerful and influential people, and should be removed from society for a long time.

The outcome of the case was worked out before it even got to court; you have only to consider the antagonism, unforgivable bias and downright bad judgement of Melford Stevenson to appreciate that. Ronnie had it right all along: no matter what was said in the twins' favour – no matter if they got a glowing testimonial from the Pope himself – they were going to go away for thirty years.

People talk about justice in this country. We hold Britain up as a shining example of democracy and fair-mindedness and the symbol of this is there for all to see in the scales of justice above the Old Bailey. How damned hypocritical!

Ronnie got thirty years for murdering a gangster before he himself was shot, yet someone who starves and tortures a child to death can get away with just one-third of that. Reggie got thirty years for killing a thug who had proved himself a despicable, woman-beating layabout, yet an evil, calculating terrorist warrants the same sentence for killing and maiming innocent men, women and children in the name of politics and religion. Where is the democracy and fair-mindedness in that?

The reason the twins got thirty years was to make an

example of them. Someone high up actually believed they were so rich and well-connected that they could get together one thousand men and try to take over the country. Ronnie in particular got a good laugh out of that, but it was no joke to the nation's leaders. They saw the twins as a real threat and that's why a Top Secret directive to nail them went out from the Home Secretary to Scotland Yard. The deals the police did with Hart, Donaghue and the others, and all that followed, were very carefully orchestrated from on high to serve as a warning to any other villains with aspirations to wealth, fame and power.

Personally, I feel the politicians and police over-estimated Ronnie and Reggie. Yes, they were amazingly tough and uncompromising, and had plenty of rows. But the only people they frightened were other hard cases in that shadowy, twilight world in which the twins moved. 'Gangland twins' reign of terror . . .' and other such awe-inspiring headlines may sound terrific to the Fleet Street sub-editors who write them but, believe me, they are a load of rubbish. I've never been able to understand all the talk about terror and neither have Ronnie and Reggie. The papers make it sound as though shopowners, stall-holders and publicans cowered in fear every time the twins came into sight. But the truth is that the East End locals – particularly in Bethnal Green – welcomed them with open arms because they were respectful, generous and spent a lot of money.

If this 'reign of terror' had been fact and not a figment of the newspapermen's vivid imagination, is it not fair to assume that a few of the supposedly terrified working people would have been queuing at the Old Bailey to drive a nail into their persecutors' coffins? If not a few people perhaps one or two? The fact that not one such person was moved to make a statement against either

Ronnie or Reggie speaks for itself, I think. Quite simply, no one could say anything because there wasn't anything to say. Much was made of the so-called protection racket the twins were supposed to have run, the money that was supposed to have been demanded under the threat of violence. But, here again, not one club owner or publican stood up and said, 'The Kray twins forced me to pay them.'

Ronnie and Reggie carried the can for certain members of their Firm who grassed them to the police as I'd warned they would. The twins won't ever say that publicly – and certainly won't moan about it – but it's true. Hart and Donaghue particularly loved the violence and enjoyed the money it brought, but they quickly changed sides when the heat was on. When the going gets tough, the tough get going, so they say. Well, Hart and Donaghue certainly got going – straight into the arms of Nipper Read and his men. As tough guys, Hart and Donaghue proved to be cowards who would have set up their own mothers to avoid going to jail.

Donaghue was one of the biggest villains around; he actually carried out the violence the twins were accused of. Yet he was allowed to walk away and begin a new life with a new identity, and because he helped the law he seems to have a licence to do whatever he likes. Some time ago he was arrested for breaking and entering, but was let off with probation after using the pressure of the trial as an excuse. Later he got away with stabbing a taxi driver by telling Nipper Read the cabbie had threatened him for grassing up the twins.

I understand the need for police to have informers, but it seems to me that they are trying to make a nation of them. In the long term, we will have a nation of traitors.

Nipper even tried to get me to go over to the other side. It happened one time when all the accused men were being taken to Bow Street for one of the committal proceedings. As we were shepherded into the huge black van I found myself at the back, which was unusual. No sooner had we joined the morning traffic than a policeman started chatting to me. I'd always got on well with the law so I didn't think too much about it, but as we neared Bow Street and prepared to get out the officer whispered something about Read wanting to speak to me on the quiet about Reggie. I knew immediately what he was getting at: he knew Reggie was the one who'd stabbed McVitie and he knew I had nothing to do with it. He was interested in persuading me to give evidence against Reggie in return for all charges against me being dropped. Nipper had no chance of that and I politely declined the opportunity to speak to him 'on the quiet' or any other time. But I didn't hold it against Nipper for trying. He had a job to do and he was doing it to the best of his ability. Throughout the whole business, I found him polite, courteous and, in a way, understanding. To me, at least, he was always a proper gentleman.

Perhaps I should not have been surprised. Although I wouldn't class any copper as a bosom pal, someone I would invite to dinner, I have enjoyed a friendly relationship with men of various ranks over the years. While most of the Old Bill seemed suspicious of everything the twins and their friends got up to they accepted that I was getting on with my own life and not part of the so-called Firm. In fact, if I was around when they pulled the twins in for questioning – like the McCowan arrest at the Glenrae Hotel, for instance – they would say, 'Stay out of it, Charlie – this has nothing to do with you.' And in the cells, during and after the Bow Steet and Old Bailey hearings, I was always the one they relied on to sort things out and calm people down. This was one of the reasons I felt confident, even after my arrest, that whatever the police had on the twins it could not have anything to do with me. The Old Bill knew I was straight and I was convinced it would be only a matter of time before I was released.

How wrong can you be!

The police had been ordered to get *all* the Krays – not just the twins – and no matter how much they believed in my innocence that is precisely what they set out to do. Whether they would have succeeded in framing me for complicity in the McVitie murder without Ronnie Hart's lies is not important now. But what still rankles to this day is the injustice of what happened a year after I was convicted.

In June 1970 Hart swore an affidavit that evidence he gave at the Old Bailey was false: neither Freddie Foreman nor I, he said, was involved in McVitie's murder in any way. The statement read: 'All I know of the night of the murder was that they (the twins) did, in fact, kill him. I don't know what happened to the body; who disposed of it.'

One would have thought such a turnabout would have been viewed as vital evidence guaranteed, surely, to warrant a close look at the case. But it was pooh-poohed by the legal brains, and although a copy of Hart's affidavit was sent to the Home Secretary, calling for the case to be reopened, nothing happened. Later, Chris and Tony Lambrianou made police statements admitting they were involved in getting rid of McVitie's body but making it clear neither Foreman nor I was. Again, it made not the slightest difference. My name, it seemed, was written on a long prison sentence and the police were going to see that I got it.

After all the blatant discrepancies in prosecution evidence which were glossed over in court I was not really surprised that the case was left unopened. But that did not stop me feeling disappointed and very bitter at the sheer injustice of it all, whether my name was Kray or not. In Britain, the judicial system appears marvellous – until it happens to you.

Ironically, I feel I've come out of it all better than Hart. I've served my sentence, and although life isn't what it might have been, I'm able to move around freely with a clear conscience. Hart, on the other hand, has got to live with the knowledge that he knowingly deprived an innocent man of nearly seven years of his life by telling blatant lies. I'm not normally a revengeful or vindictive person but I pray that Hart's evil treachery plagues his mind and affects his life as much as his perjury affected mine.

The other main prosecution witness who did nothing to help my case, Harry Hopwood, is now dead. I wonder if his wife is scarred by her husband's betrayal of well-meaning men who did nothing but help him. Hopwood talked a good fight, but when it came to it he was as cowardly as the rest who surrounded the twins, and when the chance came to sell his soul this latter-day Judas hardly gave it a second thought. Shortly after the trial his wife was heard boasting in the butcher's: 'We've never had it so good since Harry turned the Krays over. We've got everything we ever wanted.'

I could not put it better myself. That sums up Harry Hopwood and his wife perfectly.

Lots of people, I know, felt our mum was at the centre of the twins' villainy. Others who didn't still found it impossible to accept that she didn't know what they were up to. As teenagers, the twins were often out half the night; then, as young men, they would suddenly leave the country for a week or so. Surely, asked the sceptics, their mother would ask questions, demand to know what was going on. Well, the truth is that Mum *didn't* ask questions.

She was terribly naïve – all the family were, believe it or not – and honestly had no idea that the twins were involved in trouble of any kind. When the rumours about heavy violence, and, eventually, the Cornell killing, began buzzing round the East End, the twins would gloss over it to put her mind at rest. 'It's all talk, Mum, just people around the club,' they would say. And Mum always accepted it. Once she was asked on television if the stories about the twins' violent exploits were true, and she replied simply, 'I don't know.'

In all the years I've had to think about the family tragedy I've wondered whether, deep down, she did know the twins had an evil streak but turned a blind eye because she couldn't face up to the truth. If this is so it's sad, but understandable: what mother wants to accept she has a problem child or, in her case, two? But I will not have our mum blamed for the way the twins turned out. She did her best for them, as she did for me. When Ronnie and Reggie were involved in trouble as young boys, she would tell them, 'You mustn't argue with people – it's terrible.' But the twins would always make light of it, saying this person or that had done this bad thing and they had had to sort it out. Indoors, she did cut short the flare-ups between them, but how could she be expected to control them when they were outside? She tried her best to guide them, to discourage them from fighting and arguing, but as they grew into young men she could not be with them twenty-four hours a day, any more than I could.

It has also been said that the Krays salted away a fortune when the writing was on the wall. That's a laugh. We did earn a lot, it's true, but not a fortune. And what money we did have we spent or, in Ronnie's case, gave away. I wish we *had* put some of our cash away, because then I wouldn't have had to rely on the fifty pounds Mum

284

gave me when I came out of Maidstone. And certainly she would not have had to move back into a council house and do two jobs to make ends meet. If there had been a fortune around, you can bet your boots our beloved mum would have lived like a queen because that is what she deserved. Neither Ronnie, Reggie nor I can speak too highly of her. In the face of the worst publicity – indeed nationwide shame – she didn't falter, never lost faith in us, and only twice throughout the nightmare that followed our arrests did she allow us to witness the agony that was tearing her apart.

The first time was while we were in Brixton awaiting trial. A bloke told a national newspaper that he'd over-heard a phone conversation in which someone said the twins were arranging for Princess Margaret's son, Lord Linley, to be kidnapped and held until they were released. The twins were slaughtered, and Mum went spare. She wrote to the Queen saying they would never dream of doing a thing like that; they would never involve a child in any trouble. It took Mum a long time to get over that because the paper printed the story as though it was true, and she thought millions would believe it.

The other time she cracked in front of us was at the Old Bailey after we had all been sentenced. They allowed Ronnie, Reggie and me to talk to her through a glass wall, one at a time. Mum broke her heart that day. She kept saying, 'That's it. That's the end of the story. Thirty years. I can't believe it.'

The twins and I did our best to comfort her. 'We'll come out on appeal,' we said. 'In three months it'll all be over.' In our hearts we knew it wasn't true, but it was the only thing we could think of to calm her and stop her worrying. Mum was not fooled, however. 'How can I *not* worry?' she would say. 'It's the end of your lives.'

In those emotional moments in the cells below the Old

Bailey, as Ronnie and Reggie tried to stem the tide of her tears, I'm sure they came the nearest to feeling regret, if not remorse, for the murders that had brought them to justice and broken the heart of the woman they worshipped. For they, like me, had such respect for her that they could not bear the thought of hurting or disappointing her.

It is that word, respect, which is a key factor in the rise and fall of my brothers. And if one is apportioning blame for the way they turned out I, more than anyone, must stand up and be counted. As a child it was drummed into me that respect was the greatest word in the English language. If you gave that to people, Mum would tell me, you nearly always got it back. As the twins' elder brother I felt it my duty to drum it into them too, and maybe I did it too much, because that word became all-important in their lives. They were almost obsessive about it and as they grew into young men the word became part of their everyday language. As respectful people themselves, they demanded respect from others and, if they didn't get it, they were physically equipped to do something about it, which they did quite often.

Hard though it is for me to accept, I feel I may be the guilty one in the Kray story, the one to blame for making the twins so incredibly fearsome and a legend in their own time. I was the one who made them aware their fists were lethal weapons. I was the one who put on their first boxing gloves and taught them how to take care of themselves during those wartime evenings in Vallance Road. I was the one who detected how good they were and took them, at the age of ten, to a boxing club. I was the one who persuaded them to turn pro, then trained and sparred with them. I was the one who sat in their corner, advising, coaxing, encouraging them, convincing them they were uniquely outstanding, with the potential to become champions.

I was the one who made them believe they were invincible.

I don't want to apologize for what I did. My attitude to the twins was motivated by the best of intentions. Boxing was an honourable sport, and as a profession it offered two academically unqualified young men the chance to make something of their lives, to become people who would warrant the respect they wanted. But in the light of what happened I've lain awake at night wondering whether it would all have been different if I'd taught the twins a different sport; perhaps bought them football boots, not boxing gloves, and got them to vent whatever anger and frustration they had running around a field, not slugging another human being.

All through our lives I've tried to do the best for my brothers, but unfortunately they don't see it that way. I'm their human punchbag, the scapegoat who gets the blame every time something goes wrong. They even give me the impression that it is my fault they're in prison. It would be lovely to have some recognition, even gratitude, for the many things I've done on their behalf, the problems I've sorted out, the help I've given the arrogant losers they have befriended behind bars. But the twins are not made that way. The only time I've really been close to either of them is when Mum died and I comforted them in prison. They were at their lowest ebb and, perhaps, seeing things as they really were for the one and only time in their lives. Both said they were really proud of me and thanked me for everything I was doing for them and the family.

Sadly, their memories proved short. Elder brother Charlie was, alas, always a bit too soft for their liking.

They might not care to admit it, but when it comes down to it they view me as a great disappointment.

Respect, it seems, is something they will never show me.